WITHDRAWN

This is a study of writing of the seventeenth and eighteenth centuries, mainly in France, but also in Britain and Russia. Its focus is on the establishing and questioning of rational, 'civilized' norms of 'politeness', which in the *ancien régime* means not just polite manners, but a certain ideal of society and culture.

Within this general context, a series of familiar oppositions, between polite and rude, tame and wild, urban(e) and rustic, elite and popular, adult and child, reason and unreason, give the initial impetus to enquiries which often show how these opposites interpenetrate, how hierarchies are reversed, and how compromises are sought. Polite society, like polite literature, needs and desires its opposite. The ideal is often the meeting of garden and wilderness, where the savage encounters the civilized and gifts are exchanged. Professor France points to the centrality, but also the vulnerability, in classical culture, of the ideal of 'politeness', and his discussion embraces revolutionary eloquence and enlightened primitivism, the value of hyperbole, and the essay as a form of polite sociability.

Cambridge Studies in French

POLITENESS AND ITS DISCONTENTS

Cambridge Studies in French

General editor: MALCOLM BOWIE

Recent titles in this series include:

RICHARD D. E. BURTON
Baudelaire in 1859: A Study in the Sources of Poetic Creativity

MICHAEL MORIARTY
Taste and Ideology in Seventeenth-Century France

JOHN FORRESTER
The Seductions of Psychoanalysis: Freud, Lacan and Derrida

JEROME SCHWARTZ
Irony and Ideology in Rabelais: Structures of Subversion

DAVID BAGULEY
Naturalist Fiction: The Entropic Vision

LESLIE HILL
Beckett's Fiction: In Different Words

F. W. LEAKEY
Baudelaire: Collected Essays, 1953 – 1988

SARAH KAY
Subjectivity in Troubadour Poetry

GILLIAN JONDORF
French Renaissance Tragedy: The Dramatic Word

LAWRENCE D. KRITZMAN
The Rhetoric of Sexuality and the Literature of the French Renaissance

JERRY C. NASH
The Love Aesthetics of Maurice Scève

For a complete list of books in the series, see the end of this volume

POLITENESS AND ITS DISCONTENTS

PROBLEMS IN FRENCH CLASSICAL CULTURE

PETER FRANCE
UNIVERSITY OF EDINBURGH

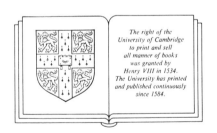

The right of the
University of Cambridge
to print and sell
all manner of books
was granted by
Henry VIII in 1534.
The University has printed
and published continuously
since 1584.

CAMBRIDGE UNIVERSITY PRESS

CAMBRIDGE

NEW YORK   PORT CHESTER

MELBOURNE   SYDNEY

Published by the Press Syndicate of the University of Cambridge
The Pitt Building, Trumpington Street, Cambridge CB2 1RP
40 West 20th Street, New York, NY 1001-4211, USA
10 Stamford Road, Oakleigh, Melbourne 3166, Australia

First published 1992

Printed in Great Britain at the University Press, Cambridge

A catalogue record for this book is available from the British Library

Library of Congress cataloguing in publication data
France, Peter, 1935–
Politeness and its discontents: problems in French classical
culture / Peter France.
p.   cm. – (Cambridge studies in French)
Includes bibliographical references and index.
ISBN 0 521 37070 1 (hardback)
1. French literature – 18th century – History and criticism.
2. French literature – 17th century – History and criticism.
3. France – Civilization – 17th–18th centuries.   4. French literature –
European influences.   5. European literature – French influences.
6. Literature and society – France.   7. Social ethics in literature.
8. Courtesy in literature.   9. Classicism – France.   I. Title.
II. Series.
PQ265.F73   1992
840.9'353'09033 – dc20   91-9105   CIP

ISBN 0 521 37070 1 hardback

WG

To the memory of Austin Gill

CONTENTS

ACKNOWLEDGEMENTS

Versions of chapters in this book appeared previously in the following publications, though many have been radically recast, amalgamated or translated. I am grateful to the editors and publishers for permission to use them here.

Chapter 1
'Equilibrium and Excess' in *The Equilibrium of Wit*, ed. D. Coleman and P. Bayley (Lexington, Kentucky: French Forum Publishers, 1982); and 'L'Hyperbole chez Racine' in *Racine, théâtre et poésie*, Actes du troisième colloque Vinaver, Manchester 1987 (Francis Cairns Publications, Liverpool, 1991).

Chapter 3
'Myth and Modernity: Racine's *Phèdre*' in *Myth and Legend in French Literature. Essays in Honour of A. J. Steele*, ed. K. Aspley, D. Bellos and P. Sharratt (London, Modern Humanities Research Association, 1982).

Chapter 4
'La Politesse en question' in *Saggi e ricerche di letteratura francese*, 29 (1990).

Chapter 5
'Sociability, Journalism, and the Essay' in *Continuum*, 3 (1991).

Chapter 6
'The Commerce of the Self' in *Comparative Criticism*, 12 (1990); and 'Rousseau, Adam Smith and the Education of the Self' in *Moy qui me voy; the Writer and the Self from Montaigne to Leiris*, ed. G. Craig and M. McGowan (Oxford, 1989).

Chapter 7
'The Writer as Performer' in *Essays on the Age of Enlightenment in Honor of Ira O. Wade*, ed. J. Macary (Geneva–Paris, 1977).

Chapter 8
'Speakers and Audience: The First Days of the Convention' in *Language and Rhetoric of the Revolution*, ed. J. Renwick (Edinburgh, 1990).

Chapter 9
'Diderot traducteur de l'anglais' in *Colloque international Diderot*, ed. A. M. Chouillet (Paris, 1985); and 'The French Pope' in *Alexander Pope: Essays for the Tercentenary*, ed. C. Nicholson (Aberdeen, 1988).

Chapter 10
'Jacques or his Master? Diderot and the Peasants' in *British Journal for Eighteenth-Century Studies*, 7 (1984).

Chapter 11
'Primitivism and Enlightenment: Rousseau and the Scots' in *Yearbook for English Studies*, 15 (1985).

Chapter 12
'Western European Civilisation and its Mountain Frontiers' in *History of European Ideas*, 6 (1985).

Note
All translations are my own, unless otherwise indicated. Spelling has been modernized throughout.

INTRODUCTION

France of the *ancien régime* has acquired a legendary aura, for better or worse. The 150 years preceding the Revolution were felt by many living at the time (or at least many of the privileged few) to be a summit of European civilization, worthy of being set alongside Pericles's Athens or Augustan Rome. Even today, they exert their ambiguous fascination on nostalgic or not-so-nostalgic observers. They can be seen as a high point of what Norbert Elias called the 'civilizing process',[1] the triumph of politeness. In the eighteenth century, Voltaire and others were elaborating the myth of the 'siècle de Louis le Grand' (as Perrault put it); later, Clive Bell was to cite Voltaire's own society as one of his examples of 'civilization', a period characterized by reason, tolerance and elegant sociability.[2] Less agreeably though, this is the time of what Michel Foucault called 'le grand renfermement', when popular and irrational beliefs were squeezed into the margins, locked away by the onward march of a repressive rationalism.[3] Or else it is the old regime, a hierarchical age when the polite orders controlled and exploited a largely peasant society.

These grand images, like most other historical generalizations, are easily disproved or subverted. Even so, they seem to me a good starting point, for they are linked to problems that continue to beset those who live in 'civilized' Western nations and produce or consume polite culture. Most modern Europeans and North Americans, for all the nostalgia they may feel for a different state, live lives shaped more or less according to the civilized norms of what the philosopher–historians of the Scottish Enlightenment knew as 'commercial society'. And yet, who does not feel in his or her life the pains of politeness? Who has not regretted the taming of the wilderness, or felt repulsion at the way European civilization has conquered the world? Jean-Jacques Rousseau still speaks to many people when he writes of the discontents of socialization:

1

Celui qui dans l'ordre civil veut conserver la primauté des sentiments de la nature ne sait ce qu'il veut. Toujours en contradiction avec lui-même, toujours flottant entre ses penchants et ses devoirs, il ne sera jamais ni homme ni citoyen; il ne sera bon ni pour lui, ni pour les autres. Ce sera un de ces hommes de nos jours, un Français, un Anglais, un bourgeois; ce ne sera rien.[4]

Such were the issues that preoccupied me when I was writing this collection of essays on French literature of the *ancien régime*. I should stress at the outset that the essays were written separately rather than as consecutive chapters in a book. My aim was therefore not to argue a single thesis, but to explore a variety of avenues whose interconnections will, I hope, be sufficiently apparent. To describe the central focus of interest, I use the word politeness in my title, taking it in its broad eighteenth-century sense to mean not only polite manners but something like what we call civilization, in other words an interrelated set of values which together define a certain ideal of modern European society and culture.

Within this general context, a series of familiar oppositions, between polite and rude, tame and wild, urban(e) and rustic, elite and popular, adult and child, reason and unreason, gave an initial impetus to enquiries which often led me to see how these opposites interpenetrate each other, how hierarchies are reversed, how compromises are sought. Polite society, like polite literature, needs and desires its opposite, and finds a place for it. Rousseau brings up his imaginary Emile to live like a savage, but the savage is then brought to live in society. The ideal is often the meeting of garden and wilderness, where the savage and the civilized meet and exchange gifts. In practice, relations between the polished and the rude are not generally so idyllic.

A further, specifically French, myth of opposition is the contrast between a monarchical, religious, magnificent and tragic seventeenth century and a progressive, secular, liberal eighteenth century. First Louis XIV, then the Enlightenment. It has not been uncommon in France for allegiance to a 'century' to be an expression of political choice – seventeenth century (often a rather short seventeenth century) to the right, eighteenth to the left. From the point of view of politeness, however, the continuities between the reign of Louis XIV and those of his successors are more striking than the contrasts. The chapters of this book, while many of them concentrate on a specific moment, were written from the assumption that the institutional division into centuries makes little sense, and that this period of about one hundred and fifty years gains from being seen as a whole. I shall sometimes call it 'classical France' – 'la France classique'.

The starting point is language, that great force for both cohesion and division. My earlier studies of rhetoric focussed on the difficulty of reconciling the demands of truth-telling and sincerity with those of persuasive communication. At the same time, it was evident that the rhetoric of classical literature – and by literature I mean all kinds of writing – was very much a rhetoric of politeness. It allowed a place for the vehemence of passion, but it was ultimately ruled by the urbanity of polite society. In the language of educated men and women of the period, and particularly in the language of their writers, one sees the constant pressure to exclude (or at least control) what could be considered vulgar. Claiming to codify the usage of good society, a Vaugelas or a Bouhours consecrated the hierarchical principle which Hugo later formulated so memorably:

> La langue était l'Etat avant quatre-vingt-neuf;
> Les mots, bien ou mal nés, vivaient parqués en castes.[5]

This meant in practice the exclusion of technical, old-fashioned, provincial or rustic ways of speaking, but also the condemnation of types of writing which were thought of as savage, puerile or excessive.

One such element is hyperbole, or exaggeration, which is the subject of Chapter 1. It is a figure associated with the language of young people, plebeians, barbarians and orientals. It also belongs to 'the lunatic, the lover and the poet'. The question of hyperbole thus raises in miniature the problem of poetry in a polite and reasonable society. Diderot wrote in 1758 that 'la poésie veut quelque chose d'énorme, de barbare et de sauvage',[6] and by this time it was quite common to think that the civilized modern age was an age of prose. Could poetry be for this sensible, discreet culture something more than a peculiarly artful form of polite communication?

Hyperbole is connected with larger questions of reason and unreason, moderation and excess. It seems clear that the strength of French classical writing cannot be accounted for in terms of 'la parfaite raison' which 'fuit toute extrémité / Et veut que l'on soit sage avec sobriété'. Only an impoverished view of many of the writers of the time could fail to see how they deal in extremes of emotion, desire, ambition, pride. Even if the characteristic move is finally to reassert the order of normality, the poem, the play or the novel has for a time allowed the emergence of something excessive or irrational. Chapters 2 and 3 are devoted specifically to the supernatural. Taking two hostile and apparently very different figures, Perrault the *moderne* and Racine the *ancien*, I examine how the stories of the one and the tragedies of the other make room for improbable elements, which might seem out of place in modern civilized society. Perrault's ogres and fairies, Racine's gods and goddesses, relics respectively of a popular and a 'primitive' culture, are admitted on sufferance; hedged about with irony and scepticism, they still carry a charge that can disturb the fragile work of civilization.

If the first three chapters are concerned mainly with the place of excess and unreason in polite culture, the group that follows is more directly concerned with the moral and literary implications of the ideal of polite sociability. Chapter 4 has a central position in the book, since it examines the discourse of politeness. *Honnêteté* and *politesse* – or their English equivalents – were essential values for the educated men and women of seventeenth- and eighteenth-century France and Britain. Round these notions eddied a debate for which *Le Misanthrope* set the terms. The polite person repeats in his or her person the work of civilization, smoothing out roughness, learning to adapt to the expectations of the group, to play a part in the concert of society. The result should be a masterpiece of harmony; it could also be experienced as a betrayal of the self and its values. By the same token, politeness could be seen as an oppressive force, taming the individual, imposing conformity and deference. Was it possible to conceive of politeness in different terms, stressing sincere feeling rather than artifice, equality rather than hierarchy? Rousseau, the inescapable Rousseau, often brings these dilemmas into the sharpest focus.

Sociability presses on writers as on others. Literature at this time is deeply engaged in social intercourse, and some of its characteristic forms, such as the dialogue and the essay, express this dependence. Writers might lay claim to being a new power in the land rather than the entertainers of fashionable society. Yet to exert an influence – and in many cases simply to earn a living – they had to play their part in the world, speaking to polite society in the language it was used to, flattering their patrons or their audiences. This sort of commerce, to use a word which was interestingly ambiguous at the time, could be felt as degrading. In some cases, to a greater or lesser degree, authors were driven to assert their independence by defying the rules of polite communication. Diogenes the Cynic is the figure who sums up most neatly the ideal of rude dignity – Jean-Jacques Rousseau is Diogenes, but so, in *Le Neveu de Rameau*, are both Diderot and his demonic *alter ego*.

It could be said that Diogenes came into his own at the end of the century. The final chapter in Part II extends beyond the end of the *ancien régime* and ventures on to a new scene. In place of the salon or academy, the revolutionary assembly. In place of the old politeness, the pathos of a new world. The real or apparent harmony of sociable living gives way to verbal battles, fights to the death. In this setting, the patterns of older rhetoric are twisted by events into something new and shocking. Excess becomes the order of the day. It is not surprising if the eloquence of the Revolution, while admired by those for whom it marked a fresh start, has been condemned and mocked for its transgression of the norms of polite reason. There is something scandalously extreme about this discourse. Now that the voices have been silent for two hundred years, it is perhaps as hard to know what to make of them as of their hyperbolic contemporary, the Marquis de Sade.

Politeness means learning to accommodate to others within a given social group. The final group of essays here moves outside this harmonious circle to observe polite society confronting the Other, and attempting to find a place for it. One aspect of this is the assimilation of foreign cultures through translation, a practice which always has to wrestle with problems of otherness and identity. Chapter 9 considers the challenge offered by some literary texts written in English. Britain might not seem very far from France, but in their different ways, Shaftesbury, Pope and Ossian-Macpheron posed problems of adaptation. Their strangeness had to be smoothed out.

Chapter 10 is concerned with a different 'other', the common people, those excluded by status, wealth or education from the polite world. Bakhtin argued that in *Pantagruel* and its sequels we see embodied the clash of different cultures and social groups, the learned humanism of the Renaissance against an older popular culture.[7] Both live together, and their dialogue gives life to a great book which contains the polite ideal of Thélème as well as the monstrous vulgarity of Panurge and the giants. In classical France, it seems clear that there was a growing segregation of popular and polite culture. 'Low' literature survived, of course, but it knew its place. The mixed praise of Rabelais that we find in La Bruyère's *Caractères* is typical:

son livre est une énigme, quoi qu'on veuille dire, inexplicable; c'est une chimère, c'est le visage d'une belle femme avec des pieds et une queue de serpent, ou de quelque autre bête plus difforme; c'est un monstrueux assemblage d'une morale fine et ingénieuse et d'une sale corruption. [...] c'est le charme de la canaille.[8]

Voltaire said much the same of Shakespeare. Rare indeed are the works of the classical period in which the popular and the polite coexist on more or less equal terms. *Jacques le fataliste* goes some way towards this, and its author invokes Rabelais as a precursor.

For of course, even if Rabelais was largely eclipsed from polite society for two centuries or more, a certain taste for popular culture survived among the elite – and was nurtured by writers such as Perrault – until the Romantic movement gave a new impetus to the collection of folk poetry, folk tales and the like. So it was also, and increasingly so, with the attraction of cultures that could be described as primitive, the distant noble savages of Tahiti or North America, but also peoples closer to home. For the polite *literati* of Paris or Edinburgh, primitivism could be a form of escapism, but also a source of literary renewal. Dubious as they were, the poems of Ossian set Europe dreaming. But primitivism – if that is the word for it – could also be a part of new anthropological thinking, as in the writings of Rousseau or the Scottish philosopher Adam Ferguson. In such cases, one realizes that enlightenment and primitivism, far from being enemies, can be two faces of the same coin.

The final chapter leaves classical France behind and looks at the confrontation of the polite and the rude over the years between James Boswell's visit to Corsica and Mérimée's novel about that island. The focus here is on the rocky fringes of Europe, which trade, education and military power were subjugating to the civilized cities of the plain – at the same time that the native peoples of North America were succumbing to European colonists. The destruction or taming of their ancient culture is a source of sadness to many whose lives are poles apart from the wild and vengeful mores of the ancient mountain peoples. Politeness needs to preserve the rude and wild ways it destroys – and re-creates them in imaginary forms, from Marie-Antoinette's Hameau to our own wilderness parks.

Such, briefly, is the trajectory followed by these essays. With the exception of Chapter 7, they were all written in the last ten years, mainly for conferences or for publication in various journals and books (as indicated in the acknowledgements). Some have been lightly revised, others have been completely rewritten, and some result from the fusion of previously separate pieces. In putting them together for this volume, I have often made the links between them more apparent, since they seem to me to belong together, but I have not attempted to recast the whole collection as a unified book.

There can therefore be no question here of a complete treatment of the topic of politeness. There are many other related topics to which I might have been led. Almost all the topics discussed here could be studied in other countries and at other periods, and it would be rewarding to explore their manifestations in cultural fields other than writing. I have stayed mainly in the area in which I have some competence, French (and, to a lesser extent, British) literature of the seventeenth and eighteenth centuries. And even here, my choice of topics is inevitably somewhat arbitrary. Within the same general perspective, it would be worth examining such subjects as 'indecent' writing or the Théâtre de la Foire and related popular entertainments, to name only two. Similarly with authors: I consider quite a number of writers here, both well-known and obscure (and several of them reappear in two or three different chapters), but clearly many others could have been chosen. My aim is to raise questions, not to cover the field.

It remains for me to thank the institutions and people who have helped me in the writing of this book. The universities of Sussex and Edinburgh, their librarians, and my colleagues and students, no doubt contributed most. I must also thank Princeton University for a lecturing invitation which brought me to think seriously about many of the issues discussed here, and the various other universities and learned societies which have invited me to lecture or give papers. The National Library of Scotland has provided not only an excellent working environment but examples of politeness in action. A grant from the British Academy allowed me to visit the Soviet Union for research on Chapter 12. And in particular, I am grateful to the Rockefeller Foundation for being able to stay at their Study Centre at Bellagio. The Villa Serbelloni, under the genial guidance of Roberto and Gianna Celli, provided a rare example of a polite world, at the same time a salon, an academy and an Abbaye de Thélème, which helped me greatly in the final stages of this book.

It is always an invidious business to single out individuals for thanks; in any case they might prefer not to be associated with this publication. I owe a great deal to the authors of the books and articles mentioned in the notes, in particular (as far I can judge) to the work of Norbert Elias, Jean Starobinski, Roger Chartier, Jacques Chouillet and Marc Soriano. Nicholas Phillipson helped me a great deal with the Scottish writers who figure quite prominently in these pages, and John Renwick provided friendship, encouragement and a fund of information on various topics. My thanks to them all, and to the many other friends I cannot mention here.

Part I

EXCESS AND UNREASON

1

HYPERBOLE

'Love is infinitely delightful to its object, and the more violent the more glorious. It is infinitely high; nothing can hurt it. And infinitely great in all extremes of beauty and excellency. Excess is its true moderation.'[1] These are the words of the English poet Traherne, writing in the mid seventeenth century about divine love. They are a far cry from the all too famous advice for human life given by Molière's Philinte:

> La parfaite raison fuit toute extrémité
> Et veut que l'on soit sage avec sobriété

or its echo in Bouhours's *Manière de bien penser*: 'Tout ce qui est excessif est vicieux, jusqu'à la vertu, qui cesse d'être vertu dès qu'elle va aux extrémités'.[2]

Philinte and Bouhours may be taken as representatives of classical French culture, a culture of reasonable, sociable men and women, and their remarks can be extended beyond the moral field to encompass art and literature. From around the middle of the century, this culture defines itself against the excesses associated with the Italian-influenced baroque art of the preceding generations. What had seemed impressive comes to seem grotesque. Extravagant behaviour, extravagant feeling, and extravagant language are mocked and outlawed by the classical critics. Excess is the enemy of the new politeness.

At the same time, however, Traherne's praise of excess corresponds to an impulse which is not easily subdued – the impetus that produces not only religion, but art. Thomas Hardy wrote that 'the real, if unavowed, purpose of fiction is to give pleasure by gratifying the love of the uncommon in human experience'.[3] Such a taste for the extraordinary may be scorned as childish or barbaric, but it remains a potent force, even in a civilized age. My aim therefore in these three opening chapters is to explore some of the ways in which extravagance persisted in the literature of Louis XIV's France. Chapters 2 and 3 will be concerned with the childish folly of ogres and giants and the irrational excesses associated with the pagan gods. In this chapter I shall concentrate on what may seem the most childish element, the element most vulnerable to abuse and ridicule, the literary use of exaggeration or hyperbole.

Properly speaking, hyperbole is a figure of speech, a trope. It is often supposed that this trope is uncharacteristic of French classical literature, which is dominated rather by litotes, 'l'art d'exprimer le plus en disant le moins'.[4] And it is not difficult to accumulate quotations from classical French poetics and criticism which express mistrust of linguistic extravagance and recommend an unobtrusive form of literary language. In this, the critics were echoing the maxims of civilized politeness. The *honnête homme* is 'celui qui ne se pique de rien'; he fits into society, shines in society even, but without going in for vulgar excess. However, such proclamations only reveal the prevalence of the 'vice' they warn against. It is misleading to say that hyperbole had little part to play in classical French literature.

To most people today, the very word is probably pejorative, and the rhetoric books of classical France were certainly reticent about this figure. A snobbish distaste for it is seen in Nicole's dictum in his short treatise on the epigram: 'Cette figure est la ressource des petits esprits qui écrivent pour le bas peuple'.[5] For many it was indeed a suspect figure; beloved of rustics, young people, savages and Asiatics, it was diametrically opposed to the good taste of civilized adults in a polite society. They were supposed to prefer restraint and sobriety. It did, however, have its defenders.

Quintilian defines hyperbole as 'an elegant straining of the truth' ('decens veri superiectio'), which can consist either in saying more than is literally true, or in exaggerating through comparison and metaphor. He makes the expected proviso: 'Although every hyperbole involves the incredible, it must not go too far in this direction, which provides the easiest road to extravagant affectation'. Otherwise, however, hyperbole is welcomed; it is 'a virtue, when the subject on which we have to speak is abnormal. For we are allowed to amplify, when the magnitude of the facts passes all words, and in such circumstances our language will be more effective if it goes beyond the truth than if it falls short of it.'[6] This is a good account of one of the basic functions of hyperbole;[7] the other one, mentioned by many theoreticians, is that it is the natural way of expressing and communicating strong feeling. And indeed, if one reflects a little, one realizes that hyperbole is one of the most indispensable figures of speech. To deny it would be to deny rhetoric – and to deny rhetoric (if this were possible) would be to impoverish communication intolerably.

To some rhetoricians, hyperbole seemed particularly appropriate to poetry. Thus Bernard Lamy, who makes the important link between this figure and that most poetic of tropes, metaphor:

Les poètes veulent plaire, et surprendre par des choses extraordinaires et merveilleuses: ils ne peuvent arriver à ce but qu'ils se proposent, s'ils ne soutiennent la grandeur des choses par la grandeur des paroles. Tout ce qu'ils disent étant extraordinaire, les expressions qui doivent égaler la dignité de la matière doivent être extraordinaires et éloignées des expressions communes. Les hyperboles et les métaphores sont absolument nécessaires dans la poésie, l'usage ne fournissant point de termes assez forts.[8]

Boileau too, though he might create for himself the image of the plain speaker, knew – and was confirmed in his knowledge by Longinus[9] – that hyperbole is essential in what he called the 'sublime'. He was conscious of the perils of grandiloquence and rarely ventured into hyperbole without putting up a guard of irony, but in theory at least he maintained the value of high poetic language against his opponents in the camp of the Moderns.[10] In his tenth *Epître*, he writes of the belittling criticism the true poet will have to meet:

> Et bientôt vous verrez mille auteurs pointilleux
> Pièce à pièce épluchant vos sons, et vos paroles,
> Interdire chez vous l'entrée aux hyperboles ...[11]

In the face of such opposition, hyperbole becomes almost the mark of a noble spirit.

Bouhours is particularly interesting on this subject. He is of his age in rejecting what is felt as the extravagance of former times, especially when it is also the extravagance of other nations. Exaggeration is the characteristic vice of the Spanish language; as against this and Italian 'puerility', French is the language of unaffected adult discourse. Perhaps, as Charles V is reputed to have said, Spanish is the language for talking to God; Bouhours retorts: 'Accordons à l'Empereur [...] que leur langage est le langage des dieux [...] le nôtre est le langage des hommes raisonnables'.[12]

This remark comes from Bouhours's *Entretiens d'Ariste et d'Eugène*; his later work, *La Manière de bien penser dans les ouvrages d'esprit*, is a more extended discussion of what the English would have called true and false wit. The book is a dialogue between Philanthe (Mr Loveflower) and Eudoxe (Mr Goodsense). Eudoxe is more or less the author's mouthpiece, and he finally convinces his interlocutor that the kinds of wit the latter admires are really false diamonds, all flitter and no solidity. The first part of the third dialogue is devoted to the vice of 'excès de grandeur'. Eudoxe's typical move is to say that a given expression may seem striking at first, but that when you look more closely you see that it has no firm basis in truth. A good example is Brébeuf's translation of a passage where Lucan writes that Pompey

> Ou n'a point de sépulcre, ou gît dans l'univers:
> Tout ce qu'a mis son bras sous le pouvoir de Rome
> Est à peine un cercueil digne d'un si grand homme.

Bouhours comments: 'Ces pensées ont un éclat qui frappe d'abord et semblent même convaincantes à la première vue, car c'est quelque chose de plus noble en apparence d'être couvert du ciel que d'un marbre, et d'avoir le monde entier pour tombeau, qu'un petit espace de terre; mais ce n'est au fonds qu'une noblesse chimérique'.

Since excess is never worthy of praise, 'les pensées qui roulent sur l'hyperbole sont toutes fausses d'elles-mêmes, et ne méritent pas d'avoir place dans un ouvrage raisonnable'. However, Bouhours immediately qualifies this: 'à moins que l'hyperbole ne soit d'une espèce particulière, ou qu'on y mette des adoucissements qui en tempèrent l'excès' (pp. 30–1). The first of these categories is like the lexicalized metaphor; there is nothing shocking about such familiar expressions as 'c'est la vertu même' or even 'il va plus vite que le vent'. But as soon as the hyperbole becomes noticeable it must be toned down, either by some qualification such as 'si j'ose parler ainsi' or, better still, by an ironical tone which makes it plain that it is to be taken as a figure. Thus the Italian Tesauro's qualifying 'par che' ('it seems that') is not enough when he writes of a firework show: 'Par che sagliano ad infiammar la sfera del fuoco, a fulminare i fulmini ed a gridar allarme contra le stelle'. He should have put his tongue more obviously in his cheek: 'S'il badinait comme Voiture, on lui passerait ses pensées toutes hardies, toutes fausses qu'elles sont' (p. 39). The urbane Voiture is Bouhours's ideal.

Nevertheless, for all their timidity, these are ways of letting hyperbole through the mesh of rational criticism. Bouhours is aware that it is sometimes needed, and quotes Quintilian to that effect. When the subject is grand enough, 'l'hyperbole la plus hardie est une perfection du discours' (p. 357). Although the book tries to trace the limits beyond which hyperbole seems excessive, the sensible Eudoxe is not always censorious. He declares that 'outre la solidité, on veut de la grandeur, de l'agrément, et même de la délicatesse'. 'Le vrai' is not enough; one also needs 'quelque chose d'extraordinaire qui frappe l'esprit' (p. 105). Moreover, the very use of dialogue allows Bouhours to express a love for the showy. His Philanthe can be thought of as the representative of youthful taste, since love of verbal extravagance was thought of as the prerogative of the young,[13] a childish toy to be put away by those who aspire to be serious adults. The book is a paradoxical show-case of false diamonds, which glitter briefly before being exposed for what they are.

What is more, many of the diamonds, which might seem false to a modern taste, turn out to be solid after all. This is particularly noticeable when Bouhours is discussing ways of praising great men, above all the King. The place of eulogy in seventeenth-century French writing is perhaps not sufficiently recognized today. It belonged to epideictic (or demonstrative) rhetoric, which was the subject of endless schoolroom exercises and occupied a great deal of space in adult poetry, prose and public speaking. In harangues of all kinds, in funeral orations, in history, in court poetry, in much religious poetry and love poetry, indeed in many of the long speeches of tragedy, there is the same urge to praise and amplify. Among the set objects of praise, the monarch occupied a privileged place.

The problems of flattery were familiar to Bouhours and his contemporaries. As he says, 'c'est un grand art que de savoir bien louer' (p. 266). This was a generation of writers who liked to think of themselves as returning to good sense after the excesses of the previous generations, but their society revolved around a king who had to be virtually deified, and who probably did produce in many of his subjects the dazzlement of the *merveilleux*.[14] In writing about Louis, if anywhere, hyperbole was surely in order. But how could this be reconciled with the demands of truth? In *La Manière de bien penser*, several interesting pages are devoted to this problem; they show their author treading a tricky path just this side of excess.

The tone is set by Eudoxe in the second dialogue, in a discussion of the 'grandeur' which is one of the characteristics of a 'pensée ingénieuse': 'Mais c'est sur le Prince qui nous gouverne [...] que nos meilleurs écrivains ont pensé peut-être le plus noblement, comme si la hauteur du sujet avait élevé leur génie' (p. 145). This 'hauteur' is such that the panegyrist is freed from the bonds of moderation. Bouhours cites a series of 'pensées' about the King, of which the following may serve as an example:

> Ton esprit que rien ne limite
> Fait honneur à la royauté;
> Et l'on ne voit que ton mérite
> Au-dessus de ta dignité.   (p. 146)

This is a 'pensée également juste et sublime', and Bouhours does not remark on the hyperbole of the first line.

Later in his book, he returns to this question when he discusses the vice of 'enflure'. Many examples are given of extravagant eulogies that go beyond the limits of acceptability. One of the worst offenders is the Spaniard Gracián, whose praise of Alexander contains those words already mocked in the *Entretiens d'Ariste et d'Eugène*: 'Grande fue el de Alexandro y el archicoraçon, pues cupo en un rincon del todo este mundo holgadamente, dexando lugar para otro seis'. Eudoxe's comment is: 'Avez-vous rien vu de plus recherché et de plus enflé!' Philanthe attempts a defence: although the 'pensée' is 'un peu hardie' and 'un peu fanfaronne', it describes well 'un grand cœur que le monde entier ne pouvait remplir'. But Eudoxe takes no pleasure in Gracián's exuberance and puts it down firmly: 'Croyez-moi, cela est énorme, et ne sied point bien' (p. 328).

It is usually Spaniards or Italians who are condemned in this way. Bouhours is ingenious in defending French authors who have praised Louis XIV. The idea that 'notre sage monarque [...]dit en ses réponses plus de choses que de paroles' is defended (not unreasonably) on the grounds that 'd'une parole on peut faire entendre plus d'une chose' (p. 251). The apparently paradoxical hyperbole is thus resolved into a sound thought, and this perception of truth in falsity is a potent source of pleasure, akin to the pleasures of metaphor and allegory as Bouhours understands them.

A slightly trickier case is provided by four lines on the crossing of the Rhine in 1672 (that great source of panegyric), which might remind British readers of the story of King Canute:

> De tant de coups affreux la tempête orageuse
> Tient un temps sur les eaux la fortune douteuse;
> Mais LOUIS d'un regard sait bientôt la fixer;
> Le destin à ses yeux n'oserait balancer.

To Philanthe these lines are quite as 'hardis' as those of an Italian poet who has just been censured, but Eudoxe protests: 'Ils ne sont point fanfarons; ils ne sont que forts, et ils ont une vraie noblesse qui les autorise'. His argument is that the poet is not claiming that 'les destins en général dépendent du Roi', but only the 'destin de la guerre'. He goes on:

Comme le système de sa pensée est tout poétique, il a droit de mettre la Fortune en jeu; et comme la présence d'un Prince aussi magnanime que le nôtre rend les soldats invincibles, il a pu dire poétiquement:

16

Hyperbole

Mais LOUIS d'un regard sait bientôt la fixer;
Le destin à ses yeux n'oserait balancer.

C'est comme s'il disait: Dès que LOUIS paraît, on est assuré de la victoire. Y a-t-il quelque chose d'outré, et toute l'Europe n'a-t-elle pas été témoin d'une vérité si surprenante? (pp. 368–70)

Of course Bouhours, like his poet, is doing his bit of flattery here (notice his hyperbolic 'invincibles'), but the essential point for our purposes is that, while doing his best to meet the demands of truthfulness, he is well aware of the value of exaggeration. Perhaps excessive moderation is a vice too.

Praising great men was one important field in which hyperbole kept its place in the age of reasonable politeness. Another was religious writing, since here, in Traherne's words, to the believer 'excess is [...] true moderation'. And a third area, which accounts for a large part of what we now call literature, was the poetry and prose of love. Hyperbole is justified here not so much because the object of speech is (as they say) beyond praise, but because extravagant language seems the natural expression of strong emotion. Bacon writes in his essay 'Of Love' that 'the speaking in perpetual hyperbole is comely in nothing but love',[15] and in Renaissance love poetry there is a powerful tradition of exaggeration ('en sa beauté gît ma mort et ma vie') and a down-to-earth counter-tradition ('My mistress' eyes are nothing like the sun'), which may in turn serve as a springboard for new flights of eloquence.

A great deal of classical French literature is devoted to excessive love. 'A quel excès d'amour m'avez-vous amenée?', cries the distraught Bérénice, and her cry is taken up and repeated a hundred times in the *Lettres portugaises*.[16] This short and successful work is almost entirely made up of a recital of mad, hopeless love, expressed throughout in vehement language which is often that of hyperbole. It may be an unusual production, but its popularity demonstrates the continuing appeal of excess to seventeenth-century readers.

In love letters such as those of the supposed nun, it is difficult to isolate particular examples of hyperbole, since the whole context is one of extravagant passion. This is clear from the very first sentence: 'Considère, mon amour, jusqu'à quel excès tu as manqué de prévoyance' – the word 'excès' will recur like a leitmotif in each of the five letters. A few lines further on, there is what is unmistakably a 'straining of the truth': 'Hélas! les miens [eyes] sont privés de la seule lumière qui les animait, il ne leur reste que des larmes, et je ne les ai

17

employés à aucun usage qu'à pleurer sans cesse' (p. 39). Even before this, there is an inverted hyperbole (of a sort easily matched in eulogies of Louis XIV by Boileau and others) whereby the speaker proclaims that his subject beggars all description: 'cette absence, à laquelle ma douleur, toute ingénieuse qu'elle est, ne peut donner un nom assez funeste' (p. 39). The words 'toute ingénieuse qu'elle est' suggest the relationship between this passionate writing and the essential movement of epideictic eloquence; one could compare it with similar turns of phrase in a very different piece of writing, a 'lettre pointue' of Cyrano de Bergerac: 'Mais que dirai-je de ce miroir fluide [...] et puis, quelle autre chose pourrais-je ajouter à la description de cette image enluminée [...]?'[17] In both cases it is a question of finding the most striking formulation possible.

So even if it is difficult to say that this or that expression in the *Lettres portugaises* is hyperbolic, the writing works constantly to magnify the experience of unhappy love. This is evident in the concentration of words and phrases which are at the border of hyperbole: 'excès', 'insupportable', 'aveuglement', 'insensé', 'fureur', 'violence', 'tyranniser', 'accabler', 'déchirer', and constant references to death. Then there are the declarations of extravagant feeling: 'Je vous ai destiné ma vie aussitôt que je vous ai vu'; 'je me flattais de sentir que je mourais d'amour'; 'je suis résolue à vous adorer toute me vie', 'je suis jalouse avec fureur de tout ce qui vous donne de la joie'. Such extreme emotion is preferred to everything else: 'Pourriez-vous être content d'une passion moins ardente que la mienne? Vous trouverez peut-être plus de beauté [...] mais vous ne trouverez jamais tant d'amour, et tout le reste n'est rien' (p. 41). 'Tout le reste n'est rien' – the world well lost. Throughout the letters, the reader is struck by the lack of 'mesure' of which the nun speaks: 'j'irais, sans garder aucune mesure, vous chercher, vous suivre, et vous aimer par tout le monde' (*ibid.*).

It is true that the five letters are shaped like the five acts of a tragedy, and the work is shaped to lead to a final movement of repentance and apparent detachment:

J'ai vécu longtemps dans un abandonnement et dans une idolâtrie qui me donne de l'horreur, et mon remords me persécute avec une rigueur insupportable, je sens vivement la honte des crimes que vous m'avez fait commettre.   (p. 67)

This might seem like a renunciation of excess, but here too the language shows the same vehemence, and the very last sentence of the *Lettres* contains the revealing words: 'je suis une folle de redire les mêmes choses si souvent'. The interest of the work lies precisely in this obsessive repetition which exceeds all measure. Indeed the excess is visible not only in the sentiments and the vocabulary, but in the rhetoric and the rhythm of the letters, the accumulation of questions and exclamations, the endless repetition of 'je', the piling of clause on clause in what elsewhere would be regarded as ill-formed sentences:

Quoi! cette absence, à laquelle ma douleur, toute ingénieuse qu'elle est, ne peut donner un nom assez funeste, me privera donc pour toujours de regarder ces yeux dans lesquels je voyais tant d'amour, et qui me faisaient connaître des mouvements qui me comblaient de joie, qui me tenaient lieu de toutes choses, et qui enfin me suffisaient? (p. 39)

Such writing shocked the taste of at least one contemporary. Gabriel Guéret, in his *Promenade de Saint-Cloud*, published in the same year as the letters, has one of his interlocutors observe: 'D'ailleurs, il n'y a même pas de style; la plupart des périodes y sont sans mesure; et ce que j'y trouve de plus ennuyeux, ce sont les continuelles répétitions, qui rebattent ce qui méritait à peine d'être dit une seule fois' (*Lettres*, p. xiii).

If, as seems probable, the *Lettres* were not the work of a nun, but of Guilleragues, then we must take this hyperbolic style, with all its excesses, to be a successful imitation of the language of emotion – successful, that is, in that it convinced innumerable readers of its authenticity. It is all the more remarkable to think of this book as the creation of the man whom Boileau addressed as an 'esprit né pour la cour et maître en l'art de plaire', the ambassador who wrote the elegant *Valentins*. No doubt the civilized Guilleragues found some obscure satisfaction in imagining himself in the skin of an unbalanced Portuguese nun – Portuguese because the inhabitants of the Iberian peninsula are given to an extravagance which French good sense repudiates, and a nun, no doubt, because the combination of female passion (as it seemed to a man) and unnatural segregation produces a violence that appealed to readers who went to fiction for the extreme rather than the normal.

From Guilleragues to Racine is a short step. If there is a writer who has been taken for a model of measured good taste, it is the author of *Bajazet* and *Phèdre*. Such is the implication, for instance, of Leo Spitzer's presentation of his 'classical soft pedal': Racine belongs to a civilization of restraint, and shows a constant effort to attenuate the direct (and no doubt impolite) expression of passion.[18] Such a muted Racine is naturally opposed to earlier, more extravagant dramatists such as Alexandre Hardy or the playwrights of Jacobean England.

It is clear, however that this sober tragedy is founded on excess and unreason.[19] Tragedy must go beyond the ordinary; why do we attend such performances, if not to satisfy the desire for the great, the exceptional, the excessive? At bottom, Racinian tragedy is entirely hyperbolic; it is a world of grandiose, often monstrous figures, whose misery, wickedness, heroism or love remain exemplary in spite of all the weaknesses their creator heaped on them. He begins with 'le sujet le plus tragique de l'antiquité' (*La Thébaïde*), and goes on to represent the opposite extremes of humanity – the god–king Alexander and the diabolical Nero. At the end of his career, having depicted a whole gallery of excessive passions, Racine will devote two plays to the God of the Jews, whose greatness is beyond all hyperbole. Nothing could be less down-to-earth than these plays, which have often been acclaimed for their discreet reason. How then are the conflicting demands of moderation and excess reconciled? What can be the place of extravagance in these plays for reasonable people? And in particular, what is the part played in Racine's dialogues by the language of excess, by hyperbole? Is it as absent from them as has sometimes been suggested?

It must be admitted straight away that at a distance of two centuries it is not always easy to know what one can properly call hyperbole, what would have seemed exaggerated to Racine's contemporaries. For one thing, as we saw earlier, hyperbole is closely associated with metaphor. Very often Racine's metaphors introduce an element of exaggeration, expressing in an extreme form emotions of fear, pain or joy. Here are a few examples from Act IV of *Bérénice*:

La force m'abandonne, et le repos me tue	(IV, i, 956)
Je viens percer un cœur que j'adore, qui m'aime	(IV, iv, 999)
Vois-je l'Etat penchant au bord du précipice?	(IV, iv, 1003)

In such cases, as in Hippolyte's 'le jour n'est pas plus pur que le fond de mon cœur', it is harder to say: 'This is hyperbole' than in such simple examples as 'D'un seul de ses regards il peut vaincre Alexandre', where the figure is more obvious, and more open to ridicule. (In this case it is in fact used mockingly.) Other types of hyperbole, more familiar and thus less vulnerable, include the conventional use of numbers such as 'cent' or 'mille', the recourse to superlatives and absolute expressions such as 'tout', 'jamais', 'toujours', 'seul', or the typically Racinian allusions to 'les yeux de l'univers', that 'plus noble théâtre' which Titus sets before himself. And in general, it must be said that while the whole basis of Racine's theatre is hyperbolic, one does not frequently perceive particular expressions as 'going too far'. Rhetoricians advised orators to keep hyperbole for the high points in their speeches. To be effective, it must not be too frequent.

Broadly speaking, the functions of hyperbole are twofold, dramatic and poetic. By the former, I mean the use of this figure as a part of a character's rhetorical arsenal, or as an indicator of his or her feelings or nature. Irony is the clearest case of the tactical use of hyperbole. Guez de Balzac, in his *Apologie pour Monsieur de Balzac* (published under the name of Ogier), had followed Quintilian in allowing that hyperbole, far from being a sign of bad taste, can be a kind of elegant raillery.[20] Racine's characters are not usually as urbane as this implies, but they certainly use hyperbole aggressively to ridicule the pretensions of adversaries. In this way Cléofile mocks Axiane and Porus in order to persuade Taxile:

> Quelque brave qu'on soit, si nous la voulons croire,
> Ce n'est qu'autour de lui que vole la Victoire;
> Vous formeriez sans lui d'inutiles desseins,
> La liberté de l'Inde est toute entre ses mains;
> Sans lui déjà nos murs seraient réduits en cendre,
> D'un seul de ses regards il peut vaincre Alexandre.[21]
>
> (*Alexandre*, I, i, 85–90)

The persuasive use of the figure is more often non-ironical, however, and is a kind of flattery. To spur their masters on to some act of will, Phoenix (in *Andromaque*) and Paulin (in *Bérénice*) set before them exaggerated images of their grandeur, past, present or to come. In the same way, the eloquent Ulysse paints for Agamemnon the glorious image of a victory that will be 'l'éternel entretien des siècles à venir' – which is perhaps accurate seen from our place in time, but which in context must be seen as hyperbole.

Not that the persuasive use of hyperbole is necessarily flattery. One may also exaggerate in order to underline the gravity of a situation, and thus convince one's interlocutor. To quote just one example from hundreds, Monime wants to escape Pharnace's attentions and speaks to Xipharès of a marriage 'pour moi plus cruel que la mort'. This can be accepted as an accurate expression of her feelings. Soon, however, her language grows stronger:

Jamais hymen formé sous le plus noir auspice
De l'hymen que je crains n'égala le supplice.

(*Mithridate*, I, ii, 155—6)

The hyperbole here is meant to sway Xipharès. It also signifies her own heightened feeling of horror and fear — and this brings us to the other main dramatic use of the figure, for the expression of emotion or character.

If hyperbole, as the theorists claimed, is the normal product of strong feeling, it is only to be expected that in the passionate world of Racine's tragedies it will be constantly coming to the surface. (I say 'coming to the surface', since it is generally discreet in its manifestations, though still perceptible to those who listen attentively.) *Bajazet*, a play set in an oriental land of hyperbole, far from the measured politeness of the Paris salons, provides a good example.

In Act I, Scene 4, Atalide has just learned of Roxane's fatal decision ('Bajazet doit périr, dit-elle, ou l'épouser'). Alone with her confidante, she is free to give vent to her feelings, her 'malheur extrême'. We are in the realm of excess. The language continually verges on the hyperbolic, without one's being able to say that it 'strains the truth' (but what is this truth?). Atalide's first words are those of absolute despair: 'Zaïre, c'en est fait, Atalide est perdue' (I am not convinced that the use of the third person here acts as a Spitzerian soft pedal). The impression is reinforced two lines later with the paradoxical 'Mon unique espérance est dans mon désespoir'. In the scene that ensues, the words 'tout', 'jamais' and 'toujours' all underline the extremity of the situation. Thus Atalide speaks of the illusory happiness she has lost in these lines:

Tout semblait avec nous être d'intelligence:
Roxane, se livrant tout entière à ma foi,
Du cœur de Bajazet se reposait sur moi,
M'abandonnait le soin de tout ce qui le touche... (I, iv, 346—9)

A little later, contrasting her situation with that of Roxane, she repeats the words 'tout' and 'toujours', which join with the hyperbolic metaphor 'accabler' and the conventional exaggeration 'mille' to create a powerful image of suffering:

Ma rivale, accablant mon amant de bienfaits,
Opposait un empire à mes faibles attraits;
Mille soins la rendaient présente à sa mémoire;
Elle l'entretenait de sa prochaine gloire;
Et moi, je ne peux rien. Mon cœur, pour tous discours,
N'avait que des soupirs, qu'il répétait toujours. (I, iv, 379—84)

Hyperbole

Here as elsewhere, strong simple statements combine with a tendency to superlative and hyperbole to create an impression of powerful emotion. The verbal 'violence' of which Racine's characters so often speak reveals the 'violence des passions' referred to in the preface to *Bérénice*. Anger in particular is conveyed in vehement outbursts where hyperbolic metaphors abound – as when Thésée's 'voix redoutable' hurls insults at his son:

> Monstre, qu'a trop longtemps épargné le tonnerre,
> Reste impur des brigands dont j'ai purgé la terre
> (*Phèdre*, IV, ii, 1045–6)

Madness is the extreme case. There is no King Lear in Racine, but sometimes, usually at the end of a tragedy, a hero or heroine succumbs to a fit of 'fureur' which authorizes a riot of verbal extravagance. Oreste, in his frenzy, returns to the hyperbolic image of cannibalism which Hermione had mocked in Act II. Apart from Créon in *La Thébaïde*, the other tragic heroes and heroines stop short of Oreste's real madness, but many of them lose all sense of proportion (an expression that sounds grotesquely out of place in this world). Phèdre, for instance, in her horror of the passion that is destroying her, speaks in her vision of hell of 'des crimes peut-être inconnus aux enfers'. The hyperbole (although attenuated by a reasonable 'perhaps') suggests the violence of the heroine's remorse – but it also communicates to the spectator a kind of sacred horror to which a more modest use of language would be inadequate.

It is here that we come to what I call the 'poetic' function (the term is to be taken in a totally un-Jakobsonian sense). Whatever its dramatic usefulness (for the creation of character), it also serves to lift the tragedy to a higher plane. One may recall the statement of Abbé d'Aubignac that hyperbole is 'convenable au théâtre, où toutes les choses doivent devenir plus grandes'.[22] Racine's heroes and heroines may often seem pathetic creatures, incapable of reaching the heights of the heroic models they set before themselves, but what he called the 'tristesse majestueuse' of tragedy demands that we feel the exceptional nature of their fate. Seen in this light, the superlatives, whether of greatness or misery, help to build up exemplary images. This is particularly visible at the end of certain tragedies. Créon takes his place with Etéocle, Polynice, Jocaste and Antigone in the black legend of the house of Laius, Oreste becomes the 'tristis Orestes' of legend and Néron the absolute monster of history.

The 'sublime' ambitions of tragedy are of course vulnerable to parody. *Alexandre le grand* is an interestingly ambiguous case.

For Racine's contemporaries, the emperor was both the essence of heroism (see the dedication of the play to Louis XIV) and a destructive maniac.[23] At a distance of three centuries, it is not easy to tell how the public of 1665 may have responded to the grand image of Alexander presented by the playwright. Ideal heroism or empty bombast? We saw how Cléofile and Taxile mock the heroic pretensions of Porus, whose own noble stature is meant to elevate that of Alexandre. They are weak figures of course, and moreover they are mightily impressed by the glory of the conqueror. It is to Taxile that Racine gives the speech of praise (III, iii, 810–22), which is evidently meant for Louis. Cléofile, for her part, opens the play with the gigantic image which is going to dominate all that follows:

> Quoi! vous allez combattre un roi dont la puissance
> Semble forcer le ciel à prendre sa défense,
> Sous qui toute l'Asie a vu tomber ses rois,
> Et qui tient la fortune attachée à ses lois? (I, i, 1–4)

(Compare the panegyric verses from Bouhours's *Manière de bien penser* quoted earlier.) Nevertheless, Cléofile's scepticism about Porus may affect Alexandre too, suggesting the hollowness of the exploits of a hero who sometimes talks like a Matamore:

> J'irai rendre fameux par l'éclat de la guerre
> Des peuples inconnus au reste de la terre ... (III, vi, 909–10)

In the last act, the sad words of Cléofile cast a shade on the grandeur of her lover. Against Alexandre's hyperboles she sets her own, conjuring up a world of nightmarish grandeur to dwarf the deeds of the conqueror of the world:

> Qu'espérez-vous combattre en des climats si rudes?
> Ils vous opposeront de vastes solitudes,
> Des déserts que le ciel refuse d'éclairer,
> Où la nature semble elle-même expirer. (V, i, 1329–32)

Alexandre is not to be deflected from his purpose, and the tragedy ends in his triumph. But seeds of doubt have been sown, and we may well remember these words as we listen to those other figures of power, Pyrrhus, the conqueror of Troy, Mithridate, 'ce roi qui seul a durant quarante ans / Lassé tout ce que Rome eut de chefs importants', Agamemnon, King of Kings, Thésée, 'l'ami, le compagnon, le successeur d'Alcide'.

Heroic hyperbole is vulnerable to irony; so too is the hyperbole of love. For the sad Oreste, the cruelty of the Scythians ('des peuples cruels / Qui n'apaisaient leurs dieux que du sang des mortels') is not so harsh as Hermione's:

> Madame, c'est à vous de prendre une victime
> Que les Scythes auraient dérobée à vos coups,
> Si j'en avais trouvé d'aussi cruels que vous.
>
> (*Andromaque*, II, ii, 502–4)

Such a hyperbolic comparison brings a sharp answer:

> Quittez, Seigneur, quittez ce funeste langage ...
> Que parlez-vous du Scythe et de mes cruautés?

Pyrrhus, too, draws an extravagant parallel between the cruelty of war and of love ('Je souffre tous les maux que j'ai faits devant Troie') – an absurd and monstrous comparison in the eyes of his captive.

Nevertheless, even if Racine regularly undermines his own heroes, I do not think that his tragedies are ultimately anti-hyperbolic. One can see this even in the apparently quiet *Bérénice*. Here, in the final scene, the queen rejects the extravagantly funereal language of the two heroes, Titus and Antiochus. One might say that she gives them a lesson in polite discretion:

> Je vivrai, je suivrai vos ordres absolus.
> Adieu, Seigneur, régnez: je ne vous verrai plus.
>
> (V, vii, 1493–4)

But this is not all. She too, before her final exit into nothingness, places herself in the world of superlatives, posing with her two companions before that 'univers' which is the indispensable spectactor of great tragic events:

> Adieu. Servons tous trois d'exemple à l'univers
> De l'amour la plus tendre et la plus malheureuse
> Dont il puisse garder l'histoire douloureuse.

Do we call this hyperbole? It is not absurd like the ravings of a Matamore, but the claim to unique and superlative status goes beyond plain truth into the realm of panegyric.

In making these remarks, I have no intention of replacing the excessively discreet Racine of a certain tradition – by now a rather antiquated tradition, it must be admitted – with a wild Racine. He is no Marlowe, nor does he fall into that kind of absurdity which tends to lie in wait for extravagant authors. The verbal hyperbole in his tragedies is for the most part motivated by a psychology of verisimilitude. It may convey vanity, flattery, irony, the desire to persuade, or else the whole range of violent passions. Such exaggeration belongs to the characters rather than the author. But in a theatre that excludes all that is prosaic, a theatre where everything turns on great interests and great passions, hyperbole belongs to the author too, and it marks a certain emancipation from the enclosing discourse of 'la parfaite raison'. It may be condemned as childish, oriental or primitive by the urbane, polite discourse of classicism — but then tragedy is not polite.

2

OGRES

Heroes may be regarded as hyperbolic; so, even more obviously, are giants and ogres. It is not possible to tell how widely or completely anyone in seventeenth-century France believed in the existence, past or present, of such monstrous beings. Travellers' descriptions of the inhabitants of distant lands may have encouraged such beliefs, and there were plenty of respected written records of giants of former days. Alongside the long-lived patriarchs, the Old Testament told of 'large-limbed Og' (in Milton's phrase) and of the great Goliath, 'whose height was six cubits and a span'. More monstrous was Homer's Cyclops, and it is worth having a look at the lines devoted to him by Bouhours in *La Manière de bien penser*.

The passage concerns not so much the probability of the existence of such a being as the way Homer leads the listener or reader to accept it. Bouhours is highly critical of a really extravagant writer 'qui en parlant de la roche que le Cyclope lança contre le navire d'Ulysse, disait que les chèvres y paissaient' (p. 359). This strains credulity. By contrast Homer makes it relatively easy for us to go along with his improbable fiction:

Il ne dit pas tout d'un coup que Polyphème arracha le sommet d'une montagne: cela aurait paru peu digne de foi. Il dispose le lecteur par la description du Cyclope qu'il dépeint d'une taille énorme, et auquel il donne des forces égales à sa taille, en lui faisant porter le tronc d'un grand arbre pour massue et fermer l'entrée de sa caverne avec une grosse roche [...] et enfin il ajoute que Neptune était son père. Après toutes ces préparations, quand le poète vient à dire que Polyphème arracha le sommet d'une montagne, on ne trouve point son action trop étrange. Rien n'est, ce semble, impossible à un homme qui est fils du Dieu de la mer, et qui n'est pas fait comme les hommes ordinaires. (pp. 32–3)

Presumably Bouhours did not believe in the literal existence of Polyphemus. Neither, one imagines, did Turner, when he painted Ulysses deriding Polyphemus and wreathed the gigantic figure of the Cyclops in mists which both aggrandize him and attenuate the straightforward image that we find in the *Odyssey*.[1] Bouhours knew, as Racine did, that 'les ornements de la Fable [...] ajoutent extrêmement à la poésie'. The giant is one figure from that land of the *merveilleux* which was mocked by rationalists, but which continued to cast its spell over a society where opera and fairy-tale, metamorphosis and apotheosis had their place alongside (and intertwined with) rational adult literature.[2]

Literal belief in giants, in the late seventeenth century as today, was probably left to children, but also perhaps to the mass of the people, particularly the peasants, who are so often assimilated to children or savages in the writings of the polite classes. Whatever people actually believed, the stories of Gargantua, taken from Rabelais or the original *Croniques*, continued to be published in the mass-consumption pedlar's literature of the Bibliothèque Bleue, together with stories from the Charlemagne cycle, where pagan giants such as Fierabras, the modern equivalent of Goliath, defied the crusading armies.[3] Probably more important was the oral tradition, including the popular stories which were to make with Charles Perrault their decisive move into children's literature. It is on Perrault and his ogres that I wish to concentrate in this chapter, since they provide a good insight into the polite use of popular culture.[4]

When Charles Perrault began to concern himself with folk tales, he was principally known as the champion of the *modernes* in the *Querelle des Anciens et des Modernes* which had begun in 1687 with the reading of his poem 'Le Siècle de Louis le Grand'.[5] Much earlier, before he clashed with Boileau and the *anciens*, he had dabbled in the burlesque, which can be seen as a disrespectful expression of impatience with the place given to classical antiquity in the culture and education of the time. Later, as well as working for the greater glory of the King and Colbert, he was to develop a more thoroughgoing critique of ancient values in the name of a modernity which was Christian, rational and polite. His own non-burlesque writings, including odes, religious epic, verse epistles, *précieux* lyrics and academic writings, all tend in this direction. In particular, the quarrel with Boileau led him to develop at great length the comparison between ancient culture and literature and the achievements of the century of Louis XIV. What is especially interesting for our present purposes is his critique of Greek literature in the *Parallèle des anciens et des modernes*.

In Perrault's eyes, ancient Greek literature is primitive. For all their genius, the ancient poets were bound to express the culture of their time, and this culture strikes a modern French person as vulgar and childish. The attack is mounted on several fronts. There is the question of pagan religious beliefs, the 'amas de chimères, de rêveries et d'absurdités' which Fontenelle denounced at about the same time in his *De l'origine des fables*.[6] In addition, Perrault stresses the immorality of Greek mythology. Then there is the accusation of 'bassesse' or vulgarity. Seen from the standpoint of the polite society of 1688, the world of Greek literature, and particularly of Homer, is distastefully crude, a world of barbarians.[7] It may be nature, but it is 'une vilaine nature qui ne doit point être exprimée' (I, Preface). The behaviour of Homeric heroes and gods is what Perrault's contemporaries associated with peasants: 'les paysans seraient bien aises de savoir ce passage, et de voir qu'ils ressemblent à Jupiter quand ils battent leurs femmes' (III, 55).

All the time comes the refrain that this is childish stuff (and to many seventeenth-century eyes, the peasant and the savage are like children). It is the moderns who are the true ancients, the adults. The Greeks fall short of adult standards of rationality and good taste. This shows in the excessively figurative, 'oriental', nature of their language, an 'incorrectness' which has been rescued by pious critics who have given 'le nom honorable de figures à toutes les incongruités et à toutes les extravagances du discours', which in a modern would be simply 'sottises' (I, 24). Pindar's writings are 'galimatias', and Plato is needlessly obscure. If the language is childish, so too is the subject matter. The *Odyssey*, in particular, is 'fort comique, à le regarder par rapport à nos mœurs' (III, 73) – and this indeed is how Perrault does regard it; there is no hint of historical relativism in his writing.

In discussing the *Odyssey*, Perrault inevitably comes to the Cyclops. His tone is dismissive. Like quite a lot of ancient literature, it resembles a fairy-tale: 'Quand on a douze ans passés, peut-on prendre plaisir à de tels contes?' (III, 84). What he objects to is apparently not so much the improbability of such a being, as the silly verbal trick (calling himself 'Nobody') by which Odysseus escapes Polyphemus – like the wily heroes of certain folk-tales, one might add. Elsewhere in the *Parallèle*, however, he does specifically criticize a gigantic allegorical figure of Discord in Homer, and this gives rise to an entertaining exchange about giants between himself and Boileau, in which the latter has no difficulty in defending poetic hyperbole, whereas Perrault declares that, improbability for improbability, he prefers the seven-league boots of French folk-tales to the fantasies of Homer.[8]

What is fascinating about this is of course precisely the fact that Perrault wished seven-league boots on French literature. The critic of the absurdities of the ancients was the person who gave their classic status to such stories as 'La Belle au bois dormant' and 'Le Petit Poucet'. This apparent contradiction has been very interestingly explored by Marc Soriano, and there is no need here to go at length into Perrault's probable motivation. It is, however, worth asking how he, as a civilized and rational modern, justifies the writing down of absurd stories which belong to the common stock of the despised peasantry – despised, that is, in that they provide a stick to beat Homer with.

The essential point is that for Perrault these stories are 'des contes que nos aïeux ont inventés pour leurs enfants' (p. 51). In reality, as we know, the tales were far from being simply children's tales, but the only oral context in which he presents them is that suggested by the 'madrigal' attributed to his niece Mademoiselle L'Héritier which figures at the end of the preface:

> Le conte de Peau d'Ane est ici raconté
> Avec tant de naïveté,
> Qu'il ne m'a pas moins divertie,
> Que quand auprès du feu ma nourrice ou ma mie
> Tenaient en le faisant mon esprit enchanté. (pp. 52–3)

As he describes them, then, they are tales told by women to amuse children, but also – and this is what distinguishes them from some of their immoral ancient counterparts – they are designed, like fables, to teach moral lessons agreeably. Perrault lays particular stress on this aspect in the preface. It was in order to insist on this childish aspect of the tales that he had the prose *Contes* dedicated to the King's young niece by his son Pierre, who did indeed almost certainly play quite an important part in their composition.[9]

It is obvious, however, from the circumstances of their publication ('La Belle au bois dormant' was first published in the *Mercure galant* for instance) and from their reception (they began a fashionable craze), that the *Contes* were destined for adults. What were these children's stories meant to do for grown-ups, and sophisticated ones at that? The terms which Perrault uses to describe them, 'bagatelles', 'agréables sornettes' and the like, seem to suggest that he does not expect them to be taken seriously at all. They are to be a pleasant distraction from business. The verse tales, which are more obviously directed at adult readers, offer in their playful verse amplification of popular subjects a pleasure akin to that provided by La Fontaine's *Fables*.[10] But I think one could apply to all of the *Contes* the passage from the introduction to 'Peau d'âne' where Perrault mocks his (*ancien*) critics. There are those, he says, who want nothing but 'le pompeux et le sublime', whereas 'l'esprit le plus parfait / Peut aimer sans rougir jusqu'aux marionnettes':

> Pourquoi faut-il s'émerveiller
> Que la raison la mieux sensée,
> Lasse souvent de trop veiller,
> Par des contes d'ogre et de fée
> Ingenieusement bercée,
> Prenne plaisir à sommeiller? (p. 97)

It is the same point made by such rationalists as Fontenelle and Karl Marx:[11] that the superior, civilized adult can take pleasure in returning temporarily to a more primitive, childish state. Formulated in such a way, this may suggest an unduly trivializing approach to folklore, myth and the like. How in practice does Perrault deal with his ogres, having scorned those of the ancients?

First of all, where does the word 'ogre' come from? In the passage just quoted, the author feels the need to provide it with the explanatory footnote: 'homme sauvage qui mangeait des petits enfants' (the imperfect tense puts it in the past of 'once upon a time'). *The Oxford English Dictionary* says that Perrault's use of the word is the first recorded use. This is not correct, though Perrault may have been the first to use the feminine form 'ogresse'. 'Ogre' is found, for instance, in Chrétien de Troyes's *Perceval*. It seems likely, moreover, to judge from the way Perrault uses it repeatedly in the *Contes* (where there are not a few old and unusual words), that it comes from popular speech, perhaps directly from the oral story-tellers who were one of his sources. The etymological derivation from 'Hungarian' is generally discredited in the dictionaries, which tend rather to see its root in the Latin *Orcus*, meaning a monstrous being. It is not synonymous with giant: as we shall see, one of the teasing questions that arises is the size of ogres.

Compared with many of the host of writers of fairy stories over the following decades,[12] Perrault is sparing in his use of supernatural elements, fairies, metamorphoses, magic spells and the like. All his stories except 'Griselidis' contain something of the sort, but it is usually fairly unobtrusive (for instance the transformations in 'Cendrillon'). Ogres do, however, figure in three of the prose tales, and Blue-Beard, although presented simply as 'un homme', shows some ogreish characteristics – which is not surprising since he takes the place occupied by the devil in similar folk-tales. Leaving him on one side, we have ogres and ogresses in 'Le Chat botté', 'La Belle au bois dormant' and 'Le Petit Poucet'.

In the first of these, the ogre is a comic character, powerful but stupid, and he easily falls victim to the cat's cleverness. He is characterized in the first place by his possessions − 'un ogre, le plus riche qu'on ait jamais vu', the owner of all the lands through which the King passes. His castle is magnificent and so is the 'collation' he offers to his fellow-ogres. In fact he seems rather like a Fouquet, an excessively rich subject who meets his nemesis. There is no suggestion that he is any larger than the next person, although he can transform himself into a lion or an elephant. Nor does he appear to eat little children. Indeed, he is not at all a frightening figure, and is capable of civility, if not politeness; the story-teller remarks mockingly: 'L'ogre le reçut aussi civilement que le peut un ogre, et le fit reposer'. As for his fellow-ogres (ogres are sociable and invite one another to dinner), we learn that on arriving at the castle, they 'n'avaient pas osé entrer, sachant que le roi y était'. In a word, Perrault appears in this story to be introducing a formidable figure from folklore only to rid him of all his terrifying qualities.

In 'La Belle au bois dormant', things are different. It is not an ogre that we see, but an ogress. She is by no means a comic character, and what is even more alarming, she is the mother of the hero. We learn quite unexpectedly in the middle of the story, when the Prince has already awakened the sleeping Princess, and their two children have been born, that he dared not tell his mother, since 'elle était de race ogresse, et le Roi ne l'avait epousée qu'à cause de ses grands biens'; what is more, 'on disait même tout bas à la cour, qu'elle avait les inclinations des ogres, et qu'en voyant passer des petits enfants, elle avait toutes les peines du monde à se retenir de se jeter sur eux'. It is a heavy burden of heredity for the young hero, to be compared perhaps with the evil weight of the past and the family of Jezebel for the young Joas in *Athalie*. Naturally, in his fairy tale, Perrault does not allow this future threat to intrude, though he does note that after the wicked mother has perished in the cauldron of serpents, the hero 'ne laissa pas d'en être fâché: elle était sa mère'.

Here again, there is no question of the ogress being a gigantic creature. All the emphasis is on her cannibalistic instincts. She calls for the flesh, first of her granddaughter, then of her grandson, and finally of her daughter-in-law, and although she can be tricked by the traditional substitution of animal's flesh, she remains an all-powerful figure in the absence of the young King. Perrault intensifies the horror of the situation with the threefold repetition of the threat to the innocent and defenceless, and brings his story to a horrifying climax:

Furieuse d'avoir été trompée, elle commanda dès le lendemain au matin, avec une voix épouvantable qui faisait trembler tout le monde, qu'on apportât au milieu de la cour une grande cuve, qu'elle fit remplir de crapauds, de vipères, de couleuvres et de serpents, pour y faire jeter la reine et ses enfants, le maître d'hôtel, sa femme et sa servante.

As in 'La Barbe bleue' (and classic melodrama), the suspense — what Perrault calls the 'horrible spectacle' — is built up powerfully before being dissipated by the hero's timely arrival. In these bloodthirsty pages, however, there is one curious detail: the ogress's desire to eat Aurore 'à la sauce-robert'. Interestingly, this phrase was omitted from the text when it was first published in 1696 in the *Mercure galant*, but reinstated for the publication in book form a year later. It introduces a note of black humour which seems to poke fun at the notion of cannibalism, though without really undermining the macabre effect of these pages.

The Queen Mother is not the only ogre in 'La Belle au bois dormant'. She is preceded by one who exists only in the minds of the people. When the Prince comes upon the overgrown castle where the Princess is asleep, he asks the local inhabitants what it means. The mystery is explained in various ways:

Chacun lui répondit selon qu'il avait ouï parler. Les uns disaient que c'était un vieux château où il revenait des esprits; les autres que tous les sorciers de la contrée y faisaient leur sabbat. La plus commune opinion était qu'un ogre y demeurait, et que là il emportait tous les enfants qu'il pouvait attraper, pour les manger à son aise, et sans qu'on le pût suivre, ayant seul le pouvoir de se faire un passage au travers du bois.

For a moment here, we seem to hear the sceptical observer, collecting examples of popular belief (as it might be the legends of Gilles de Rais). One may compare it with the lines in *Phèdre* where Théramène reports the rumoured presence of 'un dieu' at Hippolyte's death.[13] Just as Racine teases his spectator with a half-believed supernatural image, Perrault allows his ogre to flicker across his pages without entering the story, announcing the much more real ogress of the final section.

It is in 'Le Petit Poucet' that the ogre really comes into his own. In the 'story-type' ('The Children and the Ogre') to which this story belongs in the standard Aarne-Thompson classification, the part of the ogre is played by a variety of frightening beings. In the eighty-two French stories of this family listed in the compendium of Delarue and Teneze,[14] the house to which the lost children find their way is occupied by (among others) the devil, an ogre or giant, a witch or ogress, a wolf, a 'Saracen' or 'Tartaro', a werewolf, and even, in one story, a hermit. Sometimes these creatures are made more monstrous by such details as an eye in the middle of the forehead (reminiscent of the Cyclops) or the possession of one-hundred-league boots, and often the ogre or monster chases the children mounted on a magic sow. Always the presence of a monstrous being is essential to the story. As for his or her size, there is a tendency towards the gigantic, but this is more evident in the chase than the preceding episode.

Perrault himself says little about his ogre's size – just as he drops the diminutive dimensions of Poucet after the beginning of the story. When the children arrive at the house, there is nothing to suggest that its dimensions are out of the ordinary. Subsequently, we hear of the great quantity of meat stored up for entertaining the three ogre guests. But the only occasion on which the ogre seems gigantic is when he is glimpsed impressively striding from mountain to mountain – and this is thanks to the seven-league boots. It is interesting therefore to see how Gustave Doré, in his illustrations to this story, varies the size of the ogre; in some engravings he is the size of a large man, in others he is several times as big as the children. In this, as in his depiction of the frightening forest, Doré clearly felt impelled to bring out more clearly the horrific element which is present in the *Histoires ou contes du temps passé*.

For in this, the final story in his collection, it does seem that Perrault has gone out of his way to emphasize this primitive horror. Before we even get to the ogre's house, the tone is set as the children cower in the deep, dark forest:

La nuit vint, et il s'éleva un grand vent qui leur faisait des peurs épouvantables. Ils croyaient n'entendre de tous côtés que des hurlements de loups qui venaient à eux pour les manger.

Then comes the arrival at the house, the revelation that it belongs to 'un ogre qui mange les petits enfants', the sight of a whole sheep roasting for his supper, his menacing return, his threat to eat his own wife, the capture of the children and so on. As he picks up the first of them, we are back in the ancient cave of Polyphemus. The extravagant horror continues in the night scene that follows, with the cruel young ogresses, the cutting of the throats and the sinister pun ('Va-t-en là-haut habiller ces petits drôles d'hier au soir'). Even just before the denouement we see the children trembling with fear. The ending is one of relief from terror.

But of course this is not Perrault's only voice. Against the horror is set a recurrent note of humour. On being told that they risk being eaten, Poucet remarks politely that in any case the wolves would eat them, so 'nous aimons mieux que ce soit Monsieur qui nous mange'. More gruesomely, we are told that the young ogresses 'promettaient beaucoup, car elles mordaient déjà les petits enfants pour leur sucer le sang'. The same comic juxtaposition of a demure or familiar tone and grim subject matter is seen in Perrault's assurance that the ogre 'ne laissait pas d'être fort bon mari, quoiqu'il mangeât les petits enfants', in the aside that the seven-league boots 'fatiguent fort leur homme', and in the parenthesis, often omitted from modern editions of the story for children, that when the ogre's wife found her dead children swimming in blood 'elle commença par s'évanouir (car c'est le premier expédient que trouvent presque toutes les femmes en pareilles rencontres)'. What is one to make of Perrault's double tone here? There have been many who have regretted his ironic winks and asides as diluting the potential power of his primitive tale. Does this in fact reveal the impossibility for a rational subject of Louis XIV of taking seriously material of this kind? Perhaps, but it seems to me equally possible that some, if not all, of these little touches go back to the sort of oral performance that Perrault might have heard. Tellers of tales are not without a sense of humour, and an adult telling a horrifying story of this kind to a child might well want to provide reassurance at the same time as excitement. However one looks at it, this duality is absolutely characteristic of Perrault. Marc Soriano puts it well; writing of the supernatural in the *Contes*, he says:

Perrault ironise à son sujet, le renvoie à l'enfance. C'est évidemment prendre ses distances par rapport à lui, y voir une superstition [...] Mais en même temps, en notant les superstitions du temps jadis, Perrault montre qu'elles existent pour lui [...] La contradiction de sa conscience correspond assez [...] à celle de son monde culturel.   (*Les Contes de Perrault*, p. 477)

We shall see in the next chapter that in this respect at least Racine the *ancien* resembles Perrault the *moderne*. In tragedies as in fairy-tales, ancient and irrational elements exist side by side with a modern attitude that seems to contradict them. In Perrault's case, one could even argue that the irony and the distance protect the vulnerable primitive elements and allow them to survive and retain something of their force in the unfavourable environment of a polite culture.

So Perrault's attitude to what we can broadly call popular culture is certainly complex. On the one hand, he dresses it up for polite consumption, eliminating some of its more shocking elements and playing elegantly or mockingly with others. There is no question here of the romantic valorization of the primitive that is so widespread in the nineteenth and twentieth centuries. But on the other hand, he appears genuinely interested in the folklore he uses. One justification for this interest is given in an interesting passage in the dedication of the prose tales, where he writes (under his son's name) that the powerful have a duty to find out more about the life and culture of their subjects: 'ces contes donnent une image de ce qui se passe dans les moindres familles ... mais à qui convient-il mieux de connaître comment vivent les peuples, qu'aux personnes que le ciel destine à les conduire?' (p. 127).

The attitude suggested by this quotation is one of benevolent and distant superiority. Nor is Perrault's presentation of peasant life free of the supercilious mockery of the educated city-dweller. Thus the beginning of 'Le Petit Poucet' presents the woodcutter's family as surprisingly numerous because 'sa femme allait vite en besogne et n'en faisait moins que deux à la fois'. And when they suddenly receive the money owed them by the seigneur, the wife buys three times as much meat as they need – this is the sort of improvidence associated with children or savages by the prudent bourgeoisie to which Perrault belonged. One might add that in both these cases, and in others besides, it is the woman who is the target of mockery; in this the *Contes* conform to an ancient tradition, which unites men of all classes.

'Le Petit Poucet' is an interesting case, however, because for all his irony, Perrault does invite the sort of involvement with his rustic protagonists that is found in genuine folk-tales. After the somewhat flippant opening, we are plunged into the poverty and hunger which were only too familiar in seventeenth-century France: 'Il vint une année très fâcheuse, et la famine fut si grande, que ces pauvres gens résolurent de se défaire de leurs enfants'. There were famines in France in 1693 and 1694. If the theme of children abandoned in the forest is a regular folklore motif, this is partly because it corresponded to a reality of peasant existence (though no doubt there are other, psychological, motivations).[15] To make matters worse, Perrault announces casually that the local seigneur had owed the woodcutter ten *écus* – an improbable touch, one may think, but accentuating the vulnerability of the poor heroes. It would be wrong to describe this as a piece of social criticism; rather we see here what is unusual in seventeenth-century writing, a kind of identification with the fate of the common people. One might also speculate about the ogre, with his isolated house, his hunting and meat-eating habits, his dinners for his fellow-ogres and his ability to terrorize the neighbourhood – is he not a refracted image of the seigneur as he may have seemed in the popular imagination?

Perrault's attitude towards his peasant characters is a mixed one then, like his attitude to popular beliefs and superstitions. He re-creates and he smiles. But what comes across most strongly in the *Histoires ou contes du temps passé* is his love for the actual tales and the manner of popular story-telling. This easily outweighs his ironic asides and his half-serious apologies for inflicting such childish things on the reader. La Fontaine had written, somewhat ambiguously:

> Si Peau d'Ane m'était conté,
> J'y prendrais un plaisir extrême.[16]

Perrault provides this pleasure above all through the natural-seeming simplicity of his narrative.

The quality praised in 'Peau d'âne' by the madrigal attributed to Mademoiselle L'Héritier (see above, p. 30) is 'naïveté'. This is glossed by the *Dictionnaire de l'Académie* in these terms: 'Il se prend aussi pour cette grâce et cette simplicité naturelle avec laquelle une chose est exprimée, ou représentée selon la vérité ou la vraisemblance'. It is this that appealed to Perrault's fashionable audience. The *Mercure galant*, announcing the publication of the prose tales, says that the connoisseurs regard them as 'des contes originaux et de la vieille roche'. This means that they belong not just to Perrault, but to 'un nombre infini de pères et de merès, de grand-mères, de gouver-nantes et de grand'amies qui, depuis peut-être mille ans, y ont ajouté'.[17] The connoisseurs mentioned here are those who preserved a taste for national 'antiquities', as Addison would shortly do for the ballad of 'Chevy Chase' in England.[18] Such people did not disappear in classical France, and as well as romances of chivalry or folk-tales they appreciated the often despised works of a Rabelais[19] or the crude 'gaulois' tradition which Perrault also illustrates in his 'Les Souhaits ridicules'.

Stylistically, Perrault's tales are by no means all of a piece. The 'Contes en vers', or at least the first two of them, often aim, not entirely successfully, at a modern, elegant wit. At the opposite extreme is the lucid simplicity of 'Le Petit Chaperon rouge':

Il était une fois une petite fille de village, la plus jolie qu'on eût pu voir; sa mère en etait folle, et sa mère-grand plus folle encore.

The vocabulary, the rhythm and the story-telling formulas all suggest an oral telling. 'Mère-grand' is one of the rustic or slightly archaic words sprinkled through the text to give the much-appreciated flavour of a 'conte de la vieille roche'. But one has only to compare Perrault's stories with almost any of those written down later by more scientific

folklorists to realize how much this is an effect of art. And this too
was obvious to cõntemporary readers. The Abbé de Villiers notes in
1699 that the best examples of this now fashionable genre were not
the more fanciful ones, but those that imitated most faithfully the
simple style of ignorant story-tellers, and that 'il faut être bien habile
pour bien imiter la simplicité de leur ignorance'.[24]

One may compare this with the discourse on politeness which I
discuss in Chapter 4. Just as the highest politeness is marked by an
unaffected ease, which may seem spontaneous to the unthinking, so
the natural style of the folk-tale, when imitated by a truly talented
writer, becomes the highest elegance. The barrier between rusticity
and politeness is miraculously removed. And this is precisely one of
the thematic centres of Perrault's *Contes*. Several of them are
celebrations of natural, unaffected courtesy. In 'Griselidis', in line
with an old topos, the Prince seeks a virtuous bride far from the court,
in the uncorrupted woods. He finds not only virtue, but politeness.
Already in the dedication, Perrault sets his story in opposition to city
sophistication. Paris, 'où l'homme est poli' and where women are
sovereign, will find his Griselidis too rustic and old-fashioned, he says
mockingly. But his heroine, though dressed in poor clothes, is a model
of true politeness, and of elegance as well. To the ladies-in-waiting
who come to dress her in court clothes.

> cette rustique cabane,
> Que couvre et rafraîchit un spacieux platane,
> [...] semble un séjour enchanté.

And once she comes to court, like Marivaux's Marianne,[21] she has
no difficulty in picking up the appropriate manners.

The pattern is that of the poor girl who in spite of appearances
turns out to be more beautiful, more elegant, more polite than her
supposed superiors. So Peau d'Ane, who is in fact a king's daughter,
conceals 'sous sa crasse et ses haillons' not only the heart of a princess,
but the delicate white hand which fits the ring. It is the same in
'Cendrillon', where the heroine in the ashes is not only beautiful but
truly polite towards her tormentors. In 'Les Fées', imitated as it is
from Mademoiselle L'Héritier's 'Les Enchantements de l'éloquence',
the key word is 'honnête'; the younger daughter's naive *honnêteté*,
which is expressed in the simple words 'oui-da, ma bonne mère', is
rewarded with a gift which represents the summit of eloquence. In
all these cases, beauty emerges from apparent rusticity. It is of course
an old pastoral theme.

Finally we should consider another, rather different way in which the *Contes* can be seen as dramatizing the victory of politeness over its opposite. In his folk-tales, although they come from a primitive, rustic culture, Perrault finds models for the vanquishing of crude and barbarous manners. The ogres are killed or rendered harmless. The strange brutality of the King in 'Griselidis' meets its match in the young girl's courage and virtue, which win him over, not before time, to a more civilized way of proceeding. The ogress of 'La Belle au bois dormant' and the monster of 'La Barbe bleue' are both destroyed. But again it is perhaps 'Le Petit Poucet' which provides the best example.

The hero, one should recall, is a woodcutter's son, and his original place is the forest. In fact, in the seventeenth century, there had been a considerable replanting of forests initiated by Perrault's patron Colbert, to provide timber for ships after the old forests had been much diminished by the demand for firewood and industrial fuel. But the forest of this story comes from further back; it is the wild place of wolves, a place where an ogre can eat little children. Poucet's exploit, rather like that of Theseus or Odysseus, is to disarm this monster (he should kill him really, one cannot help thinking, but this would doubtless be too violent for Perrault's ideal ending). Earlier in the story, with his Ariadne's thread of pebbles, he had temporarily overcome the threat of the wild wood. At the end, he makes the forest safe for travellers by taking away the ogre's seven-league boots.[22] And in Perrault's slightly absurd alternative ending, he uses these to enter the modern world, serving as a military courier and buying 'des offices de nouvelle création' for his family. Suddenly, with a humorous jolt at the end of his last story, Perrault says goodbye to the archaic domain of the folk-tale, laying bare the gap, which he had elsewhere managed to paper over, between the fashionable world of 1697 and the ancient rustic world where ogres walk.

3

MYTH AND MODERNITY: RACINE'S *PHEDRE*

Phaedra, daughter of Minos and Pasiphaë, granddaughter of the sun, half-sister to the Minotaur, is the wife of Theseus, the slayer of the Minotaur and other monsters. Hounded by Venus (Aphrodite), she falls in love with Hippolytus, son of Theseus, and an Amazon queen. Hippolytus loves a descendant of Vulcan and Gaia (the Earth). Theseus, returning from the underworld, is misled into believing his son guilty of loving Phaedra and calls on his tutelary god Neptune (Poseidon) to avenge him. A monster emerges from the sea and causes Hippolytus to be dragged to death by his horses. Phaedra poisons herself.

Such is the subject of the play in which Racine, drawing on Euripides and others, gave his public 'ce que j'ai mis de plus raisonnable sur le théâtre' (Preface to *Phèdre*). What could these ancient and monstrous events mean to the Christian subjects of Louis XIV, to the polite contemporaries of Descartes and Fontenelle? Let me approach this subject in a roundabout manner, starting from our own century and what it has made of Racine.

At the time of the First World War the Russian poet Osip Mandelstam was a member of the Acmeist group, who proclaimed as part of their programme a belief in the traditional craft of the word. This meant a choice of ancestors. As Mandelstam put it in an essay 'On the Nature of the Word' written some years later, 'the Acmeist wind turned the pages of the classics and the romantics, and they fell open at the very place that was most needed by the age. Racine opened at *Phèdre*.'[1] What did the age need in *Phèdre*? Mandelstam wrote two poems inspired by Racine's tragedy; the first, dated 1915, reads as follows:

> I shall not see the celebrated 'Phèdre'
> In the ancient many-tiered theatre
> With its high smoke-blackened gallery
> By the guttering candles' light.
> And indifferent to the actors' bustle

40

As they gather in the harvest of applause,
I shall not hear across the footlights
Winged with its double rhyme the line:

How all these veils have grown repugnant to me ...

The theatre of Racine! A mighty curtain
Divides us from the other world;
Between that world and us a curtain hangs
And stirs with its deep furrows.
Classical shawls fall from the shoulders,
Molten with suffering the voice grows firmer
And the word white-hot with indignation
Attains a sorrowing incandescence ...

I am too late for Racine's high festival!

Again the decaying posters rustle,
And faintly comes the smell of orange peel,
And as if out of the lethargy of ages
My neighbour stirs to life and says to me:
– Exhausted by the madness of Melpomene,
It is only peace I long for in this life;
Let us go, before the jackal audience
Comes and tears the Muses limb from limb!

What if some Greek could see our games ...[2]

Racine may be a chosen ancestor, but the central idea of Mandelstam's poem is the distance between his time and ours. In fact, as is often the case with this poet, the reader is led in more than one direction here. On one reading, Racine's theatre, which can still be performed today, creates an 'other world' (nobler, more passionate), separated from the tawdry world of orange peel and decaying posters by a great curtain. But it seems to me that another meaning is more insistent: that Racine's 'celebrated' play, with its 'white-hot' language and proper accompaniment of noble gesture, costume and setting, is something which has gone for ever. It is on the same side of the divide as Greek tragedy and can be set against what Mandelstam contemptuously calls 'our games' (modern culture, but perhaps also the War?).

This is a modern view of Racine which is familiar and persuasive. *Phèdre* and most of the other plays continue to be performed and read, but many critics would suggest that this theatre belongs to a lost world. Roland Barthes, for instance, writing in his illuminating essay 'Dire Racine'[3] of the problem of diction and the difficulty of reconciling the classical-operatic mode with the psychological-realistic, concludes:

Comme pour le théâtre antique, ce théâtre nous concerne bien plus par son étrangeté que par sa familiarité: son rapport à nous, c'est sa distance. Si nous voulons garder Racine, éloignons-le.   (p. 144)

One notices that Racine is again aligned with the ancients. He belongs with an archaic world that we cannot really recover.

Such a separation is implied by another myth of our times, the Death of Tragedy. George Steiner, in his book on that subject,[4] declares: 'tragedy is that form of art which requires the intolerable burden of God's presence. It is now dead because this shadow no longer falls upon us as it fell on Agamemnon or Macbeth or Athalie' (p. 353). Again Racine's theatre is placed with that of the Greeks (and Shakespeare) on the other side of a great divide, and it is specifically the presence of myth[5] or religion that defines the difference. Much modern interpretation of such plays as *Phèdre* has sought precisely to emphasize this mythical or religious element. Steiner himself not only writes eloquently of the 'brutish ferocity of the myth' (p. 90) in *Phèdre*, but even says at one point: 'If I were to stage the play, I should have the background grow transparent to show us the dance of the Zodiac and Taurus, the emblematic beast of the royal house of Crete' (p. 93).

If one decides on such a staging (and it is not infrequent in the twentieth century), is one simply attempting an archaeological reconstruction of the lost world (because we are 'too late for Racine's high festival')? This is what might be implied by Steiner's further remark that 'the role he [Racine] plays in French life is ornamental rather than vital' (pp. 104–5). Or is it not rather, in spite of appearances, a way of updating this old theatre (otherwise imprisoned in a *grand siècle* strait-jacket)? It is certainly different from the modern-dress approach to modernization, and is founded on the assumption that at any rate the sophisticated modern audience (and who else do producers of Racine have in mind?) is sufficiently impregnated with Freud and Jung, Frazer and Artaud, to welcome the mythical as a valuable, even essential, element in literature and theatre.

Certainly, the Minoan legends have been popular in our time. The story of Phaedra and Hippolytus, for instance, has been given a relatively popular treatment in Mary Renault's *The Bull from the Sea* and in Jules Dassin's film *Phaedra*. Both of these combine a stress on the mythical aspects of the story with the attempt to make it more immediately present (in Dassin's film Hippolytus meets his death at the wheel of a sports car). *The Bull from the Sea* is a tale of human emotion and actions, but it is full of passages such as this one (where Theseus is cursing his son):

The anger that rose in me seemed the wrath of the earth itself. It flowed through my feet, as the earthfire rises in some burning mountain before it destroys the land. And then, as if my mind had been lit with a flame, I knew that it was true. It was not my anger only. The god had howled and the bird had cried, and my head had tightened; yet I had not felt Poseidon's warning; because my anger had risen in time with his. Now I felt it, and felt it soon to fall; the god my father standing by me, to avenge my bitter wrong.[6]

Of course since Theseus is the narrator, the author can introduce such ideas without committing herself to them − it is local colour, the attempt to revive a supposed archaic mentality for a modern audience. At the same time the rhythm (almost verse at the end) shows that this is also an attempt to give that audience an ancient *frisson*.

The two most interesting English versions of *Phèdre* both strengthen the mythical element in the play. Thus Robert Lowell in his *Phaedra* renders the lines:

> O haine de Vénus! O fatale colère!
> Dans quels égarements l'amour jeta ma mère!
>
> (*Phèdre*, I, iii, 249−50)

by:

> Oh, Venus, murdering Venus! love
> gored Pasiphaë with a bull.[7]

thus vigorously reminding the twentieth-century audience of the nature of Racine's decorously veiled 'égarements'. At times he also replaces Venus by Aphrodite (the two coexist in a generalized antiquity); the mythical potential of the Greek goddess is probably greater today than that of her over-exposed Roman counterpart.

Tony Harrison's *Phaedra Britannica* goes further than this. Feeling perhaps that the gods of classical antiquity, whether Greek or Roman, no longer pack sufficient punch, and wishing to update Racine's play while retaining what is felt as its archaic force, he situates it in the India of the Raj. Phaedra the Memsahib speaks to her confidante like this:

> My body froze, then blazed. I felt flesh scorch
> as Siva smoked me out with flaming torch.
> I sense the gods of India were there
> behind the throbbing heat and stifling air.[8]

Again, as with Lowell, overt physicality reinforces the power of the religious reference. The allusion to Indian religion (suggesting perhaps to British readers a similar confrontation in *A Passage to India*)

43

is an effective way of rendering what Steiner describes as the 'tremendous tension between the classical, rational form of the actual drama and the demonic, irrational character of the fable' (pp. 80–1).

If twentieth-century poets, translators and producers have been moved to bring out what I have called the mythical aspects of Racine's play, it is not surprising if critics have taken the same road. I do not wish here to survey the modern 'mythological' approaches to Racine, which spell out the implications of what has been sketched above. It is worth noting, however, that while some of the more adventurous suggestions of Roland Barthes (concerning the primal horde and 'le *tenebroso* racinien' for example) raised a small storm when they first appeared, it comes as no surprise today to be told that behind the psychological realism or civilized decorum of these tragedies there lies the perception of the world which is best described in terms of myth,[9] that Racine's theatre has as much in common with the haunting world of the *Bacchae* as with the more purely human drama of, say, *Cinna*.

'Myth criticism' is a development of our time, and the view of Racine's plays suggested above would have surprised most readers and critics of the eighteenth and nineteenth centuries. Over this long period, the author of *Phèdre* was admired above all for his success in depicting real human emotions in real human situations – also for his elegance of course. *Esther* and *Athalie* (the 'religious' plays) were perhaps special cases, and Sainte-Beuve was able to say of the latter: 'Athalie est belle comme l'*Œdipe Roi*, avec le vrai Dieu en plus'.[10] Apart from the two 'tragédies sacrées', however, I do not think Racine's theatre would have been described by most nineteenth-century readers as religious, or as 'mythical' in the sense of Roland Barthes. This appears to be true even of August Wilhelm Schlegel, when he credits *Phèdre* with being closer to the Greeks than any other contemporary French plays. What he has in mind is not any mythical significance, but rather the noble simplicity of the ancients: 'one must feel all the more admiration for a poet who could still read the ancient poets with such feeling and had the courage to follow in their footsteps, showing such purity and unadulterated simplicity in the face of the artificial taste of the day'.[11] The 'remythologizing' of Racine is perhaps the consequence of notions of poetry and drama put forward in the Romantic period, but it was left to the twentieth century to accomplish it.

What now of Racine's age, and what of the playwright himself?[12] For Mandelstam, he may have served as a bridge to the Greeks, and Racine himself wrote more than once of the continuity between his theatre and that of Euripides, but is there anything to suggest that he or his spectators valued, or even perceived, the mythical element which modern interpreters have laid bare in his work? It is a hard question, involving the history of ideas as well as the interpretation of literary texts. Contradictory answers are given by different scholars. We know that the *merveilleux* in its many forms was omnipresent in French literature of the age of Louis XIV, in opera, and ballet, in official painting and sculpture, in epic and lyric poetry.[13] Partisans of the *merveilleux chrétien* and the *merveilleux païen* did battle, but it was the latter which dominated the scene. And the various sources of mythological reference, alongside the enchantments of medieval romance and fairy story, maintained their central position. What, however, did they mean to the contemporaries of Racine and Perrault?

Jean Seznec asserted in *La Survivance des dieux antiques* that pagan mythology in the seventeenth century was 'de plus en plus érudite et de moins et moins vivante, de moins en moins sentie et de plus en plus raisonnée'.[14] Against this view, which is probably the orthodox one, it is worth considering Bernard Beugnot's thought-provoking claim that 'derrière la mythologie la plus codifiée guette encore parfois l'animisme; la difficulté à fixer les frontières de l'allégorie et l'incertitude de son statut correspondent à de secrets divorces inscrits dans la poésie classique'.[15] As far as Racine is concerned there is an even starker contrast between R.C. Knight's argument that the myth criticism practised by such writers as Eigeldinger is anachronistic when applied to a seventeenth-century French writer[16] and Steiner's contention that the very essence of Racine's plays is the felt and powerful tension between the irrational world of myth and the apparently decorous classical form.

Certainly a great many signs point in the direction indicated by Knight and Seznac. Mars, Venus and the rest of them look like tired old props and do not normally evoke the world of mysterious powers that modern critics have seen in *Phèdre*. The Jesuit Father Pomey's *Pantheon Mysticum*,[17] which served as a schoolboy's guide to what was known in France as *la fable*, is hardly sympathetic to the beliefs it categorizes. For the most part mythology is understood here as no more than a necessary code for writing and understanding literature, and at times the ancient deities are treated with heavy mockery or even indignation. The story of the birth of Bacchus or Dionysos is 'both wonderful and ridiculous, if the poets may be heard, as they must when the discourse is about fables' (p.59); Venus is 'an impudent strumpet, and the mistress and president of obscenity' (p.108);

and the whole 'Pantheon' is 'the Temple of the Heathen Gods, which the superstitious folly of all men has feigned' (p. 1).

Writing from a different perspective, and implicitly extending the criticism of the pagan gods to Christianity, Fontenelle wrote not long after *Phèdre*:

> Mais si l'on vient à se défaire des yeux de l'habitude, il ne se peut qu'on ne soit épouvanté de voir toute l'ancienne histoire d'un peuple, qui n'est qu'un amas de chimères, de rêveries et d'absurdités. Serait-il possible qu'on nous eût donné tout cela pour vrai?[18]

Although the tone of indignation may suggest that the battle was not won (as of course it was not), such arguments promote the idea, which is explicitly stated in *De l'origine des fables*, that mythology is not to be taken seriously by the enlightened adult, but is capable of giving pleasure to the reader who is willing to suspend disbelief and indulge his or her imagination:

> Quoique nous soyons incomparablement plus éclairés que ceux dont l'esprit grossier inventa de bonne foi les fables, nous reprenons aisément ce même tour d'esprit qui rendit les fables si agréables pour eux. (p. 235)

In this way, Perrault introduced the ogres and fairies of folklore to the readers of the *Mercure galant*.[19] So too Marx, in the celebrated passage in his *Grundrisse*, answers his question why we can still find pleasure in Greek art, when it is founded on outdated myth, with this rhetorical question: 'Why should not the historical childhood of humanity, where it attained its most beautiful form, exert an eternal charm because it is a stage that will never recur?'[20]

On this reading, when Racine writes in his preface to *Phèdre* of 'les ornements de la fable, qui fournit extrêmement à la poésie', we should not read anything between the lines; the allusion to Thésée's descent into the underworld is no more than a pleasing reminder of an outdated and unbelievable story — a story which incidentally is recounted in very matter-of-fact terms in Pomey's *Pantheon*: '[Theseus] went down to hell; and returned back into the world again' (p. 307). And yet, if we reread the relevant lines in *Phèdre*, it is hard to believe that 'les ornements de la fable' should be understood simply in this rather trivial sense, any more than we should underestimate the strength of 'enchanter' in Boileau's line on the mythological machinery of epic: 'Là pour nous enchanter tout est mis en usage' (*Art poétique*, III, 163).

The conversation between Aricie and Ismène is by no means the first of the many references to the underworld in the play, but it is one of the most conspicuous. Ismène prefaces her reports on Thésée's fate with the remark that these are 'd'incroyable discours' (as Pomey might have said), but her attitude is one of wonder rather than scepticism:

> On dit même, et ce bruit est partout répandu,
> Qu'avec Pirithoüs aux Enfers descendu
> Il a vu le Cocyte et les rivages sombres,
> Et s'est montré vivant aux infernales ombres,
> Mais qu'il n'a pu sortir de ce triste séjour,
> Et repasser les bords qu'on passe sans retour.[21]

(II, i, 383–88)

There is the same tone in Aricie's reply:

> Croirai-je qu'un mortel avant sa dernière heure
> Peut pénétrer des morts la profonde demeure?

(II, i, 389–90)

None of this is necessary in terms of the plot, but it is calculated to produce in the audience the same sort of feeling as Hamlet's lines about the 'undiscovered country, from whose bourn no traveller returns'. And this is reinforced of course by all the other references to the kingdom of Minos, notably by Phèdre's horrifying vision of the underworld and the judgement in Act IV, Scene 6.

As innumerable commentators have remarked, passages such as these also evoke Christian themes, as do the fires and flames of love (however conventional they often were), the fearful eye of the sun, the avenging gods, family curses, retribution and purification, and all the other elements of *Phèdre* which make it something other than a psychological drama. This is not to say that we should give a Jansenist reading (for instance) to Racine's pagan tragedies, since these elements are common to several mythical or religious systems, but simply that in evoking such fabulous subjects as Theseus's descent to Hades, he was probably awaking powerful echoes in the minds of spectators and readers for whom the Christian religion was a great deal more real than the religions of Pomey's *Pantheon*. Racine himself made this connection, though in a more stylistic context, when he congratulated himself on echoing Phèdre's 'Misérable, et je vis ...' in the lament of the damned in the second of his *Cantiques spirituels*.[22]

To this argument that Racine took his myths seriously, it may be objected that he could hardly have treated the Hippolytus theme without making some contact with the ancient myth and that he reduced this element as much as he could. One might answer to this that he was free to choose less god-haunted subjects, or else that even in the all-too-human plays such as *Bajazet* and *Britannicus* there is also a strong religious charge, in the symbolism of the closed palace for instance. Another approach is to see how the unfortunate Pradon,[23] writing on the same subject in the same year as Racine, treated that part of his material which might have been thought unacceptable to a modern, supposedly rational, audience.

Phèdre et Hippolyte, though different in plot from Racine's play, retains some of the essential mythical elements such as the appearance of the monster and Thésée's appeal to his tutelary god:

> Et toi, Neptune, et toi, dont la race divine
> De Thésée anoblit le sang et l'origine,
> Plongeant ce sang impur dans l'abîme des eaux,
> Donnez ce monstre en proie à des monstres nouveaux. (IV, vi)

(As this example shows, Pradon's play contains several of the images which have been seen as most powerfully Racinian − thanks partly to Racine's unacknowledged influence no doubt). What is more, Pradon adds some supernatural elements from the arsenal of the dramatists of the time: he has an oracle (of Delos) and 'funestes messages'. There is a good deal about irresistible fate, the Gods and the Heavens, and Phèdre describes herself (rather splendidly, I think) as 'de la race des dieux, fille de la lumière' (I, iii).[24]

On the other hand, Venus is considerably less present: in *Phèdre et Hippolyte* there is nothing like the 'Vénus toute entière à sa proie attachée' of Racine's play. More importantly, while retaining a mythological background ('la fable qui fournit extrêmement à la poésie' in the weak sense), he omits anything which defies rational explanation. There is nothing here to match the 'dieu, qui d'aiguillons pressait leur flanc poudreux' of the *récit de Théramène*. And above all, Pradon goes out of his way, in the course of the play, to mock the idea of Theseus's descent into the underworld, which Racine was later to defend in his preface. In the first scene he has Hippolyte reply to his confidant, who has mentioned this rumour:

> Prétends-tu m'éblouir des fables de la Grèce?
> Peux-tu croire un mensonge? Ah! ces illusions
> Sont d'un peuple grossier les vaines visions.

This is confirmed by Thésée, who explains:

> A cent autres j'ai peint le Styx et le Cocyte [...]
> Mais je crois vous devoir un récit plus sincère;
> Votre esprit est guéri des erreurs du vulgaire.
> J'ai dû par politique en répandre le bruit. (II, vii)

Reminiscent as it is of Fontenelle's debunking of *la fable*, this looks like a deliberate attack on Racine, Boileau, and the camp of the *anciens*. Similarly Minos, who is seen in Racine's *Phèdre* as the redoubtable judge of the dead, is here brought down to earth, and figures simply as a rival king who is a threat to Theseus. Instead of myth, politics. And as for heroes, Pradon gives his Hippolyte these words:

> Quoiqu'au-dessus de nous, ils sont ce que nous sommes;
> Et comme nous enfin les héros sont des hommes. (I, i)

In brief then, one sees in *Phèdre et Hippolyte* the not unskilful use of the old machinery, but much less sign than in *Phèdre* that the old myth is being taken seriously. Pradon's play is resolutely this-worldly, though with archaic local colour. It seems a good deal nearer to the enlightened eighteenth century than Racine's.

In *Phèdre*, finally, much stress is placed on Thésée's role as a killer of monsters:

> Procruste, Cercyon, et Scirron, et Sinnis,
> Et les os dispersés du Géant d'Epidaure,
> Et la Crète fumant du sang du Minotaure. (I, i, 80–2)

In eliminating these relics of an archaic age, Thésée (like 'le petit Poucet' one might say) founds a new modern order. He is the creator of civilization. Under him, Athens can expand confidently, or so it seems. But as Aricie warns him:

> Vos invincibles mains
> Ont de monstres sans nombre affranchi les humains.
> Mais tout n'est pas détruit; et vous en laissez vivre
> Un ... (V, iii, 1443–6)

Phèdre's passion is a monstrous eruption of the dark forces which Thésée had thought to subdue. It is this eruption that gives its power to the play, but at the end, Thésée would prefer to erase it altogether:

> D'une action si noire
> Que ne peut avec elle expirer la mémoire? (V, vii, 1645–6)

His concluding words to Aricie seek, in the face of disaster, to establish a new order; they represent a turning away from the dangerous world of myth.[25]

For Racine's tragedy is at a dividing point, which we may mark symbolically with Fontenelle's *De l'origine des fables*. Janus-like it looks back to the ancient world of Greek myth which modern interpreters have sought to resuscitate in it, and looks forward to two centuries (or more) of psychological drama. It is the same with the biblical plays. *Athalie*, as William Stewart showed in a most illuminating article,[26] is balanced between human tragedy and sacred drama, the latter element being manifested above all in the chorus. It seems significant that while Handel wrote an oratorio called *Athalia*, *Athalie* was always performed at the Comédie Française in the eighteenth century without the chorus, and was admired by Voltaire as a fine political tragedy.

When all is said and done, though, we cannot hope to know for sure what Thésée's descent to the underworld, the curse of Venus or Neptune's 'vengeance meurtrière' meant to Racine and his contemporaries. It is hard enough to understand what they mean to us. Even if Racine had something quite superficial in mind when he wrote of 'les ornements de la fable', that would be no reason why modern producers, readers, and other interpreters of Racine's text should not attempt to bring out more fully the mythical element in *Phèdre*, using it as a stepping stone to Euripides and beyond. On the other hand, it may be doubted whether most twentieth-century Europeans (or at any rate most audiences for Racine) can do more than play with mythology in the manner suggested by Fontenelle or Marx. C.S. Lewis, thinking more of the Romantic poets, wrote beautifully of the way in which allegory kept the pagan gods alive so that they can be born again into a purely poetic existence.

The gods must be, as it were, disinfected of belief; the last taint of the sacrifice, and of the urgent practical interest, the selfish prayer, must be washed away from them, before that other divinity can come to light in the imagination. For poetry to spread its wings fully, there must be, besides the believed religion, a marvellous that knows itself as myth.[27]

This may sound bland, and far removed from the more violent terms in which Racine's myths, among others, have often been revived in our time, but I do not think it gives a false idea of our attempts to make a lost world live again. As Mandelstam wrote,

> Between the world and us a curtain hangs
> And stirs with its deep furrows.

Part II
ENLIGHTENED SOCIABILITY

4

POLISH, POLICE, *POLIS*

On 24 February 1989, referring to the relations between British higher education and the Conservative government of Mrs Thatcher, the *Times Higher Education Supplement* published a leader entitled 'The Pitfalls of Rudeness'. It argued that in the management of higher education in Britain, an old public order of civilized discussion, aiming for at least the appearance of dialogue and consensus, had been replaced by a new order, that of *diktat* from on high:

Today politeness is out of fashion. Rudeness is chic. The prevailing ethos of British society is now of confrontation rather than accommodation. Edge not ease. In this the Government which has matched its spirit to that of the 1980s is both a trend setter and a follower of fashion. It is certainly very rude. It never says sorry. It is not interested in the other side of the question. It lectures rather than listens.

The nostalgia for a more democratic consensus is perhaps based on an illusion — do universities really listen rather than lecturing? But these remarks do have the merit of reminding one that politeness can be a political matter.

Such is the point of my title, based as it is on a word-play, a confusion of two similar, but unrelated word families.[1] The first set is made up in English by the series: *polish, polite, politeness*, and in French: *poli, polir, politesse*. The second, stemming from the Greek *polis*, includes *politics, policy* and *police*, and in French *politique, police, policer*. The two groups are easily confused. The aim of the present chapter is to explore some threads of this semantic web in seventeenth- and eighteenth-century France.

Similar explorations can be — and have been — carried out for other countries,[2] but France is a case of particular interest in that for contemporary observers in Europe it was 'indisputably the seat of the Graces'.[3] So said Lord Chesterfield, who had written to his son some weeks earlier:

53

You want nothing now, thank God, but exterior advantages, that last polish, that *tournure du monde*, and those graces which are so necessary to adorn and give efficacy to the most solid merit. They are only to be acquired in the best companies, and better in the best French companies than in any other.

(pp. 183–4)

Similar views were being expressed all over Europe. David Hume, for instance, after three years studying at La Flèche, made it his business to bring the benefits of French *politesse* to his native Scotland.[4] The French, for their part, were fully conscious of their superiority in this domain. In his *Dictionnaire*, Furetière echoed the general opinion when he noted that 'on ne saurait voir plus de politesse qu'il y en a à la cour de France', and Voltaire wrote in his dedication of *Zaïre* to the English merchant Fawkener: 'depuis la Régence d'Anne d'Autriche, ils ont été le peuple le plus sociable et le plus poli de la terre'.[5]

Foreigners sometimes resented this superiority. Their resentment surfaced in endless jests at the expense of the mannered Frenchman, the dancing master, the fop – a witty and agreeable companion, perhaps, but without the solid virtues possessed by certain neighbouring peoples. In a letter of 1733, for example, the poet James Thomson noted ironically: 'The gallant French this year have made war upon the Germans (I beg their politeness's pardon) like vermin'.[6] More seriously, later in the century, Kant was to oppose polite *Zivilisation* to *Kultur*; as Norbert Elias explains it, the latter expressed the aspirations of a national bourgeoisie to throw off French cultural predominance.[7] And well before that, Jean-Jacques Rousseau, in his *Discours sur les sciences et les arts*, had shown a highly ambiguous attitude to the refined politeness of his adopted country.

If foreigners mocked or distrusted a set of codes whose authority they grudgingly accepted, the French too were divided in their attitudes and judgements. In the period that goes roughly from 1660 to 1760, one witnesses a long and highly repetitive series of arguments, conducted in dictionaries and dissertations, plays and novels, essays and dialogues, about the nature and value of politeness. What is 'true' politeness? The crown of social virtues, or a convenient mask for the self-seeking individual? The cloak and agent of tyranny, or the promise, in an unequal society, of equal relations between citizens? I shall try to trace the main elements of this vast question as they surface in a number of different texts, chosen from a chorus of confusing and contradictory voices. To give some shape to the discussion, I shall structure it round the three words of my title, *polish*, *police* and *polis*, which between them encompass the main directions taken by the argument. 'Polish' draws attention, etymologically, to a decorative, aesthetic view of politeness, 'police' indicates its role as an instrument for social and political control, while under 'polis' I consider the attempts to redefine politeness, both morally and socially, along more enlightened lines. The division is unrealistically clear-cut, of course, but it allows one to get some purchase on a rather Protean entity.[8]

Polish

The literal meaning of *polir* suggests an aesthetic view of the subject. One starts with a rough, untreated material, and by rubbing and similar processes one transforms it into something smooth and agreeable to the touch and sight. A common dictionary example is that of marble – which allows La Bruyère to write sardonically: 'La cour est comme un édifice bâti de marbre; je veux dire qu'elle est composée d'hommes fort durs, mais fort polis'.[9]

Polish is thus opposed to roughness. On the level of manners, this means for instance the ability to talk, listen and bear oneself in a way which is pleasant to others – 'et cela avec des manières et une façon de s'exprimer qui aient quelque chose de noble, d'aisé et de délicat', as Abbé Trublet put it in his essay 'De la politesse'.[10] The individual learns such behaviour essentially from living in what is called *le monde*. And at the centre of *le monde*, on some views at least, is the court. Furetière, in the 1690 edition of his dictionary, gives the following example for *polir*: 'La Cour polit bien les gens de province'. Many other writings on politeness confirm the central role of the court; to give just one example, Abbé Gédoyn, in his dissertation 'De l'urbanité romaine', notes that *urbanité* is different from *politesse*, 'cette politesse n'étant le privilège d'aucune ville en particulier, pas même de la capitale, mais uniquement de la cour'.[11] Such an exclusive definition, as we shall see, is far from being universally accepted, but for almost all commentators it is at least clear that, as Furetière puts it, provincials are the people who need polishing. They have to be cleansed of what Abbé de Bellegarde in his *Réflexions sur la politesse* describes as 'la crasse de la province'.[12]

Let us consider another example of usage, taken from the *Dictionnaire de l'Académie Française* (1694): 'La cour, l'étude, la conversation des honnêtes gens, des dames, polit l'esprit, polit les mœurs'. This time it is a differentiated process; the polishing concerns *l'esprit* and *les mœurs*. By the former we should understand above all the ability to converse; conversation is the essential testing place for the polite, although their *esprit* might also be shown, for instance, in their taste in literature or the arts. As for *les mœurs*, the word is ambiguous; it probably refers to manners and bearing rather than morals here, but this ambiguity is an essential element in the discourse of politeness. How deep does the polish go? We may observe in any case that the polishing agency here is wider than the court; politeness is located equally in the world of *les honnêtes gens. Honnêteté* is of course another ambiguous word, which overlaps significantly with *politesse*. Its history has been amply documented by Magendie for the period 1600–60.[13] Here it means essentially good breeding.

The location of this polite society is not indicated in the Académie's example, but the presence of 'les dames' suggests that we are talking of the world of the salons. If there is one constant feature of politeness discourse in France, it is the place it gives to women. For the most part, the discourse itself appears to be addressed more to men, but women are given a central role in the process from which men benefit. Trublet, in his compilation of standard views, notes that 'le commerce des femmes' is the best school of politeness, and in a 1768 addition to his essay he writes: 'La nation où les hommes vivent le plus avec les femmes doit être par cela seul la plus polie' (p. 185).

For some writers, such as Bellegarde, this is because women are themselves more polite – more beautiful, cleaner, more accommodating, more anxious to please. They thus provide a positive model. For others, such as Trublet, it is rather that the desire to please women forces men to act and talk in a less coarse, more polished way. Marivaux's title, *Arlequin poli par l'amour*, is emblematic. The hero, with his hirsute half-mask, is a figure of animality before being polished into full humanity by the force of love. But even when there is no question of love, the woman, enthroned in the indoor world of the salon, has the task of taming men, wooing them away from the brutality that goes with their outdoor – and often military – pursuits. Rousseau, among others, was very hostile to woman-dominated salon politeness, which, in polishing men, robbed them of their manly virtues.

A third polishing agency is 'l'étude'; one of the examples from the *Dictionnaire de l'Académie* is: 'l'étude des belles lettres polit les jeunes gens'. Politeness calls for learning, but it must be learning of a certain type – generally known as *belles lettres*, and eventually literature. School learning is not enough; indeed it may well work against politeness. For one regular feature of this discourse is its hostility to what it called pedantry. The wrong sort of learning engenders a desire to display one's obscure erudition, an excessive attachment to particular opinions, and in some cases a misplaced philosophical contempt for politeness itself. Polite letters, on the other hand – e.g. octavos in French rather than folios in Latin – chime in easily with worldly conversation. Thus the novel, from *L'Astrée* onwards, offers models for agreeable behaviour and talk. There are a host of literary genres which reflect the sociability of the salons – dialogue, essay, letter, portrait, maxim, not to speak of *bouts-rimés* or *impromptus*. All helped to introduce young people to polite existence and reinforced the polishing effects of life in *le monde*. The theatre occupied a particularly important position. Not only was it a place of fashionable meeting, but, in some cases at least, it was a source of models of politeness.

A special place must be given to the academies, both the central Parisian institutions (notably the Académie Française and the Académie des Sciences) and the many provincial academies whose creation was so crucial a part of the movement of Enlightenment – and which have been well studied by Daniel Roche.[14] All of these establishments had serious purposes – some more than others – but their role was also a sociable one. The provincial academies, for instance, generally included members of the local elite, whose presence helped to make the proceedings more distinguished. They were of course different from the salons in being all-male institutions with fairly formal rules, but their deliberations seem to have been in many ways closer to salon conversation than to a modern academic conference. In them, it was not so much a case of *belles lettres* polishing the young, as of learning being cast in a polite mould.

What I have said so far has been mainly concerned with the polishing of the individual, but *politesse* was a term applied to nations as well as to individuals. Furetière gives among his examples 'polir les barbares' and 'des peuples polis et civilisés'. *Politesse*, in other words, means much the same as the newer word *civilisation*[15] when it is applied to a nation. It may be connected with the prestigious courts of the past (in Italy for example), but may also, like *civilisation*, imply a vision of progress, whereby humanity as a whole is seen as emerging from crude barbarism into the polished existence of modern times. So *politesse* (or politeness) may be a part of what one could call a political programme for backward nations (such as Scotland).[16]

Politesse, with its etymological connotations of polish, is more than *civilité*. The fortunes of these interrelated words have been excellently traced by Roger Chartier.[17] Basically, *civilité*, which takes over from *courtoisie* as a keyword in the sixteenth century, is downgraded in the following two centuries in relation to *honnêteté* and *politesse*. The *Encyclopédie* article 'Politesse' notes that 'la civilité est bonne, mais moins excellente et moins rare que la politesse'. The former was the subject of the popularizing manuals of correct behaviour (those of Courtin and La Salle being the best known).[18] It included such fundamental matters as table manners and modes of address, and was something that could be taught to most people, including children, with a view to helping them succeed in society.

Politesse, like *honnêteté* and *urbanité*,[19] implied something altogether classier. A peasant might be civil, only an *homme du monde* could be polite − and his politeness was marked by its difference from the stiffer, less 'natural' forms of taught *civilité*. In the writings of a Méré (who speaks more of *honnêteté*) or a Bellegarde, the polite person is a polished performer in upper-class circles. His or her achievement is largely aesthetic. Chartier notes, however, that civic-minded thinkers such as Montesquieu and certain of the French revolutionaries placed greater value on the more necessary *civilité* at the expense of inessential *politesse*; if the latter is the *brioche*, the former is the bread. But this was *civilité*'s last hour of glory; from the early nineteenth century on it has generally been synonymous with elementary etiquette.

As this last example shows, *politesse* can be thought of as a *supplément* − in the phrase of Madame de Lambert 'un supplément à la vertu'.[20] It is possible to lead a decent life without it. But in certain social situations merit and virtue are not enough. In Lord Chesterfield's view, the aspiring man of the world will not be content to be a rough diamond, he will aspire to 'that last polish, that *tournure du monde*, and those graces which are so necessary to adorn and give efficacy to the most solid merit'. As we know, however, supplements are of two kinds. Politeness may be an additional polish which brings out the real value of a man or woman − a value that might be concealed by boorish behaviour. But it may also take the place of that value.

In moral terms, the essential notion of politeness is constant consideration for others, a desire not to shock and hurt them, but gratify and please them. It is perhaps best expressed by La Bruyère's often quoted dictum: 'l'esprit de politesse est une certaine attention à faire que par nos paroles et par nos manières les autres soient contents de nous et d'eux-mêmes' (p. 164). Notice however the last few words: 'de nous et d'eux-mêmes'. Altruism and egoism mingle here. The desire to please and to create a favourable impression can perhaps be satisfied by a mask better than by a real face.

What if the polish in politeness is merely a superficial and deceptive surface?

This is a hoary old topos. Even those most favourable to politeness were aware of the difficulty. Madame de Lambert, for instance, notes that in cruder times there was perhaps less politeness, but more virtue. 'On a douté', she writes, 'si elle tenait plus du vice que de la vertu' (p. 93). Furetière and the other lexicographers offer in their examples abundant evidence of the common association of *politesse* and falsity, from Madeleine de Scudéry's 'La politesse est d'ordinaire une espèce d'hypocrisie' to Fléchier's 'La société n'est qu'un commerce de mensonges officieux, où l'on fait une politesse de tromper, et un plaisir d'être trompé'. Seen thus, the polite world is a world of illusion, of flatterers and dupes. Such, in *Le Misanthrope*, is Alceste's vision of *le monde*.

The uncertainty about the value of 'polish' may be compared to that surrounding eloquence. The last years of the seventeenth century saw a resurgence of the old 'querelle de l'éloquence' in France; rhetoric and eloquence, which were often presented as the crowning glory of humanity, were now attacked as amoral instruments of deceit.[21] The particular area of conflict was religious persuasion – and Christian writers were also among those who were suspicious of politeness. Naturally, other Christians tried to reconcile their faith with eloquence, and with politeness.

An interesting, if trivial, example of this debate is furnished by the exchange in the pages of the *Mercure* in 1731–2 between Abbé Trublet, whose 'Réflexions sur la politesse' were published there in June 1731, and his critic Simonnet, 'Prieur d'Hurgeville'. The critique is Jansenist in tone; Trublet is accused of insisting too much on 'la manière', on the external polish which he sees as the distinguishing feature of politeness. Simonnet, on the other hand, sees 'le solide, l'essentiel de la politesse' in its moral aspects, charity and consideration for others. What is more, Trublet's conception is hostile to excessive frankness. Simonnet, acting out the part of Molière's Alceste (like so many others), exclaims: 'Voilà donc la candeur, la bonne foi, la sincérité exclue nécessairement du commerce du beau monde et des personnes polies!'[22] How much better things were in the crude old days! Trublet, who is after all a Christian and a moral man, defends himself by saying that he was simply describing worldly politeness, not recommending it. On the question of sincerity, however, he sticks to his guns. It may be a natural human characteristic, but it is 'un grand obstacle à la politesse' (p. 154).

Police

The word 'police' draws attention to the role of politeness in promoting peace, order and security in society. This it does by enforcing self-control and deference to others – particularly to one's social superiors. Aggressive feelings and behaviour are tempered by rituals which allow members of a human (or animal) group to live together harmoniously.[23] If, as many believed in the eighteenth century, the present age was more polite than previous ones, this probably meant that it was better governed (*mieux policée*).

The point of Trublet's critique of sincerity is that for him, as for many others, politeness did not come naturally. It was a conquest over nature. Social harmony, like the harmony of music, was the result of discipline. And indeed one not infrequently finds musical performance – or theatrical performance – used in the manuals as an analogy for polite behaviour.[24] 'Pour ceux qui composent un cercle', as Bellegarde puts it (*Politesse*, p. 24), sacrifice is essential. Under the direction of the *maîtresse de maison* (if they are in a salon), all must be willing to play their part, to shine where this is required, but without stealing the limelight, to accommodate themselves to the performance of the group.

Politeness is therefore a heroic achievement. In their urbane way, its champions anticipate Nietzsche's remarks in *Beyond Good and Evil* about the great violence that had to be done over the centuries to the human animal in order to teach it to keep its word. Likewise, to be polite means repressing our instincts, which are fierce, brutal and selfish. However, if, as Pascal puts it, 'la nature de l'amour propre et de ce *moi* humain est de n'aimer que soi et de ne considérer que soi',[25] the politeness proposed by a Méré can only be superficially akin to real charity. It conceals the self, rather than transforming it. And it depends absolutely on the suppression of sincerity. To quote Pascal again, 'si tous les hommes savaient ce qu'ils disent les uns des autres, il n'y aurait pas quatre amis dans le monde' (p. 146).

This is the point of *Le Misanthrope*, the play which was an almost inescapable point of reference for discussions of politeness. Molière's comedy shows a homogeneous worldly environment where personal relations are ruled (in principle) by a code of politeness which Alceste refuses in the name of sincerity. Ignoring the social function of this code, he describes it as

> les contorsions
> De tous ces grands faiseurs de protestations,
> Ces affables donneurs d'embrassades frivoles,

60

Ces obligeants diseurs d'inutiles paroles,
Qui de civilités avec tous font combat   (I, i, 43–7)

At the same time, he has interiorized the rules he attempts to ignore – whence his own contortions as he tries to speak his mind to the offended Oronte. Philinte, on the other hand, has no illusions about the possibility of sincerity, or indeed about the goodness of humanity. For him, social exchange in *le monde* must inevitably mean the suppression of our true opinions or feelings. Nor is there any alternative world this side of the convent or Alceste's *désert*. The *honnêtes gens* of the play must therefore try to play the game by the rules. Philinte is not immoral or unfeeling, but the insincere politeness he accepts in Célimène's society is dictated purely by the need to fit in. It does not make people more loving, but at least it tames them, bringing peace, if not happiness.

Trublet and his predecessors such as Vaumorière and Bellegarde all give an image of polite conversation as a difficult exercise in self-control, poles apart from the easy effusions of friendship. Such conversation, as everyone repeats, is the acme of civilized living, and one of the great achievements of modern French society.[26] But for those taking part in this social and aesthetic art-work, it can be agony, or at least, in Philinte's words, 'un moyen d'exercer notre philosophie'. All human beings are impelled by self-love to seek their own satisfaction in conversation at the expense of others. The polite person has to do the opposite, at least in appearance. True politeness, in Bellegarde's words, 's'accommode de tout' (*Politesse*, p. 7); it enables us to live with coarse self-centred people, to put up with boredom, to accept insults with a disarming smile.

'Une grande partie de la politesse consiste à souffrir l'impolitesse', writes Trublet (p. 178). If all were polite, politeness would be less of an effort. The problem is particularly acute for the sensitive and intelligent person, who has to learn to listen patiently to stupid bores, and to resist the temptation to display his or her own superior knowledge or cleverness – nothing being worse than the person who is always right. And of course the essential thing is to avoid talking about yourself, which is what everyone really wants to do. But it is not enough to put yourself down and flatter others. *Complaisance*, which Alceste repudiates, is an essential element of politeness, but it must not be overdone. It is not simply that we should not tell unnecessary lies; equally important is the need to avoid 'fadeur'. Conversation being like a piece of music, a little dissonance is needed from time to time if it is not to become insipid. So the polite person

61

has the further duty to master the art of delicate raillery, throwing a pinch of Attic salt into the pot from time to time.

Given all these difficulties, it is not surprising that the writers on politeness come back often to the notion — which is already present in Méré's writings on *honnêteté* — that truly polite people are few and far between. The reader of these disquisitions can easily receive the impression that polite conversation, demanding as it does 'de la gêne et de l'attention sur soi' (Bellegarde, *Ridicule*, p. 10), can be experienced as a continual torture. Consequently, for some people, it was an activity whose pains exceeded its rewards. Marivaux is a good example. Although he provided models of politeness in his fiction and his plays, he seems to have found its constraints irksome. Trublet, in his memoirs, describes his unsociable singularity in Madame de Tencin's salon. Whereas the polite person is easy to deal with, Marivaux was disagreeably prickly and did not take the trouble to express himself clearly:

La société de Monsieur de Marivaux, agréable à plusieurs égards, est quelquefois désagréable par cette obscurité, fatigante même et ennuyeuse; de plus gênante par la crainte où l'on est de le blesser. En général il exige beaucoup d'égards, d'attention; il faut s'occuper de lui, l'écouter, lui applaudir.[27]

In his writings, Marivaux portrays the uncouth person in the guise of Arlequin (in *La Double Inconstance*), who is impatient with the pointless etiquette of upper-class society. In *L'Indigent philosophe*, he goes one stage further, adopting the persona of a free-spirited down-and-out who rebels against the mannered politeness of the *beau monde*: 'Ce n'est pas le plaisir qui l'a inventée; au contraire, je ne doute pas qu'il ne la chasse quelque jour'.[28] Here we are close to the position of Diogenes the Cynic, a figure who has an interesting life in polite eighteenth-century France. He represents the choice of freedom and humanity as against the enslaving manners of civilized society; his greatest incarnation is Jean-Jacques Rousseau.[29] Now among the anecdotes which cluster round Diogenes, is the famous one where he rudely defies Alexander the Great, asking him to get out of his sun. Alexander represents power. One may ask then what the relation is between politeness and authority. In what ways does it serve or reinforce the existing power structures and hierarchies? Two or three answers seem possible.

Firstly, there is the argument that polite manners are an adornment that distracts attention from the realities of inequality and domination. This is the view suggested by the passage near the beginning of Rousseau's *Discours sur les sciences et les arts*, where the advances of civilization, having been lauded as contributing to the progress of the human species, are suddenly described as garlands of flowers over the chains of oppression.[30] So the nobility at the court of Louis XIV, having lost much of its real power, found alternative satisfaction in participating in a cultural ritual that embellished its self-image.

A somewhat different thesis is that associated with the name of Norbert Elias. In his pioneering work of 1939,[31] Elias described the long process by which Europeans learned to control their bodily functions, speech and attitudes over the period from the Middle Ages to the time of the French Revolution and beyond. His argument is that in France, which played a leading part in this process, the main agency of civilization was the absolutist court. This was an institution for 'taming and preserving the nobility'; the codes of civility and politeness enforced habits of self-control (and of dissimulation) which were needed by those who had to play a subordinate part in an increasingly centralized political system. Politeness is an instrument of non-violent social control, which is gradually accepted and internalized by all layers of society.

This could be put in stronger terms. A good deal of the politeness teaching of the period we are considering insists on the proper respect to be accorded to rank. Orest Ranum, discussing the period of the Fronde, has written of the enforcement of deference to the King, or to his representatives the *intendants*, who demanded respect in peremptory fashion.[32] Seen in this light, the Fronde is an explosion of discourtesy. It is followed by a gradual acceptance by the formerly turbulent nobility of what Ranum calls the 'courtesy code'. So he can speak of an 'emasculation by courtesy' under Louis XIV — a process which left the British and Dutch with a lasting distrust of courtesy imposed from above 'for purposes of emptying society of its political rights'.

There is perhaps some exaggeration in this sinister story. Even so, it is clear that the codes of politeness could be used to humiliate (as in Molière's *George Dandin*) or to control. The civility books are strong on deference, though they warn against flattery. Courtin's popular *Nouveau Traité de la civilité* (1671), which is directed primarily at young people, teaches outsiders how to behave in *le monde*. He distinguishes between the way one behaves with one's social superiors, equals and inferiors. The most important lessons concern 'la conversation d'un inférieur avec un supériéur' — for instance, a young person in the presence of 'un grand'. The inferior must avoid any hint of effrontery, and will take particular care to adopt the right modes of address: 'Vous eûtes la bonté de me faire cette grâce', and so on. It is true that this is an elementary manual for the upwardly mobile, and concerns civility rather than politeness. Even so, a similar conception of hierarchy is to be found in such works as Madame de Lambert's *Avis d'une mère à son fils*, which is by no means meant for the social climber. The polite person is aware of hierarchy and respects it, outwardly at least.

A somewhat different point about the socio-political function of politeness involves the notion of *distinction*.[33] Unlike the elementary treatises on civility, the books on politeness were mainly concerned with the relations between inhabitants of the fashionable world. In the salons, if not in court, considerations of rank might be suspended. In such cases, *politesse* legislated for the exchanges between people who were supposed to be on a roughly equal footing. So much is true, and we shall see shortly how this might lead to a modified conception of *politesse*. Nevertheless, even if hierarchy might be ignored within the salon, politeness retained its politically conservative role in establishing a clear, almost unbridgeable gap of distinction between the polite and the not polite.

As we saw, a peasant might learn *civilité*, but *politesse* was a much rarer thing: 'un homme du peuple, un paysan, peuvent être civils, mais il n'y a qu'un homme du monde qui puisse être poli' (Trublet, p. 149). Roger Chartier has demonstrated the close connection between the widespread divulgation of the lessons of *civilité* and the creation of new frontiers to divide the elite from the rest.[34] Much stress is laid in the seventeenth- and eighteenth-century treatments of *politesse* on the superior ease, the apparent effortlessness which distinguishes the truly polite person from the merely civil. Needless to say, this ease is one of the hardest things to acquire. It is not automatically to be found among the socially privileged, but it is certainly more accessible to the well born than to the rest. There are exceptions, no doubt, but the general run of writings on the question suggest that *politesse*, like that other ineffable quality *goût*,[35] served among other things to keep people in their place.

Polis

What I have written so far presents politeness as a conservative force, giving lustre to the elite of a hierarchical society. I want now to explore alternative views of the matter, views which challenged the court-centred *politesse* with its stress on polished manners, and tried to envisage a more inward politeness ('la politesse du cœur'), and one that was more appropriate to free relations between equals – a politeness for the *polis*. Such a development also moves away from the local forms of politeness associated with particular socio-political conditions, and aims for a more universal view, just as Enlightenment thinkers aimed to formulate universal ideas of truth and justice.

An interesting argument on this question has been put forward by Daniel Gordon, who suggests, against Elias, that the salon (as opposed to the court) provided a locus for the development of egalitarian forms of dialogue.[36] In this setting, he says, are to be found the beginnings of that new social force, public opinion. One might see this sort of polite exchange as constituting what Habermas calls 'civil society', in opposition to the exercise of hierarchical power. Seen from this angle, politeness has a quite different role from those I have discussed so far. It can become an important element in an enlightened political programme.

Elements of this kind of development are found in the various writings I have quoted so far – those of Trublet, Bellegarde and others. None of these was content to propose a confessedly specious and amoral conception of his subject; all presented it at times, if not in political terms, then at least in strongly moral ones. Bellegarde, for instance, wrote that 'la politesse est un précis de toutes les vertus morales'.[37] Nevertheless, in this final section, I wish to concentrate on the work of four better-known writers, all of whom can be described in one way or another as *philosophes*. I shall ask how successful they were in freeing *politesse* from its less acceptable associations and recasting it in a new, more enlightened mould.

We can begin with La Bruyère's *Les Caractères*, an extremely influential work, which is in part at least a manual of politeness. La Bruyère shares many of the conventional views we have been considering. For him France is 'le centre du bon goût et de la politesse' (p. 173). He accepts the need for a basic politeness – or perhaps one should say civility – which means avoiding impropriety, coarseness and affectation. The country-dweller and the provincial need polishing. And if the provinces imitate Paris, Paris models itself on the court, which retains its position at the summit of the hierarchy. But in saying this, La Bruyère gives his thought a neat and rather cryptic twist: 'La ville dégoûte de la province; la cour détrompe de la ville, et guérit de la cour' (p. 253). Why is this so? Because the court, for all its superior aesthetic appeal, cannot satisfy important emotional and intellectual needs. The author's personal bitterness is visible in 'De la cour', which offers a critique of superficial court politeness that goes beyond what we find in *Le Misanthrope*. For Molière, the 'contorsions' of the fashionable world were primarily ridiculous, whereas La Bruyère insists on the harsh egoism hidden beneath the polished surface.

Nor does his exposure of false politeness stop at individual behaviour. Polite societies were conventionally contrasted with barbarous ones, but he brings out the real barbarity of polished nations such as France: 'Avec un langage si pur, une si grande recherche dans nos habits, des mœurs si cultivées, de si belles lois et un visage blanc, nous sommes barbares pour quelques peuples' (p. 358). So politeness is linked with oppression. Polished vice triumphs over simplicity. It is the same with class relations, when La Bruyère contrasts 'le peuple' and 'les grands: 'là se montrent ingénument la grossièreté et la franchise; ici se cache une sève maligne et corrompue sous l'écorce de la politesse' (p. 262). He concludes: 'Je veux être peuple'. Is this to refuse politeness or to aspire to another kind of politeness, far from the court?

One reason for this hostility to 'les grands' is no doubt their contempt for learning. Not that La Bruyère condones pedantry; he is too much of an *honnête homme* for that. But he deplores the low value placed on erudition and philosophy by polite people. Against this attitude, he praises the 'genuine' politeness of the Lamoignons, the Pellissons, the Condés or the Contis, who 'ont su joindre aux plus belles et aux plus hautes connaissances et l'atticisme des Grecs[38] et l'urbanité des Romains' (p. 354). Ordinary politeness calls for 'très peu de fonds' (little knowledge or education), whereas 'la politesse de l'esprit' demands a great deal.

What is important here is the distinction made within the concept of politeness between a superficial, worthless version and a true politeness of the mind (*l'esprit*). Or better still of the heart, since 'l'on est plus sociable et d'un meilleur commerce par le cœur que par l'esprit'. What is involved is not the ability to play a part gracefully, but the effort that is needed to make social life pleasanter for all.[39] This does indeed require effort. The chapter entitled 'De l'homme' begins with a terrible catalogue of human characteristics: hardness, ingratitude, pride, injustice, self-love, lack of concern for others. At times, La Bruyère seems to envisage a victory over human selfishness, where *politesse* would mean not a polished mask, but a genuine transformation of human nature. But his thought, like that of a Bellegarde, remains uncertain and far from optimistic: 'La politesse n'inspire pas toujours la bonté, l'équité, la complaisance, la gratitude; elle en donne du moins les apparences' (p. 164). For all his attack on false *politesse*, his vision remains tied to a hierarchical world; he does not go very far along the road to an alternative politeness.

Marivaux is less pessimistic. In his comedy *La Double Inconstance*, the rustic Arlequin – whose rusticity is his charm – is at odds with the polished world. His naive gaze allows the author to satirize in a light-hearted way the false politeness of the court. *Politesse* wins in the end, however; the heroine Sylvie, who is by nature more truly polite than the court ladies, recognizes the superiority of the Prince, in whom elegant manners accompany delicate feelings. The end of the play conforms to an old pattern, reconciling civilization and nature. Arlequin, who has not yet been 'polished' and so retains his clumsy sincerity, is to remain with the Prince as an antidote to a world in which court *politesse* suppresses the truth.

The discovery of polite society by a person from another world is a common theme in eighteenth-century literature. Generally there is a double movement: on the one hand the satire of fashionable hypocrisy through the innocent eye, but on the other acceptance of the superior value of true politeness.[40] This is how Marivaux's *La Vie de Marianne* works: it contains a critique of snobbish affectation, but also an idealized portrait of a truly polite society. Marivaux himself frequented the salons of Madame de Lambert and Madame de Tencin, who appear in his novel as Madame de Miran and Madame Dorsin. The latter in particular represents politeness as it should be. This is how Marianne describes her circle:

> Ils me mettaient à mon aise; et moi qui m'imaginais qu'il y avait tant de mystère dans la politesse des gens du monde, et qui l'avait regardée comme une science qui m'était totalement inconnue et dont je n'avais nul principe, j'étais bien surprise de voir qu'il n'y avait rien de si particulier dans la leur, rien qui me fût si étranger, mais seulement quelque chose de liant, d'obligeant et d'aimable.
>
> Il me semblait que cette politesse était celle de toute âme honnête, que tout esprit bien fait trouve qu'il a en lui dès qu'on la lui montre.[41]

Paradoxically, the politeness that distinguishes this elite circle is available to all. Or rather – and this restriction is essential – it is available to 'toute âme honnête' (the adjective is as usual ambiguous, but must have a strongly moral connotation here) and to 'tout esprit bien fait'. It seems to be a gift of nature. Marivaux knows that many people prefer their selfish interests to it, but even so, his vision of politeness remains more optimistic than that of Bellegarde or La Bruyère. There is no call for painful effort and self-sacrifice here. It is easy to be polite; all that is needed is for someone to point the way.

And in the novel, Marianne, who has none of the advantages of a fashionable education, displays a natural politeness which wins all hearts. Distinction does not depend on class now, but on a moral hierarchy.

One should not exaggerate Marivaux's radicalism. He does not envisage a form of politeness which would thrive among peasants or artisans. Nor does his 'politesse du cœur' imply any overturning of the existing social order. The moral equality of naturally polite people does not abolish distinctions of rank. It may, however, ease the mingling of different groups from the nobility and the bourgeoisie, and the infiltration of these privileged groups by at least some individuals from the lower orders. And above all it makes social hierarchies more acceptable, since it accords more importance to consideration for others than to distinguished manners.

In the generation following Marivaux's, many *philosophes* expressed discomfort at their relation with the *beau monde*. While the salons provided them with a forum for discussion, the rules of politeness could be felt as a brake on free intellectual activity. D'Alembert, for instance, in his interesting *Essai sur la société des gens de lettres avec les grands*, warns against the debilitating effects of a politeness which in order to make science and philosophy more accessible, subjects them to the trivial laws of decorum.[42] For others, the problem was moral rather than intellectual. Toussaint, in *Les Mœurs*, while endorsing the social value of politeness, insists that sincerity is a law of nature which suffers no exception. For him, therefore, it is essential to steer a middle course between boorishness and flattery. He makes it sound rather easy: 'tout autre qu'un misanthrope ou un flatteur sait concilier la franchise avec la politesse'.[43] More challenging are the pages on the subject in Charles Pinot Duclos's *Considérations sur les mœurs*,[44] which appeared not long after Toussaint's book.

Whereas many Enlightenment thinkers (Hume, for instance) saw a natural connection between the progress of polite civilization and moral and political improvement, Duclos draws a disturbing distinction between them. 'Les peuple policés', he says, 'valent mieux que les peuples polis' (p. 12). One may have to choose between corrupt politeness and rude integrity. This does not lead Duclos to a primitivist refusal of civil society; for him, savages and barbarians are neither pure nor innocent. No, what he favours, like many of his fellow-*philosophes*, is a golden mean between rude pre-civilized anarchy and the corruption of a society where surface polish usurps the place of virtue: 'Les mœurs simples et sévères ne se trouvent que parmi ceux

68

que la raison et l'équité ont policés, et qui n'ont pas encore abusé de l'esprit pour se corrompre' (p. 12).

In his chapter entitled 'De la politesse', Duclos is therefore very critical of what he calls 'la politesse d'usage', which is no more than 'un jargon fade, plein d'expressions exagérées, aussi vides de sens que de sentiment' (p. 34). Against those who saw in it the distinguishing quality of an elite, the result of a difficult process of training in self-control, he replies that difficulty does not confer value. What is more, 'il serait à desirer que des hommes qui, de dessein formé, renoncent à leur caractère, n'en recueillent d'autre fruit que d'être ridicules' (p. 35). Nor is politeness as rare as people say. In fact, it is becoming shop-soiled and therefore ineffectual; it is 'si ridicule et si vil, qu'il est donné pour ce qu'il est, c'est-à-dire pour faux' (p. 32). Whence the reaction of those who prefer to behave crudely in order to show their sincerity.

All this is vigorous enough, but Duclos is not entirely hostile to politeness. For one thing, like Philinte or Pascal, he knows that absolute sincerity would destroy friendship. More importantly, like Marivaux, he favours a politeness of the heart, founded on mutual respect. In a way, this is an anti-politeness, since it does away with all the little falsehoods and frills which society normally demands. This is how he describes it:

Le plus malheureux effet de la politesse d'usage est d'enseigner l'art de se passer des vertus qu'elle imite. Qu'on nous inspire dans l'éducation l'humanité et la bienfaisance, nous aurons la politesse, ou nous n'en aurons pas besoin.

Si nous n'avons pas celle qui s'annonce par les grâces, nous aurons celle qui annonce l'honnête homme et le citoyen; nous n'aurons pas besoin de recourir à la fausseté.   (p. 37)

Notice the appearance of the word 'citoyen', which points towards a different kind of society. Duclos seems to be hesitating between two courses: either to abandon the futile and harmful politeness of existing society, or else to attempt to give it a new, less exclusive form, compatible with civic virtue. The latter would no longer be located in the court or the salon, but in a place where citizens might meet. It would (or would it?) be available to peasants as well as to *honnêtes gens*.

It is not surprising that this passage from Duclos is cited in Rousseau's *Emile* (it is one of the few books to obtain that honour). Duclos and Rousseau were friends, and apparently resembled each other in their brusque way of behaving in society. Rousseau quotes his friend's words out of context, which gives them a more radical tone than in the original. And, naturally enough, the Citizen of Geneva goes further still in seeking to reshape the idea of politeness on egalitarian or republican lines. His writings were immensely influential and pose a similar question to Duclos's *Considérations*: does Rousseau want to discard the very notion of *politesse* or to transform it? In Chapter 11, I discuss the more general question of his primitivism; here I shall concentrate on *Emile*, where he attempts to derive a model of education from his philosophy of human nature.[45]

For the Rousseau of *Emile*, whatever he may have written elsewhere of the pleasures of solitude, it is friendship, affection and sociability which are the essence of human happiness. The point of Book 4 of the work, after three books devoted to developing the boy hero's powers independently of society, is to propose a form of socialization (Robinson Crusoe returning from his island) which will avoid as far as possible the disadvantages of existing society. In particular Rousseau is putting forward an alternative to the manners of polite society, so *politesse* naturally has a place in his discussion.

One thing is clear, and this is that the author of the *Discours sur l'inégalité* will have nothing to do with the idea of distinction. As he puts it, 'c'est le peuple qui compose le genre humain; ce qui n'est pas peuple est si peu de chose que n'est pas la peine de le compter' (p. 509). Writing of taste, he affirms that it consists in knowing 'ce qui plaît ou déplaît au plus grand nombre' (p. 671). Naturally, therefore, the exclusive world of the salons cannot be a model. In other works, notably the *Lettre à d'Alembert* and *La Nouvelle Héloïse*, Rousseau compares Parisian high society unfavourably with the cruder, more homely world of Switzerland, the Genevan *cercles* for instance. A particular bugbear of his is the place of women in the Paris salon world; he sees female preponderance as a danger to the 'manly' virtues (frankness, courage, etc.) which a free society needs. Politeness is thus associated with oppression.

This might suggest that in talking of the socialization of Emile, Rousseau would turn his back on *le monde*. This is not in fact the case. 'Emile n'est pas un sauvage à reléguer dans les deserts, c'est un sauvage fait pour habiter les villes' (p. 484). A compromise with politeness is needed, and he comes to this towards the end of Book 4. 'Comme il y a un âge propre à l'étude des sciences', he says, 'il y en a un pour bien saisir l'usage du monde'. And what he seeks to show is how the twenty-year-old Emile, in spite of his solitary upbringing, will be 'plus aimable et plus judicieusement poli que celui qu'on y aura nourri dès son enfance' (p. 654). The important thing is precisely that this politeness is not the result of a long period of training and indoctrination. Earlier in the book, Rousseau had warned against the mechanical inculcation of formulas of politeness; this is not only pointless, but harmful, since it gives children the habit of saying what they do not mean. The hero of Books 1 to 3 is noticeably lacking in concern for others and shows it. But in Book 4, thanks to the onset of puberty, he is ready to be socialized. Rousseau may be hostile to the excessive power supposedly exercised by women in polite society, but he is ready to go along with the idea that love and the desire to please bring the young man to experience such social affections as benevolence, pity and friendship. Emile comes to feel for others, and wants to be loved by them; it is these feelings that are the origin of genuine politeness, which is as appropriate in the salons as in quite different walks of life.

The essential difference between this politeness and that of a Trublet is that it comes naturally. Emile 'ne connaît ni gêne ni déguisement' (p. 665). He says what he thinks, simply, neither quarrelling nor flattering. He does not try to stand out, and is happy to go along with the norms of the society he is in: 'Loin de choquer les manières des autres, Emile s'y conforme assez volontiers, non pour paraître instruit des usages, ni pour affecter les airs d'un homme poli, mais au contraire de peur qu'on ne le distingue' (p. 666). Rousseau, doubtless remembering his own awkwardness in society, his difficulties in reconciling sincerity and politeness, presents this here (in this dream of compensation) as the easiest thing in the world – for someone who has had the right education. His reflections on 'l'usage du monde' are very close to those of Marivaux's Marianne:

On nous fait un grand mystère de l'usage du monde; comme si, dans l'âge où l'on prend cet usage, on ne le prenait pas naturellement, et comme si ce n'était pas dans un cœur honnête qu'il faut en chercher ses premières lois! La véritable politesse consiste à marquer de la bienveillance aux hommes; elle se montre sans peine quand on en a. (p. 669)

It is true that immediately after this Rousseau writes: 'C'est pour celui qui n'en a pas qu'on est forcé de réduire en art ses principes' – which seems to leave the door open to the false politeness that he repudiates. Perhaps this is why Emile, who is not concerned to be admired, is described as 'plus affectueux que poli' (p. 669). Elsewhere, we read: 'S'il n'a pas les formules de la politesse, il a les soins de l'humanité' (p. 666). One is tempted to ask if this does not render the concept of politeness superfluous. Because he was writing a treatise on education for upper-class readers, Rousseau no doubt felt the need

71

to say something on the topic. He therefore attempted, following the line of Marivaux, to outline a more acceptable version, a 'politesse du cœur', free from the old connotations of insincerity. In doing so, like Duclos, he came close to suggesting a politeness for the citizens of the *polis*, a type of 'manly' politeness that could be accepted by the French revolutionaries for instance. But his heart was not really in it. What he calls 'la véritable politesse' might be better named 'l'humanité'. If politeness is confined to *le monde*, humanity belongs to *tout le monde*.

In a word, neither Jean-Jacques nor his predecessors really resolve the contradictions associated with politeness. Conflicting moral, social, political and aesthetic connotations cluster round the term. It is sufficiently highly regarded (unlike 'urbanité' for instance) to make it worth fighting for. On the other hand, it is too closely bound up with a particular social order to be easily converted into a universal moral value. Even in the late twentieth century, when its field of application has shrunk, it has not lost all its ambiguity.

This chapter has indicated how politeness was envisaged as a victory over animality and savagery – a positive value akin to the ideal of civilization. The other side of the coin was its association with falsity, snobbery or oppression. This latter view led some thinkers to prefer cruder but more virtuous manners, to adopt the model of Diogenes the Cynic. Between the two one can locate the attempt of certain *philosophes* to bring politeness more in line with the values of the Enlightenment, tolerance, humanity, social affection. In the confused chorus of voices one can certainly trace a gradual movement here between two ideal types, from the deferential court politeness of 1660 to the values proposed by a Duclos a hundred years later.

Not that one should exaggerate oppositions between the *philosophes* and those, such as Bellegarde or Trublet, who gave more direct expression to the outlook of the fashionable world. None of them was ready to preach an amoral politeness, but neither did anyone – even Rousseau – reject the need for some sort of art of pleasing. The *Encyclopédie* article 'Politesse', by the Chevalier de Jaucourt, offers a characteristic middle view (or muddled view?). It begins with praise; politeness is exalted over civility and seen as a compendium of the social virtues. So far, so good. At the end, however, comes an unexpected twist, and we suddenly hear the voice of a primitivist critic: 'Elle n'a guère lieu au fond des forêts, entre des hommes et des femmes nus et tout entiers à la poursuite de leurs besoins; et chez les peuples policés, elle n'est souvent que la démonstration extérieure d'une bienveillance qui n'est pas dans le cœur'. Politeness was too strongly linked to the idea of distinction to be easily reconquered by the moralist or the republican.

In this chapter I have confined myself almost entirely to the realm of ideology. In order to know what went on in the world of practical action, one would need to look at the mass of evidence contained in private letters, memoirs and the like, and it may be doubted if these would lead to any simple generalization. One might also seek to explain the change in the conception of politeness by reference to shifts of power and influence within the privileged classes, but this complex task goes beyond my present purposes. One thing is clear however: the evolution I have suggested, if it affected practice as well as theory, was confined to a small elite group. As the Encyclopedist puts it, 'elle n'a guère lieu au fond des forêts'. Except perhaps in the thought of a Rousseau, the common people of peasants, artisans and beggars remained excluded from the world of politeness. They may have begun to be influenced by the elementary civility of a Courtin, and of course they had their own forms of sociability, their own politeness,[46] but at least until the time of the Revolution, the debates about *politesse* concerned only a small proportion of the French population. In their confused way, however, these debates expressed certain discontents of a triumphant yet vulnerable civilization.

5

THE SOCIABLE ESSAYIST: ADDISON AND MARIVAUX

The politeness discussed in the last chapter finds an expression in some characteristic kinds of writing. These are the so-called minor genres (far from minor in reality) which embody in their very form something of the ideal of polite communication. There are salon genres such as the portrait or the maxim, but the three central forms are the dialogue, the letter and the essay. All of these are much beloved of French and British authors of the late seventeenth and eighteenth centuries. All are capable of embracing subjects from the trivial to the grandiose, from the commonplace to the abstruse. And in all of them the matter is poured into a specifically social mould, where the polite values of ease and unpretentiousness (*le naturel*) are paramount. The enemy is pedantry, dogmatic self-assertiveness. The ideal is well expressed in a fine passage from the introduction to Hume's *Dialogues concerning Natural Religion*:

Reasonable men may be allowed to differ, where no one can reasonably be positive, opposite sentiments, even without any decision, afford an agreeable amusement, and if the subject be curious and interesting, the book carries us, in a manner, into company, and unites the two greatest and purest pleasures of human life, study and society.[1]

Hume is writing about dialogue here, but his ideal marriage of study and society suits the serious essay equally well. In fact he did write a short essay 'On Essay-Writing' which makes similar points. This is a youthful piece, which may well reflect his experience and reading in France between 1734 and 1737. It was included in the 1742 edition of his essays, but thereafter excluded from the definitive edition.[2] Apart from the title, it contains no specific mention of the essay as such, but is concerned with the relation between 'study' and 'society' among 'the elegant part of mankind, who are not immersed in animal life'. Hume remarks that 'the separation of the learned from the conversable world seems to have been the great defect of the last age'. Such a separation meant that social intercourse was reduced to

74

triviality while learning remained barbarously pedantic. But Hume is pleased to note that 'in this age' the old divide has been eroded, society has become more literate, learning more social. And his own role as essay-writer is to be an 'ambassador from the dominions of learning to those of conversation'. The latter, moreover, are under the rule of 'the fair sex'. So although essays may be written by men, one of their characteristics is to be addressed to women, who are 'much better judges of all polite writing than men of the same degree of understanding'. This is particularly true of 'a neighbouring nation' – France of course.

What comes out of Hume's remarks is thus the mediating role to be played by the essay. This raises an interesting question, and one which concerns the dialogue also. The word essay (*essai*) implies a trial. This etymology was present in the minds of Hume's contemporaries as it had been in Montaigne's. In this view the writer of an essay is one who is not sure of himself, who is thinking aloud, trying out his ideas among equals, suggesting but not asserting, starting thoughts rather than delivering a doctrine. But Hume's remarks also make it clear that this unpedantic form (like the dialogue and the letter) is very suitable for popularization. The writer of a treatise (such as Hume's ill-fated *Treatise on Human Nature*) may thus turn to the essay as a dress that will make unfamiliar ideas more acceptable to amateurs. The essay, in fact, can move (or be torn) between discovery and pedagogy.

Such a tension is visible in the two 'Spectators' which I shall discuss in this chapter, the original *Spectator* of Addison and Steele, and Marivaux's *Spectateur français*. Both texts, but particularly that of Addison and Steele, point to a crucial element in the development of the essay, and that is the role of the periodical press. Journals such as the *Mercure galant* or the *Gentleman's Magazine* clearly played an essential role in the creation and maintenance of a polite culture of sociability. Before the *Tatler* and the *Spectator*, however, the essay was not an important ingredient in such journalism. With the latter, in particular, we see the appearance of the issue of a newspaper devoted to one single subject. In other words, the subscriber to the *Spectator* could expect to receive every day between March 1711 and December 1712 a 'paper' which was more or less an essay. The essays in question are short – a far cry from Locke's *Essay concerning Human Understanding* – though the same subject may be treated in a succession of issues. They are also extremely varied in character, ranging from disquisitions on serious topics, by way of exchanges of real or fictional letters, to anecdotes and satirical or picturesque descriptions of contemporary life. It is therefore hard to make any valid generalizations about them. In this discussion I shall concentrate on the first 100 numbers.[3]

The best starting point is No. 10, in which Addison sets out the aims of the authors. He begins by speaking with modest irony of the success of his 'morning lectures'. Then, without abandoning the bantering tone, he makes the serious declaration:

It was said of Socrates that he brought philosophy down from heaven to inhabit among men; and I shall be ambitious to have it said of me that I have brought philosophy out of closets and libraries, schools and colleges, to dwell in clubs and assemblies, at tea-tables and in coffee-houses.   (I, 44)

One can see how this anticipates what Hume has to say in 'On Essay-Writing'. The world of the essay, or at least of the *Spectator* essay, is the sociable world. Alongside the coffee-house, stronghold of male sociability, we have the female tea-table, and Addison is quite plain, here and elsewhere, that he is writing very largely for a female public ('There are none to whom this paper will be more useful than to the female world' (I, 46)). What Addison and Steele offered their readers, both male and female, was a new model of polite conversation, not the frivolous or immoral conversation of courts, but a proper blend of seriousness and ease, Christianity and worldliness. In this they were extraordinarily successful. The *Spectator* was read, discussed and imitated by a relatively broad public all over Britain and beyond. It has been claimed for instance that one of the main planks of the Scottish Enlightenment was the introduction of 'Addisonian politeness' into a provincial society.[4] '*Spectator* clubs' sprang up likewise all over England, one of the best documented being that of Spalding in Lincolnshire, where a group of gentlemen formed to meet, read and discuss the *Spectator*.[5]

The journal is presented from the outset not as the writings of two authors, but as the emanation of a club − and this club is connected with the main London coffee-houses. In the second number we meet the individual members of the club in all their variety; they represent both town and country and such different social types as the lawyer, the merchant, the soldier and the man about town. The *Spectator* thus incorporates in its text some of its typical readers, even if only the male ones; as Addison writes in No. 34, 'my readers [...] have the satisfaction to find that there is no rank or degree among them who have not their representative in this club' (I, 142). The essay invites imaginary participation. And soon after the first issue, actual readers began to respond to the invitation to write to 'Mr Spectator'. Their letters were incorporated in an increasingly polyphonic text. In this way the essay can become a kind of dialogue, or a concert of voices, in much the same way that the *Lettres persanes*, that nearly contemporaneous work, combines various voices and subjects in a succession of short pieces which could almost be numbers of a periodical.

While the *Spectator* thus contributes to a new kind of sociability, its authors are far from tender towards many existing forms. No. 9 for instance begins: 'Man is said to be a sociable animal', and launches into a satirical description of 'those little nocturnal assemblies which are commonly known by the name of clubs' (I, 39) (comic examples being the club of fat men or the Humdrum Club of boring silent men). In the same way the *Spectator* contains much ridicule of fashionable society, its theatres, operas and assemblies. On the whole, sociability is no doubt a virtue, if it can be properly formed. But it is interesting to note that although the *Spectator* is supposed to represent a social group, the spectator figure himself is shown in a distinctly anti-social light. He may be a member of the club, but he plays no part in it. The essay-writer, rather than being Hume's ambassador from the realms of learning to the fashionable world, is more like a spy. Or rather, his *persona* is close to that of the traditional isolated philosopher as he is seen in La Bruyère's *Caractères* – less a misanthropist, perhaps, than a proponent of the true virtues which keep society together, but perforce something of an eccentric and an outsider in society as it is.

This comes out most clearly in No. 12, where the portrayal of the essayist is the main subject of the essay. We have previously learned (in No. 1) that Mr Spectator is a middle-aged man, learned and rather odd, distinguished for his silence, a traveller among men and societies, known to few, neutral in politics, 'a spectator of mankind rather than [...] one of the species' (I, 4). (Much later, in No. 264, he will reveal that, like Marivaux's *spectateur*, he has been crossed in love.) Hardly the most sociable of men. And in No. 12 this solitary eccentricity is carried to the point of grotesque oddity. He recounts his first arrival in London:

I then fell into an honest family, and lived very happily for above a week; when my landlord, who was a jolly good-natured man, took it into his head that I wanted company, and therefore would frequently come into my chamber to keep me from being alone. This I bore for two or three days; but telling me one day that he was afraid I was melancholy, I thought it was high time for me to be gone, and accordingly took new lodgings that very night [...] I am now settled with a widow woman, who has a great many children, and complies with my humour in everything. I do not remember that we have exchanged a word together these five years. (I, 52)

There seems to be a strange contradiction here between the drive to sociability that characterizes the *Spectator* essay and the character chosen to embody it. The two can perhaps be reconciled in a type of Stoic detachment which goes hand in hand with the proper performance of social duties — the Ciceronian model for the English gentleman as against the French courtier. No. 10 describes such people, Mr Spectator's 'brothers and allies':

the fraternity of spectators who live in the world without having anything to do in it, and either by the affluence of their fortunes or laziness of their dispositions, have no other business with the rest of mankind but to look upon them. (I, 45)

Could we not see the essay precisely as a genre designed for this sort of person, privileged to lead a life of contemplative leisure? If so, one essential element in its poetics is the creation of the appropriate type of spectator *persona*.

When we consider the actual form of the *Spectator* essays, one of the main questions is that of order. It is not easy to generalize here. Addison's Saturday semons are very different in nature from the more picturesque and comic pieces, and are on the whole constructed more in accordance with traditional rhetorical norms. But in all cases, a balance is struck between chaos and the excess of method which (according to Diderot)[6] destroys the life of a piece of writing, removing it from the coffee-house to the study. It will be helpful here to analyse just one essay, even though a single one cannot stand for all.

No. 94, dated Monday June 18, 1711, and written by Addison, is in fact the continuation of the preceding essay, a well-organized discourse on the paradox of the shortness of our lives and the difficulties we have in filling them. In it Addison has proposed various 'useful and innocent' ways of filling up our time, including the pursuit of knowledge, which he leaves for fuller discussion in No. 94. This begins, like all the rest, with a Latin tag, and throughout the essay Addison intersperses his own reflections with those of other writers. After Martial, we have a brief reminiscence of Boyle and then a long quotation from Locke's *Essay* and a reference to Malebranche's *Recherche de la vérité*. The first part of the essay moves quickly from the initial question (Addison declines to engage on such 'beaten subjects' as the usefulness of knowledge) to a related speculation that is 'more uncommon, and may therefore perhaps be more

entertaining'. This concerns the subjective nature of our perception
of time and the way in which it can be modified by the perceiver's
concentration on one subject to the exclusion of all others – or
conversely by our moving very rapidly from one subject to another.
At this point, Addison feels the need to shift from philosophy to story-
telling, and recounts one after another two marvellous stories from
the *Turkish Tales*. In each tale, however, the philosophical import
is clearly indicated, and the second story concludes with a theological
moral. Having taken his readers off into the realms of legend,
Addison then returns them explicitly to the original subject, but leaves
them to spell out the connections:

I shall leave my reader to compare these Eastern fables with the notions of
those two great philosophers whom I have quoted in this paper; and shall
only, by way of application, desire him to consider how we may extend life
beyond its natural dimensions by applying ourselves diligently to the pursuits
of knowledge.   (I, 401)

The essay then concludes with a paragraph of echoing maxims about
the wise man and the fool and a final paragraph in which a leisurely
comparison likens their respective views of past life to a desert and
a garden. This highly philosophical piece can thus end on the words
'some beautiful plant or flower'.

Several things strike one about the construction of this essay.
In the first place, its unity: there is nothing in it which is not relevant
to its central theme. In the second place, to counterbalance this, its
variety, narrative against philosophy, direct statement against
quotation, maxim against comparison. But above all, the unobtrusive
and easy way in which it unfolds. The connections between para-
graphs are well marked, but without any sense of overbearing
organization. Take the beginning of the second story:

There is a very pretty story in the *Turkish Tales* which relates to this passage
of that famous impostor Mohammed, and bears some affinity to the subject
we are now upon. A Sultan of Egypt [...]   (I, 400)

Addison does not allow his reader to lose sight of 'the subject we are
now upon', yet the primary impulse seems to be that of story-telling.
The opening has the kind of directness we might expect in conversation. By the end of the essay, the reader feels that he or she has been
led on a leisurely and entertaining walk through the realms of high
philosophy and exotic legend, without ever losing sight of the author's
main concern.

A final point is the mix of story (or description) and reflection in
the essay. The proportions of these can vary infinitely, as indeed

they can in fiction. Story may be no more than a brief illustration
in a predominantly discursive text, or it may virtually take over. In
almost all cases, though, the point of the essay emerges not so much
from rational deduction as from the reader's ability to relate example
and idea. We shall see with Marivaux how the essay fares in the hands
of a moralist who is above all a dramatist and story-teller.

Other numbers of the *Spectator* are certainly less well ordered than
No. 94, but Addison and Steele never give way to the temptations of
coq-à-l'âne – or even the relative disorder of a Montaigne. No. 46
is an interesting case, for here Addison speaks directly of the rhetoric
of essay-writing, and in particular of its *inventio*, the gathering of
copy. He creates a comic scene out of his journalist's notes, 'a whole
sheetful of hints that would look like a rhapsody of nonsense to
anybody but myself'. As he puts it, 'they are my speculations in the
first principles, that (like the world in its chaos) are void of all light,
distinction and order'. Like Pope's Newton, Addison will bring light
from dark, order from chaos. The list begins like this:

Sir Roger de Coverley's country seat. – Yes, for I hate long speeches. –
Query, if a good Christian may be a conjurer. – Childermas-day, salt-cellar,
house-dog, screech-owl, cricket. – Mr Thomas Inkle of London in the good
ship called the Achilles. Yarico. – *Aegrescitque medendo.* – Ghosts. – The
ladies' library. – Lion by trade a tailor. – Dromedary called Bucephalus.

(I, 196–7)

It is as if Addison were setting a puzzle to his readers: make a text
of that if you can. But in fact about half of the list is no more than
a table of contents for some preceding issues of the *Spectator*. Taken
together, the collection of essays is indeed a pot-pourri, but in each
individual piece the original notation has been drawn out into a
satisfying ordered whole. Nevertheless, this essay is placed under the
sign of chaos, and Addison feels free to conclude with two quite
separate letters, two little vignettes which have no connection with
each other or with the rest of the essay. Here the *Spectator* is closer
to the medley principle which governed its predecessor, Steele's *Tatler*.

Perhaps the aspect of the *Spectator* which won greatest praise from
eighteenth-century readers was its style. There are many testimonies
to the fact that contemporaries took Addison and Steele's easy
elegance as a model.[7] It was above all in language that the essayist
was able to imitate and propagate the ideal qualities of good polite
conversation and writing, witty but not ostentatious or absurd,
reasonable without being boring. Addison himself often reflects
at length on such matters, for instance in the series of papers

(Nos. 58–63) devoted to true and false wit. His doctrine will seem bland to a present-day taste, not unlike that of one of his models, Bouhours.[8] Once again, it is not easy to illustrate the practice of the *Spectator* from any one example, but here is a passage from Steele's witty moralizing (a more formal and impersonal piece than some). It comes from No. 64:

> The general affectation among men of appearing greater than they are, makes the whole world run into the habit of the court. You see the lady, who the day before was as various as a rainbow, upon the time appointed for beginning to mourn, as dark as a cloud. This humour does not prevail only on those whose fortunes can support any change in their equipage, not on those only whose incomes demand the wantonness of new appearances; but on such also who have just enough to clothe them. An old acquaintance of mine, of ninety pounds a year, who has naturally the vanity of being a man of fashion deep at his heart, is very much put to it to bear the mortality of princes. He made a new black suit upon the death of the King of Spain, he turned it for the King of Portugal, and he now keeps his chamber while it is scouring for the emperor. He is a good economist in his extravagance, and makes only a fresh black button upon his iron-grey suit for any potentate of small territories; he indeed adds his crape hatband for a prince whose exploits he has admired in the *Gazette*. But whatever compliments may be made on these occasions, the true mourners are the mercers, silkmen, lacemen and milliners. A prince of a merciful and royal disposition would reflect with great anxiety upon the prospect of his death, if he considered what numbers would be reduced to misery by that accident alone. He would think it of moment enough to direct that in the notification of his departure the honour to him might be restrained to those of the household of the prince to whom it should be signified. He would think a general mourning to be in a less degree the same ceremony which is practised in barbarous nations, of killing their slaves to attend the obsequies of their kings. (I, 276)

Several characteristics of the *Spectator* style can be seen here: the reference to accepted commonplaces (men affect to appear greater than they are), the illustration with examples which are both general ('the lady') and particularized ('an old acquaintance of mine'), the use of the personal pronouns 'you' and 'I' ('we' is also common, as one might expect, but does not appear here), the taste for nicely balanced sentences ('This humour [...] clothe them'). A playful, ironic wit pervades the passage, surfacing in the vision of the lady 'as various as a rainbow' and 'as dark as a cloud', in the contrast between the 'mortality of princes' and the financial embarrassment of men of fashion, in the comic physical detail of the transformations undergone by the mourning clothes, and in the ironic lessons to princes contained in the last three sentences, culminating in the extravagant – yet thought-provoking – comparison between the killing of slaves and the ruining of subjects. The sentences are all well formed, not casual, yet pompous only in a tongue-in-cheek way. The language is quite plain in places ('[he] is very much put to it'), but never vulgar. Nothing here is abrupt or shocking, obscure or demanding. The essayist is present, but not aggressively so; he offers his reader an easy but agreeable entertainment. It is not exciting, but it is polite.

The *Spectator* was immediately much admired, translated and imitated on the Continent. In 1717, the *Journal littéraire de la Haye* noted that the French had nothing to equal it.[9] In 1721, Marivaux rose to the challenge in his *Spectateur français*.[10] This was not his début in journalism; as well as several burlesque plays and fictional texts, he had by 1721 written a number of pieces for the *Mercure galant*, notably the *Lettres sur les habitants de Paris* (1717–18). These sketches of Paris life, inspired largely by La Bruyère's *Caractères*, anticipated the *Spectateur* in being a deliberately disjointed medley of jottings, anecdotes, portraits and reflections. They are cast in the form of a one-sided correspondence, and Marivaux maintains the pretence of real letters, continually addressing his provincial lady, and exploiting to the full the potential disorder of the genre. It is also worth noting that in 1719–20 he published in the *Mercure* his *Lettres concernant une aventure*, which foreshadow some of his later plays and novels, and that his comedy *Arlequin poli par l'amour* (1720) precedes the *Spectateur*, while *La Surprise de l'amour* (1722), *La Double Inconstance* (1724), *Le Prince travesti* (1724) and *La Fausse Suivante* (1724) all received their première during the publication of the journal. In other words, the *Spectateur français* is the work of a man who was actively pursuing a career as playwright and novelist.

Marivaux launched his journal in May 1721, announcing his intention of publishing one number a week. In this aim he failed pitifully: the public, impatient or not, had to wait over six months for the second issue, and thereafter the *Spectateur* came out at very irregular intervals – twenty-five numbers in all, the last appearing in January 1724. Subsequently Marivaux returned to this type of periodical publication with *L'Indigent philosophe* (seven numbers at fairly regular intervals between March and July 1727) and *Le Cabinet du philosophe* (twelve numbers, probably all written in advance and published at weekly intervals in the spring of 1734). All of these works were gathered up into collective volumes, and that is how the modern reader tends to approach them. In what follows, I shall concentrate primarily on the *Spectateur*, since the clear indication of an English model invites us to compare the two. What happens to the periodical essay in Marivaux's hands?

In the first place, the extremely sporadic nature of the publication meant that it was quite impossible for him to build up the kind of relations with the public that Addison and Steele had achieved. In France there could be no *Spectator* societies like that of Spalding. It is true that Marivaux does follow the English model by including letters in his 'feuilles', but these are for the most part manifestly the work of the author. Rather than being a sign of the public's participation, they are the product of the story-telling verve which was to produce *La Vie de Marianne* and *Le Paysan parvenu*. Nor is there the slightest fiction of a club whose conversation is echoed in the essays. The *spectateur* moves in a world of salons, theatres and similar public gatherings, but hardly seems to belong there. No. 10, for instance, begins like this:

Je me souviens qu'un jour, dans une promenade publique, je liai conversation avec un homme qui m'était inconnu. L'air pesant et taciturne que je lui trouvais ne me promettait pas un entretien fort amusant de sa part; il éternua, je lui répondis par un coup de chapeau; voilà par où nous débutâmes ensemble. Après cela vinrent quelques discours vagues sur la chaleur, sur le besoin de pluie, qui n'étaient qu'une façon de se dire avec bonté l'un à l'autre: *Je n'oublie pas que vous êtes là.* (p. 160)

The scene is a far remove from a convivial coffee-house. Two strangers find themselves together by chance; together they will watch and discuss the spectacle of the fashionable world. In the two or three pages that follow, after a sticky opening to the conversation, we see the *spectateur*'s chance acquaintance belie his ponderous appearance and launch into an animated speech on feminine coquetry and virtue; the *spectateur* himself plays less and less of a part, for his interlocutor says what Marivaux wants to say. The conversation is instructive, both in its subject matter and in the contradiction between the main speaker's appearance and his true character, as Marivaux notes at the end:

Il se leva là-dessus et me quitta, en me souhaitant le bonsoir. Je le conduisis des yeux, tout aussi loin que je pus, et depuis ce temps-là, j'ai toujours été sur le qui-vive avec les physionomies massives. (p. 162)

So the two characters separate, and the *spectateur* turns his attention from the 'promenade publique' to the story of unhappy love which is told in letters over three successive numbers by a fictitious female correspondent. The conversation between the two men has in fact been a general commentary on the psychological picture painted in the letters. Marivaux's intention is less to give a model of polite sociability than to investigate areas of private emotion.

Addison and Steele created their own public, providing it with examples of polite moral discourse. Marivaux's aim is different. He assumes the existence of a reading public, much the same social group as the readership of the *Mercure galant*, and he uses the periodical essay largely as a means of pursuing a series of social and psychological enquiries. His (or his spectator's) attitude towards his readers seems less pedagogical than Addison's. But he is, of course, like all essayists, very aware of the relations between writer and reader. The first number sets the tone: 'Lecteur, je ne veux point vous tromper, et je vous avertis d'avance que ce n'est point un auteur que vous allez lire ici' (p. 114). The amateurish 'honnête homme' stance is a time-honoured one, reminding French readers of Montaigne or of Pascal's famous 'On s'attendait de voir un auteur, et on trouve un homme'. Like many essayists, Marivaux cultivates the impression of a man talking informally to his fellows, on terms of equality. He involves the reader in the discussion with phrases such as 'j'en conviens', 'dira-t-on', 'voici comment', or with questions and answers. There is a kind of button-holing orality about a passage such as the following:

Supposons à présent que cet homme ait de l'esprit. Croyez-vous en vérité que ce qu'il sent en se retirant ne valût pas bien ce que l'auteur le plus subtil pourrait imaginer dans son cabinet en pareil cas? Allez l'interroger, demandez-lui ce qu'il pense de ce grand seigneur   (p. 116)

It is interesting, however, to see that almost immediately after the passage just quoted we find a quite different 'vous' being addressed, and in a quite different tone:

Grands de ce monde! si les portraits qu'on a faits de vous dans tant de livres étaient aussi parlants que l'est le tableau sous lequel il vous envisage, vous frémiriez des injures dont votre orgueil contriste, étonne et désespère la généreuse fierté de l'honnête homme qui a besoin de vous. Ces prestiges de vanité qui vous font oublier qui vous êtes, ces prestiges se dissiperaient, et la nature soulevée, en dépit de toutes vos chimères, vous ferait sentir qu'un homme, quel qu'il soit, est votre semblable.   (p. 116)

Note the oratorical repetition of 'ces prestiges'. Here, and elsewhere in the subsequent numbers, Marivaux drops the *persona* of the easy-going observer to become the eloquent preacher. Apostrophe takes the place of polite conversation, as Marivaux becomes the champion of true politeness against worldly manners.

In fact, one of the characteristics of Marivaux's *Spectateur* is the absence of a single controlling voice. Not only are there such striking shifts of tone on the part of the man who is supposed to be speaking to us, but this author figure himself disappears for long stretches, handing over discursive responsibility to a whole variety of other speakers or writers (all invented, one presumes). There are, in the first place, those whose conversation is recorded – such as the casual acquaintance of No. 10, the young female victim of No. 4, or the philosophical shoemaker of No. 5. Then there are the numerous authors of letters, the young woman who fights temptation in No. 2, the unhappy woman of Nos. 9, 10 and 11, the author of the comic letter on Homer in No. 9, and several more. In the later numbers, journals or memoirs tend to replace letters. Nos. 15 and 16 give us the supposed journal of a Spanish visitor to Paris, Nos. 17–19 the 'Mémoire de ce que j'ai fait et vu pendant ma vie' of a wise old lady, Nos. 21, 22, 24 and 25 the autobiography of an *inconnu*. The *spectateur*'s own voice is increasingly drowned out by others. In Addison and Steele's essays, it is true, there are many voices, but all of them are subordinated to the continuing presence of Mr Spectator, who introduces them, discusses them and speaks lengthily in his own right.

In this respect the *Spectateur français* reminds one of the contemporary *Lettres persanes*. Like Montesquieu, Marivaux uses the letter-form to bring in female speakers and narrators. A considerable part of his work is concerned with women's experience of love in contemporary society. Even if the essayist is normally male, this device allows for at least the semblance of an alternative perspective. But one also notices how often the other speakers of the *Spectateur* echo the attitudes and the tone of the original author figure, particularly in their taste for philosophical reflections. Thus the old lady of Nos. 17–19, like the narrators of Marivaux's novels, mingles narrative and commentary. As for the Spaniard of Nos. 15–16, he is in part a convenient device like Montesquieu's Persians, allowing an outsider's view of Paris. We first see him at his window, looking down on the street scene and noting the comic effects of wind on hair. But his text quickly comes to sound like the *spectateur*'s own compositions, with their typical mingling of scenes, conversations and reflections. The 'journal' is addressed to a 'vous' (or 'mon cher'), to whom the writer speaks just as the *spectateur* does to his readers ('Ajustez cela comme vous pourrez; je vous rends compte de mes impressions'). In No. 16, Marivaux complicates things yet further; first we are taken by the Spaniard on a business call, we read his description of the people he meets, but then, within his journal, he speaks lengthily and heatedly to a French friend who eventually cuts short his 'discours édifiants'. And the journal continues with an overheard conversation, the thoughts it provokes, and then the account of a dinner, at which the behaviour of the children provokes him into a didactic passage on education which sits awkwardly with the fiction of the traveller's diary. Marivaux finds it necessary to make his writer apologize:

Pardon, mon cher, de toutes mes réflexions; j'avais un père qui m'apprit à réfléchir, et qui ne prévoyait pas que je dusse un jour faire un journal et le gâter par là. (p. 205)

Clearly here the insistent voice of Marivaux the spectator has over-ridden the fictional voice behind which he was hiding.

As for the spectator *persona* itself, Marivaux dwells less on this than Addison and Steele, but he follows the main lines proposed by his model. His *spectateur* is middle-aged, disappointed in love, solitary in his habits. He has the philosophical detachment that goes with the part: 'mon âge avancé, mes voyages, la longue habitude de ne vivre que pour voir et que pour entendre, et l'expérience que j'ai acquise, ont émoussé mon amour-propre sur mille petits plaisirs de vanité, qui peuvent amuser les autres hommes' (p. 117). In No. 5, we see him in the role of philosophical observer, watching the spectacle of the streets with scientific curiosity:

J'ai voulu parcourir les rues pleines de monde, c'est une fête délicieuse pour un misanthrope que le spectacle d'un si grand nombre d'hommes assemblés; c'est le temps de la récolte d'idées. Cette innombrable quantité d'espèces de mouvements forme à ses yeux un caractère générique. A la fin, tant de sujets se réduisent en un; ce n'est plus des hommes différents qu'il contemple, c'est l'homme. (pp. 132–3)

One may be reminded too of the Baudelairean *flâneur*.[11] Idleness is a characteristic of Marivaux's observer. He has no work to do, no desire to subject himself to any kind of discipline: 'je n'ai jamais pris la peine de soutenir une conversation, ni de défendre mes opinions, et cela par une paresse insurmontable' (p. 117). It may well be asked, indeed, whether this affectation of laziness does not remove the *spectateur* from the sphere of the *honnêtes gens* into something distinctly more anti-social. Idleness is the mark of the aristocrat, to be sure, but also of the savage – Rousseau's natural man, or Man Friday as opposed to the industrious Robinson. The point is that this stance allows the maximum distance from the pretensions of the social world which it is one of the essayist's main tasks to satirize. So the spectator may become Diogenes – that figure who challenged and fascinated the polite eighteenth century. One may recall the philosopher figure in *Le Neveu de Rameau*, who begins in calm contemplation of men's foibles, but is driven by the dialectic of his argument into the role of root-eating cynic.[12] Perhaps Marivaux provided Diderot with a model here, for it is fascinating to see how his *Spectateur français* is followed by the *Indigent philosophe*. The speaker in this latter work is no longer the respectable if solitary man of the world, but a happy *clochard*, begging for a living hundreds of miles from Paris, the centre of politeness, and flaunting his freedom from the constraints of society and literature alike. In Nos. 5 and 6 the Diogenes mask is clearly indicated by the repeated leitmotif: 'Je cherche un homme', and in the opening number we read this proclamation of the unsociable life-style of the *gueux*:

Je n'ai point d'amis qui me viennent voir, mais en revanche je vais voir tout le monde dans les rues, je m'amuse des hommes qui passent, et quand je vois passer un coquin que je connais, je le méprise, sans avoir la peine maudite de lui faire encore des compliments, et de le traiter comme un homme estimable, comme je ferais si j'étais dans le monde. (p. 278)[13]

With this freedom, the essayist can obviously write as he pleases, following his whims rather than his audience's expectations. Like the *spectateur*, he wants to be a man, not an author: 'je ne vous promets rien, je ne jure de rien; et si je vous ennuie, je ne vous ai pas dit que cela n'arriverait pas; si je vous amuse, je n'y suis pas obligé' (p. 311). It is hard to say whether this should be read as an agreeably anti-pedantic manner, or as a flouting of the norms of politeness – more probably the former.

Not only is the principal speaker in *L'Indigent philosophe* a beggar; in Nos. 2, 3 and 4 he introduces another character, a Rameau-like adventurer who tells the picturesque story of his life. The result is a doubly cynical perspective on the society of the times; two outsiders joining forces to shock and mock the reader. Between them they take the essayist's detached *persona* to the limit. But it should not be thought that the adoption of a Diogenes mask means the abdication of the moralist's task. Far from it. The *indigent* is in fact, like Jean-Jacques or Diderot, an inveterate moralist. Marivaux enjoys playing games at the expense of serious people and happily jests at his own moralizing, yet the traditional moral lessons come across loud and clear: 'je leur apprends, moi, de dessus mon escabeau, qu'il n'y a rien de si simple que ce qu'on appelle vertu, bonne morale, ou raison' (pp. 278–9).

Of course the beggar of *L'Indigent philosophe* is not the same figure as the *spectateur*, but he develops the apparently anti-social (though in reality virtuous) qualities already possessed by the earlier character. Like him, the *spectateur* is a good-hearted person, sensitive, alive to the sufferings of others. He moves quickly from mockery of false virtue and false grandeur to indignation at injustice. When Marivaux has his narrator call himself a 'misanthrope' at the beginning of No. 5, he is no doubt alluding to the ambiguous Alceste, but there is never any question of the *spectateur* becoming a ridiculous figure. It is essential, to use a rhetorical term, that the *ethos* of the essayist remain positive. The polite public must be able to trust him.

We have seen how Marivaux's essay-writing figures flaunt their indolence, making of it a natural virtue. In formal terms, this leads to a *laisser-aller* which we find equally in all of his journals, and which separates him from the more methodical Addison and Steele. He is closer to the Montaignean model. There is no doubt that this corresponds to a deliberately chosen aesthetic of *bigarrure*.[14] Marivaux returns to this idea repeatedly. The *spectateur* claims to write without a plan, letting chance dictate what he writes and how he writes about it: 'Je ne destine aucun caractère à mes idées; c'est le hasard qui leur donne le ton' (p. 117). When he feels like changing the subject, he changes the subject. In No. 23, in answer to a friend who exhorts him to do as much, he replies willingly, and in words whose disconnected syntax seems to mime the freedom he is claiming:

Changeons donc [...] aussi bien je sens que cela me divertira moi-même, car enfin, il faut que le jeu me plaise, il faut que je m'amuse; je n'écris que pour cela, et non pas précisément pour faire un livre; il me vient des idées dans l'esprit; elles me font plaisir; je prends une plume et les couche sur le papier pour considérer plus à mon aise et voir un peu comment elles feront.

(p. 245)

There are two justifications for this disorder. As well as avoiding tedium for the audience, it allows the writer to follow his own thoughts more freely and thus more productively. The avoidance of method is rhetorically effective, as Diderot observed, but it can also be an aid to discovery. In Marivaux, I think it corresponds more to the latter aim. He gives his fullest defence of disorder, together with a critique of formal method, in No. 6 of *L'Indigent philosophe*. Here, looking back over the preceding issues, the writer notes the 'plaisante bigarrure', the apparently incongruous contrast between the moralizing of No. 5 and the picaresque cynicism of the previous numbers: 'Cela fait un ouvrage bien extraordinaire, bien bizarre: eh! tant mieux, cela fait naturel, cela nous ressemble' (p. 310). Nature, then, is the

authority for disorder – the relative disorder of the English landscape
garden as against the formal parterre. Marivaux continues:

Regardez la nature, elle a des plaines, et puis des vallons, des montagnes,
des arbres ici, des rochers là, point de symétrie, point d'ordre, je dis de cet
ordre que nous connaissons, et qui, à mon gré, fait une si sotte figure auprès
de ce beau désordre de la nature; mais il n'y a qu'elle qui en a le secret, de
ce désordre-là; et mon esprit aussi, car il fait comme elle et je le laisse aller.

So he disregards rules, he disdains the method that involves sticking
to a single subject and a plan: 'je veux être un homme, et non pas
un auteur'. It is the old leitmotif of the essayist – a man, not an
author – but the advantage of this stance is not just social, nor even
aesthetic, but epistemological. Following nature leads to truth.

In practice, Marivaux's journalism is less of a patchwork than all
this might suggest. The exception is *Le Cabinet du philosophe*, which
is presented as a collection of jottings, fragments from a philosopher's
notebook, 'des morceaux détachés, des fragments de pensée sur une
infinité de sujets' (p. 334). Even here, though, the medley principle
is not carried very far, and the last five numbers are devoted to a continuous narrative, the voyage to the 'monde vrai'. In the *Spectateur
français*, the lack of unity is less visible if we consider the individual
feuilles than if we regard the collection as a whole – and a remark
at the beginning of No. 23 about the possibility of reading all the texts
together 'dans le volume' makes it clear that Marivaux had both
possibilities in mind. Certainly, the group of twenty-five issues does
have something of the 'plaisante bigarrure' that he refers to in
L'Indigent philosophe. As for the essays taken separately, quite a
number of them are given at least the unity of continuous narrative,
which in some cases (e.g. Nos. 17–19) may remain virtually uninter-
rupted over more than one issue. Not that narrative continuity is any
guarantee of coherence – the autobiography of the musician in
L'Indigent philosophe has all the diversity of the picaresque or comic
novel. This type of *dérive* through different situations and the
reflections they provoke is found equally in the Spanish journal of
Nos. 15–16 of the *Spectateur*, or in two early essays, No. 3 and No. 5
which are good examples of Marivaux's open type of construction,
as compared with Addison's disquisitions. Let us take No. 5.

The piece begins with a declaration of freedom, the freedom not
to keep a promise previously made to the public. The *spectateur* will
follow his inclinations: 'Je me sens aujourd'hui dans un libertinage
d'idées qui ne peut s'accommoder d'un sujet fixe' (the connection of
errant thought and 'libertinage' reminds one again of *Le Neveu de*

Rameau). So he wanders the Paris streets watching the crowds on the day when the Infanta who is to marry the young Louis XV enters the city; the essay takes the form of a series of encounters and the thoughts that arise from them, as follows:

(a) general reflections on humanity;
(b) meeting with a shoemaker; his down-to-earth philosophy;
(c) analysis of the people's admiration for the street decorations;
(d) the relativity of aesthetic values;
(e) people are like pictures, wrongly valued because of their situation in society;
(f) the king goes by, acclaimed by the crowds;
(g) apostrophe to the 'princes de la terre': do good and be loved;
(h) comic conversation: the vanity of the amateur politician;
(i) moral reflections on carping criticism.

The essay comes to an end not because any conclusion has been reached, but because it risks becoming boring: 'je pense que je ferai bien de quitter la plume; je sens que je m'appesantis' (p. 137).

This piece has the unity of a day in Paris, but the narrative changes direction sharply on at least two occasions, and Marivaux marks these breaks quite clearly in his text (e.g. 'Quelqu'un que j'ai entendu parler alors, d'un ton de voix extrêmement haut, a mis fin à mes réflexions' (p. 136). It is certainly possible to see some guiding threads which link the different sections – above all the question of value, both aesthetic and moral – but there is no sense of methodical development. Nor does it seem to be the disorder that conceals a persuasive intention. No doubt the author's own values do emerge from the text, but one feels, as Marivaux claims, that one has been reading the jottings and reflections of a man, not the discourse of a preacher. The essay seems like a personal barometer rather than an exercise in pedagogy.

In this case, what enables Marivaux to avoid the appearance of philosophizing is the fact that the essay is given the form of a narrative – and the most striking feature of the *Spectateur* and its successors is indeed the predominance of the narrative over the discursive. It is true that in the work of many essayists, story-telling, whether in the first or the third person, figures prominently. Even the most philosophical essays will generally find room for some illustrative narrative. But in most essays, as we saw in the English *Spectator*, this is subordinated to the reflective voice of the essayist. He may become a story-teller, but only temporarily; before long the discursive mode reasserts itself. In relation to this model, it may well be asked whether Marivaux is really writing essays at all, so frequent and lengthy are his excursions into narrative (or dramatic scenes in *Le Cabinet du philosophe*). Of all the pieces in the *Spectateur*, only a small minority can really be best described as a series of thoughts rather than a sequence of events: Nos. 1, 7, 8 and 23 (Nos. 3 and 5 being *promenades* in Rousseau's sense of the word). Interestingly, all of these are concerned with the business of essay-writing and with questions of style and criticism.

As one would expect, No. 1 is introductory, giving readers an idea of what is to come. Yet here too narrative quickly makes an appearance. The first page is a defence of the random, natural style of composition, but retrospectively it too is presented as the result of a chance encounter: 'Tout ce que je dis là n'est aussi qu'une réflexion que le hasard m'a fourni. Voici comment [...]' Whereupon the *spectateur* launches into the description of a scene from society, in which a poor but honest man is made to suffer from the insolent arrogance of a rich *seigneur*. The story in its turn is constantly interwoven with the *spectateur*'s thoughts. The sight of the poor man immediately provokes an eloquent generalization after the manner of La Bruyère:

Hélas, disais-je en moi-même, l'honnête homme est presque toujours triste, presque toujours sans biens, presque toujours humilié; il n'a point d'amis, parce que son amitié n'est bonne à rien; on dit de lui: C'est un honnête homme, mais ceux qui le disent, le fuient, le dédaignent, le méprisent, rougissent même de se trouver avec lui; et pourquoi? C'est qu'il n'est qu'estimable.   (p. 115)

So too with the rich man. These reflections are part of the narrative; they are presented as what the *spectateur* thought at the time ('c'était donc dans de pareilles pensées que je m'amusais avec moi-même'), but they are barely distinguishable from the general authorial observation which surfaces soon after: 'Quand on demande des grâces aux puissants de ce monde, et qu'on a le cœur bien placé, on a toujours l'haleine courte' (p. 116).

Finishing off this little scene, Marivaux launches directly into a discussion with his reader and an apostrophe to the 'grands de ce monde' (quoted above, p. 84). The story which was meant to illustrate the value of real life experience in generating interesting ideas has in fact also given rise to moral reflections on power and wealth. Only when he has indulged himself in these does the *spectateur* return to his original point – with what seems like a parody of philosophical language:

Je conclus donc du plus au moins, en suivant mon principe: Oui! je préférerais toutes les idées fortuites que le hasard nous donne à celles que la recherche la plus ingénieuse pourrait nous fournir dans le travail.

What this example shows is that narrative and discourse are virtually inseparable for Marivaux. More normally, the author of the *Spectateur* hands over the narration to another character, but in all cases, his thoughts cannot be maintained within the limits of the discursive essay. His journalistic texts occupy a border territory between the essay as it is normally understood and the novel. It is customary to classify these genres separately, the one belonging to what is called 'imaginative literature' and the other to discursive prose.[15] Marivaux's example brings out the fragility of such distinctions. His *spectateur* says: 'Tout me devient matière à réflexion' (p. 117). All general maxims imply narrative, all narrative can be seen through the categories of moral thought.

This position, incidentally, is further illustrated by some of the most interesting texts of eighteenth-century literature; examples include Rousseau's *Emile* and Diderot's philosophical tales and dialogues, not to mention such English classics as *Tom Jones* or *Tristram Shandy*. The question we can ask of all such texts concerns the authority that can be accorded to any voice that presumes to draw general conclusions from the actions that are recounted. If the traditional essayist presents himself not as a figure of authority, but as a private person, trying out his own ideas on an intelligent public, this 'experimental' approach is even more evident when the essay becomes predominantly narrative in character, and particularly so when this narrative is attributed to a narrator who is distinguished from the essayist. Here the reader is drawn into a web of social observations and fictional adventures which call on him or her to embark on personal thought rather than following the persuasive discourse of a homely philosopher.

Because the French spectator speaks less in his own name than his English counterpart, it is more difficult to discuss Marivaux's language than that of Addison and Steele. Or, to put it another way, his language is that of a dramatist, speaking almost always by proxy. Even so, the *spectateur* and his various narrators do write or speak in a fairly distinctive manner, and it is worth saying a word or two about this, since it impinges directly on the question of polite sociability.[16] The first point is that Marivaux is just as self-conscious about language as Addison and Steele. More so, in fact, for he is aware that his style will seem odd to some readers. In a number of passages he seeks to rebut hostile criticism on this front and stakes out an individual position. The main issue is that of affectation. A typical hostile view can be found in the *Mélanges historiques et critiques* for 15 February 1722 (quoted on pp. 686–7 of the edition under discussion); the reviewer comments on the letter of the distraught woman in No. 2 of the *Spectateur*:

Il n'y a pas eu deux voix sur cette lettre. L'affectation s'y fait sentir à chaque mot, et ce n'est jamais ainsi que s'exprimera une femme partagée entre des sentiments si différents. Dans cet état on ne court point après l'esprit, on ne recherche point les antithèses.

Similar remarks continued to be made over many years, to Marivaux's great annoyance; he particularly resented the accusation of 'chasing after wit'. He defends himself not only in Nos. 7 and 8 of the *Spectateur*, but in an article 'Sur la clarté du discours' included in the *Mercure*, and again in No. 6 of *Le Cabinet du philosophe*. His defence is interesting.

The essential point is a protest against the tyranny of convention, which dresses itself up as a demand for clarity. For Marivaux clarity means rather 'l'exposition nette de notre pensée au degré précis de force et de sens dans lequel nous l'avons conçue'. What is more, 'si la pensée ou le sentiment trop vif passe toute expression, ce qui peut arriver, ce sera pour lors l'exposition nette de cette même pensée dans un degré de sens propre à la fixer, et à faire entrevoir en même temps toute son étendue non exprimable de vivacité' (p. 52). Writers should not be intimidated by those who accuse them of trying to be too clever. In most countries, writes the *spectateur*, 'la plupart des auteurs nous ont moins laissé leur propre façon d'imaginer que la pure imitation de certain goût d'esprit que quelques critiques leurs amis avaient décidé être le meilleur' (p. 145). Once again, Marivaux is proclaiming his right to be himself, to be natural, even if his way of being natural strikes readers as unnatural. It is, moreover, obvious how this attitude differs from that of the English *Spectator*. For Addison and Steele writing is closer to the ordinary language of good company; the writer will want to amuse his public, but sensibly, without shocking the common taste. Marivaux's stance is more individualistic, more subversive even. Like his theatrical dialogue, his journalistic style, far from being frivolously playful, often surprises the reader with the strangeness of unexpected discovery.

It is not easy to show briefly what this involves in practice. Frequently, when the relationship of writer and reader demands it, Marivaux's narrators adopt a vigorous, even a hectoring style.

At other times they banter playfully. Only comparatively rarely do we find the measured tones of Addison's 'sermons'. The most original passages are perhaps those in which complex attitudes and motives are subtly analysed. Such passages are of course common in his fiction and have their equivalent in the comedies; here is a brief example, worthy of a Nathalie Sarraute, from an anecdote of which the *spectateur* is the narrator. He is trying to mollify the hurt vanity of a would-be *bel esprit* whom he has just contradicted:

Il était une heure sonnée, c'est l'heure à peu près où l'on dîne, j'étais à jeun, lui de même peut-être, mais il ne sentait plus cela; il s'agissait de venger son esprit, cet interêt-là était plus pressé que celui de son estomac, et je n'avais pas lieu d'espérer qu'il pût s'apercevoir qu'il avait appétit.

D'un autre côté, je n'avais point de poitrine à commettre avec la sienne; mais comment quitter cet homme? Quoi, lui dire que le cœur me manquait d'inanition, que le dîner m'attendait? et lui dire cela, dans quelle conjoncture, au milieu d'un raisonnement qu'il allait faire, qu'il faisait déjà, et où il n'y allait pas moins pour lui que de se purger auprès de moi du reproche de n'être pas le plus judicieux de tous les hommes, d'un raisonnement en vertu duquel il attendait réparation, d'un raisonnement dont la justesse et la force devaient faire taire tous mes besoins; non, je ne voyais point de moyens honnêtes de m'esquiver; j'avais blessé mon homme dans son amour-propre, et le laisser là sans lui donner secours, c'etait l'assassiner, lui ôter son honneur, c'était être barbare. D'ailleurs une autre réflexion m'embarrassait encore: s'il allait m'induire aussi à prendre le parti de mon esprit, que sait-on qui peut arriver? il y a quarante ans que je fais le métier de philosophe, et que je persécute mes faiblesses, mais je n'en suis pas plus sûr de moi; l'état où je suis, c'est comme une santé de convalescent, il ne faut presque rien pour causer une rechute. (pp. 248–9)

The ironic use of strong language ('barbare', 'assassiner') may remind one of Steele's jesting about mourning clothes, but what marks the whole passage as Marivaux's is the prolonged and witty description of the feelings of the two characters involved (this being merely an extract from a considerably longer passage). One is struck by the way in which the long sentences, with their accumulation of clauses, wind their way into the minds of the interlocutors, by the beautiful interplay of the physical and the psychological, by the careful and clever use of the unexpected and prolonged metaphor of 'faiblesses' at the end. Should one say, like Marivaux's critics, that 'il court après l'esprit'? If so, he finds it. A passage like this is more demanding and more rewarding than the easy common sense often associated with the language of the essay.

We return again to the question of sociability. In the essays of the *Spectator*, while the fashions of society are entertainingly mocked, there is the distinct attempt to create a social morality in which politeness and elegance are reconciled with Christian virtues and middle-class values. The style and composition of the essays fit them for their role as a daily stimulus for discussion and a model for polite behaviour and conversation. The authors assume with a good grace the part of entertaining educator, Hume's ambassador from the study to the coffee-house, club and tea-table. This clearly met a need; Addison and Steele were in their way what Gramsci might have called the organic intellectuals of Augustan Britain.

Such was not the case for Marivaux. His periodical essays, if indeed we can call them that, have a different tone and function from their apparent model. His moral values are certainly sociable ones, and if his *spectateur* is a 'misanthrope', it is not out of indifference to the well-being of society. But the *persona* of the essay-writer here is much less clubbable; Marivaux accentuates the detachment of the writer which is already present in the English spectator, pushing it towards the traditional role of the isolated philosopher, a Diogenes in the fashionable society of the day. The stress on narrative, while it satisfies the eminently social taste for anecdote, does tend to shift the essay further away from sententious wisdom, and toward the exploration of psychological peculiarity. And the language is idiosyncratic in a way that shocked contemporaries. Not that one should view Marivaux as outsider or rebel. He continues to operate within the norms of polite culture (even Jean-Jacques will do that). But rather than being a factor in the constitution and consolidation of this culture, his journalism tends to work as a critical and dissolving ferment.

Is this difference (which I have no doubt exaggerated for the sake of argument) to be explained simply in terms of individual temperament? Certainly Marivaux was a remarkable and original writer as Addison and Steele were not. Nor was there a lack of more conventional social essayists in France. Nevertheless, I should like to propose one final, very tentative hypothesis – an absurdly broad hypothesis, that would be hard to prove or disprove (but of such is the essay made). In Britain, which had quite recently known civil strife on a scale unknown in seventeenth-century France, there was a drive towards the creation of a post-1688 consensus culture, moderate, practical, civilized and polite, and in this the essayist could play his part. France, by contrast, was a relatively stable society with a court-dominated polite culture which had been in place for some time. In such a culture was it not more tempting and worthwhile for the writer to adopt the more independent critical role which is embodied − or at least adumbrated − in Marivaux's journalism?

6

THE COMMERCE OF THE SELF

At a certain moment in Nathalie Sarraute's novel *Les Fruits d'or*, a fairly typical moment from this writer's work, we see a male character trying to deal with an unexpected challenge. The passage goes like this:

> Et voilà que la masse inerte en face de lui se met à remuer, se soulève: 'Mais dites-moi, qu'est-ce que ça peut bien vous faire, au fond, tout ça?'
> L'énorme remous l'entraîne, il roule, perdant pied. Il se débat comme un insecte qu'un souffle a renversé et qui bat l'air de ses petites pattes affolées, cherchant à se raccrocher ... 'Mais ... mais comment ... comment qu'est-ce que ça me fait?'[1]

The extravagantly metaphorical rendering of the disarray provoked by a sudden question is one example of Sarraute's exploration of the hidden continents of self. She is working here in the modern line of Dostoevsky, James Joyce and Virginia Woolf, for one of the dominant features of modern fiction (alongside the interrogation of the very conditions of representation) is the ever more penetrating representation of the inner self. But at the same time, the reader is made aware, here as elsewhere in Sarraute, of the way in which, however feebly, this devastated self attempts to face the world, to 'se raccrocher', to present itself to others, to find a successful strategy for survival and success. And in this Sarraute harks back to more ancient concerns, for in older literature, while the representation of self certainly has its place, one is probably more concerned with the presentation of self.

This is originally a rhetorical concern, though the rhetorical model of speaker addressing audience is easily transferred to most forms of writing. One of the principal points dealt with by the rhetoric manuals was indeed the way in which the orator presents himself to his audience.[2] The technical word for this is *ethos*. From Aristotle onward this is seen as one of the principal means of persuasion, and has its place alongside *logos* (the various proofs and arguments that can be adduced in support of a case) and *pathos* (the appeal to the passions of the audience). What is meant by *ethos*? We must imagine a speaker facing a possibly indifferent or hostile audience. One of his first tasks is to create a positive impression of his own character in his hearers' minds, to predispose them in his favour, so that they will more easily give credence to what he has to say. This does not necessarily mean talking about himself – the essential thing is that his good character should shine through. This should be achieved above all at the start of his speech, in the exordium, where he engages in the *captatio benevolentiae*, striving to appear modest, prudent, full of zeal for the common good. Quintilian provides good examples of this *ethos* teaching:

As the authority of the speaker becomes thus of the highest efficacy, if, in his undertaking the business, all suspicion of meanness, or hatred, or ambition, be far removed from him, so it is a sort of tacit commendation to him, if he represents himself as weak, and inferior in ability to those acting against him [...]

We must also take care not to appear insolent, malignant, overbearing, reproachful [...][3]

One notices here the words 'represents himself' and 'appear'. From the beginning the orator had been compared to the actor (and had often been advised to learn from him); he too had to put on a mask, a *persona*.

For 'orator' in all this one can – with certain modifications to which I shall return – read 'writer'. But of course more or less artful self-presentation was by no means confined to public speaking and writing. It was – and is – an essential part of everyday life, and as such has been represented in literary works of all kinds, novels, plays, histories, memoirs, essays, and in other less canonic genres such as the books on how to make friends and influence people, or (to put it in a more literary–historical way) in those prescriptive manuals of civility which so flourished in early modern Europe. More recently, these questions have become the concern of another genre, the manual of social psychology, where the prescriptive is ostensibly – though perhaps not really – dominated by the search for a scientific account of the way people negotiate personal relations. For non-specialists, the most familiar work here is probably that of Ervin Goffman, with his *Encounters* and *The Presentation of Self in Everyday Life*. Goffman likes to use the analogy of games-playing to characterize many other forms of social interaction, which are seen as forms of ritual play, in which participants engage in complex 'face work' of which they may well not be conscious.

Other analogies beside that of games are common. Theatre and music are often pressed into service. Most important of all is probably the military analogy (as we see it in Sarraute for instance); encounters are seen here as battles, and the presented self is both armour and weapon. But the analogy which will concern me here is a different one, also very widespread, that of commerce. The word is to be understood in a broad sense, meaning not only buying, selling and exchange, but more generally the process of negotiation, haggling and bargaining, the 'trucking and bartering' that Adam Smith saw as an essential part of the human make-up.

If I choose to concentrate on commerce here, it is not simply because the spirit of the present age, and the politicians who express it, encourage us to see social life in terms of the market, where everything, the self included, is up for buying and selling. It is more that some thinkers of the eighteenth century saw themselves already as living in a relatively new type of society, to which they gave the name 'commercial'. I am thinking in particular of the Scottish philosopher—historians (Smith, Ferguson, Millar) and their four-stage theory of human development.[4] The last of these four stages, after the savage, the pastoral and the agricultural, was that in which the dominance of commerce was beginning to alter the social and moral conditions of existence. The Scots viewed this development in different ways, and with mixed feelings. The advantages, in terms of security, comfort and civilization, were obvious. But there were drawbacks and dangers. In spite of his reputation, Adam Smith has passages on the alienation of the commercial world which prefigure what we find in Marx − and Ferguson is much more emphatic in his condemnation.

In any case, it is important in considering the commercial model of self-presentation, to realise that the notion of 'commerce' was a complex and ambiguous one. In Latin, and later in English, French and other languages, the word has two main types of meaning: on the one hand, etymologically, buying, selling and exchange of goods, but on the other, metaphorically, social intercourse of all kinds, including one's dealings with God or with the opposite sex. In France, from the sixteenth century onwards, the second of these two meanings seems to take precedence over the former. Montaigne's essay *De trois commerces* concerns his relations with friends, women and books, and has no truck with money. However in 1676 'commerce' was still apparently perceived as figurative in this sense and described as 'very elegant' by Bouhours.[5] (Since then of course this elegant usage has largely disappeared.) In English the double possibility offered by the word can be seen in two quotations from Goldsmith; in *The Traveller* we read

> And Honour sinks where Commerce long prevails   (l. 91)

whereas a character declares in Act 1 of *The Good-Natured Man* that 'friendship is a disinterested commerce between equals; love, an abject intercourse between tyrants and slaves'.

The word is ambiguous, and provokes ambivalent feelings. The old noble disdain for trade often tarnishes the idea of commerce, and means that the word, when used metaphorically, is taken in bad part. It would be easy to accumulate examples to show how the commerce of self is portrayed as unacceptable. In this view the mercantile values of self-interest are seen eroding the older values of honour, friendship and duty. So in the theatre we see two of Lear's daughters shamelessly trying to outbid one another in the auction for inheritance, or we find the naive but honest Britannicus saying of Nero's court:

> Mais que vois-je autour de moi que des amis vendus
> Qui sont de tous mes pas les témoins assidus,
> Qui choisis par Néron pour ce commerce infâme
> Trafiquent avec lui des secrets de mon âme?
>
> (*Britannicus*, I, iv, 329–32)

In France a crucial text is Molière's *Misanthrope*. The central issue here is the nature of proper sociability, reconciling the autonomy of the self with the necessary accommodation to society. The unreasonable Alceste denounces:

> Ce commerce honteux de semblants d'amitié   (I, i, 68)

which he sees as the truth behind the polite face of Parisian society, but his more realistic friend is willing to accept the commerce which he describes so cynically:

> Lorsqu'un homme vous vient embrasser avec joie,
> Il faut bien le payer de la même monnoie,
> Répondre, comme on peut, à ses empressements,
> Rendre offre pour offre et serments pour serments.
>
> (I, i, 37–40)

The aristocratic condemnation of commerce is somewhat eroded in the century following Molière. Hirschman has indicated how money-making, that innocent passion (as Hume saw it), comes to be preferred to the violent passions associated with aristocratic life (honour, ambition, etc.).[6] Commerce is seen by progressives as conducive to peace, harmony and security, and the stock phrase, *le doux commerce*, a phrase sufficiently shop-soiled to be mocked by Marx and Engels a century later, is used both to give a golden image of trade and to describe pleasant social intercourse. There is an assimilation of good commerce and good sociability, so that when Jefferson speaks enthusiastically of 'peace, commerce and honest friendship between nations' it is difficult out of context to guess that he is in fact thinking primarily of trade.

The books on politeness published in France, Britain and elsewhere, all contribute to inculcating the ideal of *doux commerce*. They stress the need for negotiation between selves, and do not eschew the talk of buying and selling that figures somewhat negatively in Philinte's discourse. Abbé Trublet can serve as an example. His best definition of politeness is 'sacrifier sans cesse son amour-propre à celui des autres',[7] not simply out of altruism, however, but because this is the best rational calculation of self-interest (though to be fair to Trublet, he does display a worried awareness of the moral dangers involved). Having spent some time on the politeness manuals in Chapter 4, I should like now, however, to concentrate on *The Theory of Moral Sentiments* (1759),[8] the work in which Adam Smith, who was later to achieve fame as the champion of modern commercial society, gives an illuminating account of what I am calling the commerce of the self.

It would be wrong to describe this work as a politeness manual – indeed Smith is far from well disposed towards French *politesse*. His aim is rather to give an empirical account of how people actually behave in society, a contribution to the new science of man which was to stand alongside Newton's physical science. Nevertheless, *The Theory of Moral Sentiments* is the record of Smith's lectures to young students, for the most part teenagers, at the University of Glasgow. Naturally, therefore, his 'scientific' analysis of moral behaviour is also aimed at instilling proper values in the future educated classes. All the time he appeals to a consensual 'we', while proposing as a model to his students the behaviour and attitudes of adult males of a certain rank in a specific society.

Since Smith is principally known as the author of *The Wealth of Nations* (1776), which shows how the self-interest of individuals is directed by the Invisible Hand to work for the general good, it is natural to ask how far his picture of social relations between individuals is based on the human 'propensity to truck, barter and exchange one thing for another', which is the 'principle which gives occasion to the division of labour' and thence to the whole economic system of *The Wealth of Nations*.[9] At first sight the answer is that *The*

Theory of Moral Sentiments, with its stress on the importance of 'sympathy', gives a much less egoistic account of human nature than the later work, and this apparent opposition has become known as the 'Adam Smith problem'. Scholars have by turns dramatized this problem and sought to lay it to rest. Recently, in an illuminating article, Laurence Dickey has suggested how it may be 'historicized' and more fully understood if we examine how Smith changed his first work for its sixth edition in 1790.[10] I do not want to venture into this argument here, nor to try to situate Smith in relation to a highly complex tradition of moral thought, but simply to ask how in the *Theory* Smith envisaged the mechanisms, difficulties and dangers of social intercourse in a modern commercial society.

He does not seek to deny the importance of self-interest in human action, but is at pains to refute 'licentious systems' (such as that of Mandeville) which would reduce all our actions to narrowly selfish motives. The counter-weight to egoism is provided by Smith's master-principle, sympathy. In his account, this principle enables us to 'bring home to ourselves' all the different feelings of our fellows – not just their sorrow, but equally their joy or their anger. The operation of sympathy depends crucially on imagination; on the basis of our own experience, we mentally put ourselves in the place of others. Such sympathy brings pleasure, a pleasure felt equally by those who extend sympathy and those who receive it.

In such relations of sympathy Smith finds a stimulus to social cooperation different from that of 'trucking and bartering'. He admits, it is true, that even without such 'generous and disinterested motives', society may still 'subsist among different men, as among different merchants, from a sense of its utility, without any mutual love or affection ... by a mercenary exchange of good offices according to an agreed valuation' (p. 86). But this minimal commercial society is not what he is seeking to explain or promote; happy social relations depend on mutual 'gratitude [...] friendship and esteem' (p. 85). One is struck, however, on reading the first book of the *Theory*, by the problems that can beset the workings of sympathy. We do not always naturally feel the sympathy that others believe to be their due. Either we fail to imagine their situation, or their feelings seem to us excessive in relation to the reality of their situation. The result, as often as not, is a process of negotiation between individuals.

'Proper' and 'propriety' are the terms Smith uses to describe a mutually acceptable level of emotion. Successful and harmonious social living depends on learning 'propriety' in the feelings we express and our expression of them. This may not be an easy education; one learns by hard experience. Smith's description of the process is interesting, and in particular his use of a musical analogy:

Mankind, though naturally sympathetic, never conceive, for what has befallen another, that degree of passion which naturally animates the person principally concerned [...] The person principally concerned is sensible of this, and at the same time passionately desires a more complete sympathy. He longs for that relief which nothing can afford him but the entire concord of the affections of the spectators with his own. [...] But he can only hope to attain this by lowering his passion to that pitch, in which the spectators are capable of going along with him. He must flatten, if I may be allowed to say so, the sharpness of its natural tone, in order to reduce it to harmony and concord with the emotions of those who are about him.   (p. 21)

Here we are not far removed from the ancient *ethos* teaching. The approach is not without its dangers.

In his critique of Mandeville, Smith takes great care to rebut the suggestion that the desire to be loved, admired and approved (which must be the basis of proper social behaviour) is no more than a form of self-love or vanity. One senses however in this section that his position is a delicate one. There is, he admits, a 'certain remote affinity' between disinterested love of virtue, love of true glory, and vanity, and this has allowed Mandeville to 'impose upon his readers' (p. 310). But how is one to draw the line? The problem is like that faced by Alceste. Given the desire for approval, is it not probable, in the commerce of society (the 'great school of self-command', as Smith puts it), that individuals will learn to play parts for applause? Consider the picture of the 'upstart', his attempts to ward off envy:

Instead of appearing to be elated with his good fortune, he endeavours, as much as he can, to smother his joy, and keep down the elevation of mind with which his new circumstances naturally inspire him. He affects the same plainness of dress, and the same modesty of behaviour which became him in his former station. He redoubles his attention to his old friends, and endeavours more than ever to be humble, assiduous and complaisant.

(p. 41)

Is this presentation of the self to be called virtue? Yes, if the upstart really does suppress his natural feelings. But more probably 'we suspect the sincerity of his humanity, and he grows weary of this constraint'. And things are obviously even worse if the approval of the particular spectators surrounding the individual is based on values which to the philosopher appear corrupt or unacceptable. Here it seems that the self is at the mercy of public opinion. And it is at this point in the argument that Smith has to bring in his famous 'impartial spectator', that 'man within' or 'representative of mankind' (p. 30), his equivalent of the voice of conscience.[11] This imagined judge, unlike the actual spectators of our actions, knows the truth of our inner selves and provides us with a truly objective standard. Thus, in theory at least, we are rescued from the potentially corrupting effects of the commerce of the self. We are no longer 'slaves of the world' (p. 131). Smith may be seen here making the same sort of defensive moves as the theorists of rhetoric (and therefore of *ethos*) had so often felt obliged to make in the face of attacks on their apparently amoral discipline.

What I have said so far might be said to belong to the history of ideas rather than to literature. However, the commerce of the self that I have been outlining – the negotiation, bartering, giving and taking of feelings, attitudes, gestures and words – and the relation of all this to 'true' feeling is one of the constant subjects of all kinds of literary works, from the treatises of moralists to plays, novels and fables. A great deal of the literature of the seventeenth and eighteenth centuries is concerned with offering positive or negative models of sociability for a privileged society in which 'commerce' in the sense of conversation and social intercourse is probably what matters most. As the quotations I gave earlier suggest, Molière's *Misanthrope* is all about this. One hundred and fifty years later, it seems to me that we can see in Jane Austen's novels a critical illustration of Adam Smith's ideas about propriety, sympathy and the necessary negotiation between selves. In *Persuasion*, for instance, we see the good Anne Elliot making the necessary moves to preserve harmony and sympathy:

Anne smiled more than once to herself during this speech, and entered into the subject, as ready to do good by entering into the feelings of a young lady as a young man [...] She said all that was reasonable and proper on the business; felt the claims of Dr Shirley to repose as she ought; saw how very desirable it was that he should have some active, respectable young man, as a resident curate, and was even courteous enough to hint at the advantage of such resident curate's being married.[12]

All this produces the desired effect, and Henrietta is 'very well pleased with her companion'. This is not a mercenary commerce, however, and the sacrifice of sincerity is done in the best of causes, to make the other happy. Not so with the scheming Mrs Clay or the plausible Mr Elliot. The latter's manners are pleasing in 'their propriety and correctness, their general politeness and suavity' (p. 452), but this is purely a façade adopted out of self-interest and conceals an unscrupulously selfish nature. In the behaviour of the two cousins, Jane Austen is exemplifying the difference between a praiseworthy and an immoral commerce of the self.

The novel is perhaps the best place for an exploration of these matters, and in France at least it shades off into the conversation manuals of Bary, Vaumorière or Mademoiselle de Scudéry – the last of these producing a book of *Conversations nouvelles*, which are like a distillation of the ideal conversations in her long novels. Nor is it surprising that the dialogue should be such an important literary form at this time. It is often used as a polite, sociable garb for ideas which might otherwise be rebarbative to the worldly reader – so in Shaftesbury, Berkeley, Hume or Diderot. But it is not only the philosophical subject which matters in such works. They can be seen also as models of an appropriate commerce of the self. Hume, for instance, presents his *Dialogues concerning Natural Religion* as bringing together 'two of the greatest and purest pleasures of human life, study and society'.[13] The work shows reasonable men negotiating their differences in a polite yet lively manner, until one of them, Demea, breaks the unspoken rules and is, in a manner of speaking, expelled from the *doux commerce* of his fellows into an outer darkness of fanaticism.

Diderot's *Entretien avec la maréchale* does a similar job in making of religious belief the subject of reasonable discussion, even if in it we witness what could be described in commercial terms as a hard sell for unbelief. What is interesting here is that the writer puts himself into his book, as a character. What happens therefore is that the speaker negotiating with his interlocutor merges with the author selling his wares to the reader. And this reminds us that even in apparently non-dialogic works, where the presentation of the writer's self is less overt than here, it is still vital. In this perspective the writer is seen not so much as one who represents the commerce of selves (as Jane Austen does), but as one who is engaged in this commerce. He or she is negotiating with an audience, presenting the self in the most winning, the most persuasive light possible. The writer is salesman.

It might seem, of course, that compared with the orator, who has to woo an audience before whom he stands exposed, the writer enjoys a certain freedom. He or she has no immediate public. There is a gap in time between writing and reading which not only gives the reader a certain independence of response, but also allows the writer to forget the demands of the public. It has to be said, however, that this distance between author and reader was less great in the seventeenth and eighteenth centuries than it has been for many writers since then. Polite writing in a country like France was still close to orality; speech was often seen as the model for writing and was preferred to it. In the Parisian salons it was common for new writing to be read aloud to a select audience. That this entailed a type of negotiation can be seen in the quotation from Marmontel's memoirs discussed in Chapter 7.[14] In such a *doux commerce*, the writer appears as a person of good company, deferring readily to the taste of his or her interlocutors, not pretentious or pedantic, but adapting to the expectations of an audience and through what Adam Smith might have called propriety winning approval, an approval that was necessary if he or she was to persuade the public – or simply to earn a living.

For of course we should not forget that many writers were quite literally engaged in the commerce of self – as in previous and subsequent centuries. The age of patronage, like the following age of commercial publishing, invited writers to sell themselves, sometimes in ways which seemed to them, as they may seem to us, degrading. The dedication is where this shows most clearly. In France the classic example is that of Corneille dedicating his tragedy *Cinna* to the financier Montoron with the grossest flattery. Reading this piece, one observes how the writing self is implicated in the operation: 'J'ai vécu si éloigné de la flatterie, que je pense être en possession de me faire croire quand je dis du bien de quelqu'un'.[15] In other words, my goods are not shop-soiled (the standard tactic of the flatterer).

There were many sincere dedications, no doubt, but the notion that the writing self is prostituted in the commerce of society is one that haunts many writers of this period. This is the problem that Diderot, for instance, wrestles with in *Le Neveu de Rameau*, where he puts himself into conversation with a devilish *alter ego*. Rameau envies the writer his gift, not because he can speak the truth or express his feelings eloquently and persuasively, but because his talent allows him to 'tourner une épître dédicatoire, bien enivrer un sot de son mérite'.[16] Rameau and his philosophical interlocutor agree with one another – and would no doubt have agreed with Adam Smith – that what was needed for the right commerce of the self was 'une bonne éducation'. But this apparent agreement rests on totally opposed views of human nature, which lead to quite different consequences for the man and for the writer.

Rameau sees humanity in jungle terms; beast preys on beast, and a good education teaches young human beings to hold their own and

106

obtain their pleasures in this savage world. For those who are not powerful (the great majority) this means flattery, hypocrisy, treachery and similar arts. Nor is this easy. Rameau says at times that his so-called vices, so essential for social success, come naturally to him, in which case we should have a Mandevillean harmony in which private vices bring mutual satisfaction. Elsewhere, however, as he speaks of his 'dignity', it is evident that the human animal has to be broken in to social conformity. This is emblematically represented by the stiff hand of the violinist, which has to be painfully forced into flexibility:

Ces dix doigts, c'étaient autant de bâtons fichés dans un métacarpe de bois; et ces tendons, c'etaient de vieilles cordes à boyau plus sèches, plus roides, plus inflexibles que celles qui ont servi à la roue d'un tourneur. Mais je vous les ai tant tourmentées, tant brisées, tant rompues. Tu ne veux pas aller; et moi, mordieu, je dis que tu iras; et cela sera. (p. 97)

The *philosophe*, on the contrary, is not flexible, and fights to defend the independence of the writer 'qui n'a rien et qui ne demande rien' (p. 192), a writer outside the normal commercial circuits.

Fascinating links connect Rameau with Diderot's 'frère ennemi' Jean-Jacques Rousseau, who was of all the writers of his time perhaps the one who lived the commerce of self most dramatically.[17] Not that he was necessarily hostile to commerce as such. This would have been an impossible position for the proud citizen of a Republic whose prosperity depended on a progressive attitude to trade. Nevertheless, in Rousseau's scale of values it would appear that Lycurgus's Sparta ranks higher than Geneva, where commercial corruption was already making itself felt. In any case, even if commerce had its necessary place, Rousseau was unremittingly hostile to any commercialization of human relations (in particular friendship, one of his great subjects), and equally to the commercialization of writing. He always insisted that he was not a professional writer (a 'livrier', as he put it scornfully). Writing, as he saw it, meant speaking directly from the self, with no thought for reward, payment or success. Sincerity, which endangers commerce of all kinds, is opposed to the accommodation of self to others which Molière's Philinte and Adam Smith favoured. Not that this is a straightforward business. Modern advertisers know the virtues of the more sophisticated sell that flouts the norms of salesmanship. Jean-Jacques too knew that independence can be a paying tactic: 'Mon métier [i.e. music-copying] pouvait me nourrir si mes livres ne se vendaient pas, et voilà précisément ce qui les faisait vendre' (I, 403).

Now Rousseau notoriously insists that writing is derived from, and inferior to, speaking. His model of good communication (outlined for instance in Book 4 of the *Emile*) is face-to-face speech, in which, as we have seen, *ethos* is an element of the first importance. Rousseau did not himself actually speak in public; his talent did not run this way, for he lacked a ready wit and was easily abashed. As he put it in the *Confessions*, 'le parti que j'ai pris d'écrire et de me cacher est précisément celui qui me convenait' (I, 116). Nevertheless, as a writer, he holds strongly to the oral model; he wants to be thought of as a man addressing his fellow-men. It follows from this, and from his exacerbated self-consciousness, that the presentation of self is an inescapable concern of his. We can see something of this if we consider his openings, his *exordia*.

His first successful work was in fact couched in the form of a written speech, a discourse designed to be read aloud to the Academy of Dijon. This *Discours sur les sciences et les arts* is typical of Rousseau in the complexity of its opening. It shows what I should describe as his characteristic 'double entry' in which two conflicting types of *ethos* follow one another, the 'commercial' and the 'non-commercial'. The 'Discours' proper begins with a traditional *exordium* in which Rousseau negotiates with his judges in the time-honoured way:

Le rétablissement des sciences et des arts a-t-il contribué à épurer ou à corrompre les mœurs? Voilà ce qu'il s'agit d'examiner. Quel parti dois-je prendre dans cette question? Celui, Messieurs, qui convient à un honnête homme qui ne sait rien, et qui ne s'en estime pas moins.

Il est difficile, je le sens, d'approprier ce que j'ai à dire au tribunal où je comparais. Comment oser blâmer les sciences devant une des plus savantes compagnies de l'Europe, louer l'ignorance dans une célèbre académie, et concilier le mépris pour l'étude avec le respect pour les vrais savants? J'i vu ces contrariétés; et elles ne m'ont point rebuté. Ce n'est pas la Science que je maltraite, me suis-je dit; c'est la vertu que je défends devant des hommes vertueux.   (III, 5)

Flattery is evident here, together with modesty (a little dinted by the end of the first paragraph perhaps). Rousseau is making the necessary moves to secure the benevolence of his audience, to 'approprier' his words to his hearers. But in the printed book, this *exordium* is preceded by a preface whose tone is distinctly less conciliatory. Drawing back from face-to-face negotiation, Rousseau launches a challenge, seeking to create his own audience rather than do business with the audience he has:

Je prévois qu'on me pardonnera difficilement le parti que j'ai osé prendre. Heurtant de front tout ce qui fait aujourd'hui l'admiration des hommes, je ne puis m'attendre qu'à un blâme universel; et ce n'est pas pour avoir été honoré de l'approbation de quelques sages que je dois compter sur celle du public. Aussi mon parti est-il pris; je ne me soucie de plaire ni aux beaux-esprits, ni aux gens du monde. [...] Il ne faut point écrire pour de tels lecteurs, quand on veut vivre au-delà de son siècle. (III, 3)

Posterity is the escape route from the commerce of the writing self. The Rousseau we see here makes no allowances. He is the Diogenes figure defying his polite audience, the author who chose as his epigraph the Ovidian 'Barbarus hic ego sum, quia non intelligor illis'. Not surprisingly, perhaps, this impolitic stance proved very successful.

Many of Rousseau's later works display the same complex entry. Often something like a traditional *exordium*, stressing the author's modesty, is interwoven or juxtaposed with a defiant declaration of independence that apparently leaves no room for bargaining. In the *Emile*, for instance, the 'double entry' is in a way reversed. The text proper begins with uncompromising paradoxes, calculated to shock:

Tout est bien sortant des mains de l'auteur des choses: tout dégénère entre les mains de l'homme [...] Sans cela tout irait plus mal encore, et notre espèce ne veut pas être façonnée à demi. (IV, 245)

Before this opening, however, comes a preface where the author tempers his confident tone with an eye to the possible reactions of his audience, explaining, negotiating, apologizing: 'Ce recueil de réflexions et d'observations, sans ordre et presque sans suite, fut commencé pour complaire à une bonne mère qui sait penser' (IV, 24). It is true that at the end of this first paragraph he does describe himself as 'un homme, qui de sa retraite, jette ses feuilles dans le public'. This seems closer to the 'take it or leave it' of Diogenes, perhaps, but the basic stance is still that of the modest human being, not the dogmatic author.

In the letters too, and particularly such public letters as the refutation of the Archbishop of Paris, one can see the difficulty Rousseau experienced in finding the appropriate tone for this particular form of commerce. He was indeed very conscious of such problems. The letter-form, like conversation, makes specific demands of propriety in a given society. The problem, exacerbated for a poor man with rich protectors, is how to remain true to oneself while engaging in this potentially debasing commerce.

Such problems press in unusually strongly on the autobiographer. Here Rousseau is not just the salesman, he is the commodity too.

As he writes his life, he presents his own self as object, but equally as subject; he is the person who writes/speaks just as much as the person described. *Ethos* is central to successful autobiography. And Jean-Jacques offers a fascinating series of solutions to these problems. In the *Confessions*, the *Dialogues* and the *Rêveries*, he fabricates images of both his past and his present self, even if he is not necessarily entirely conscious of the image of the writing self that his reader will derive from his text. The represented self goes beyond the deliberately presented self.

In 1764, Rousseau drafted an introduction to his *Confessions* which is now called the 'préambule de Neuchâtel'. It is a fairly long text in which the author, while maintaining his own special distinctiveness, appears to be trying to do a deal with his potential readers, explaining the value of what he has to offer, engaging them in reasonable terms in a joint scientific enterprise of psychological investigation. But a few years later, as he rushed towards a provisional conclusion to his autobiography, he rejected this earlier text in favour of the definitive opening, the famous page which flouts Quintilian's rules for an *exordium*:

Je forme une entreprise qui n'eut jamais d'exemple, et dont l'exécution n'aura point d'imitateur. Je veux montrer à mes semblables un homme dans toute la vérité de la nature; et cet homme, ce sera moi.

Moi seul. Je sens mon cœur et je connais les hommes. Je ne suis fait comme aucun de ceux que je connais. (I, 5)

A mad, daring opening, which has worked powerfully on some readers, but has turned many against the author from the start.[18] It is a good *exordium* in being eye-catching and stressing the exceptional importance of the subject, but it hardly conforms to traditional *ethos* teaching. Flaunting his own self in a society where good breeding insisted that 'le moi est haïssable',[19] Rousseau is as far removed as he could be from the habits of *doux commerce*.

It is all the more interesting to note therefore that, unlike most of Rousseau's writings, the *Confessions* were in fact intended for oral performance; large sections of the work were indeed read aloud in Parisian salons in 1770. The final lines of the book present this dramatic confrontation of writer and public in a vertiginous *mise en abyme*. Going right back to his opening audacity, Rousseau again challenges his audience:

Pour moi je déclare hautement et sans crainte: Quiconque, même sans avoir lu mes écrits, examinera par ses propres yeux mon naturel, mon caractère, mes mœurs, mes penchants, mes plaisirs, mes habitudes et pourra me croire un malhonnête homme, est lui-même un homme à étouffer.

And then, pulling back and addressing the reading public, he adds the following despairing coda:

J'achevai ainsi ma lecture et tout le monde se tut. Madame d'Egmont fut la seule qui me parût émue; elle tressaillit visiblement; mais elle se remit bien vite, et garda le silence ainsi que le reste de la compagnie. Tel fut le fruit que je tirai de cette lecture et de ma déclaration.

(I, 656)

Throughout the work, Rousseau has attempted to engage his reader in reasonable conversation, asking questions, joking, explaining himself. But here we witness the apparent[20] breakdown of the commerce between writer and audience. The autobiographer seems to be burning his boats, abandoning all negotiation in an ultimate challenge – which is itself an attempt to appeal over the heads of the actual Parisian audience to a better-disposed posterity.

After the relative failure of the reading of the *Confessions*, Rousseau returned to the task, attempting to find a different way of communicating. The result is the extraordinary trio of dialogues known as *Rousseau juge de Jean-Jacques*, where he splits himself into two, and shows a typical Frenchman and a reasonable Rousseau (people of good commerce) talking about the pariah Jean-Jacques. But again there is prefatory material. The text entitled 'Du sujet et de la forme de cet écrit' seeks to involve the no doubt posthumous reader in a kind of bargain. Or perhaps it would be more accurate to speak of a contract in which the reader is established as the 'dépositaire' of a sacred trust.[21] This is not so much the commerce of the self, as the entrusting of the self to others. And this is why Rousseau was so scandalized by Condillac's reaction when he was given the text to read. Instead of receiving it as the truth of the author's self, he treated it as a book and gave the author advice for improving it – for marketing it, one might say. Even so, Rousseau is of course preoccupied with the best way of presenting himself. His prefatory text shows him still wrestling with the old problems.

Celui qui se sent digne d'honneur et d'estime et que le public défigure et diffame à plaisir, de quel ton se rendra-t-il seul la justice qui lui est due? Doit-il parler de lui-même avec des éloges mérités, mais généralement démentis? Doit-il se vanter des qualités qu'il sent en lui, mais que tout le monde refuse d'y voir? Il y aurait moins d'orgueil que de bassesse à *prostituer* ainsi la vérité.

(I, 665, my italics)

111

In the end though, as this second attempt to enter into proper relations with an audience seems to be breaking down, we see Jean-Jacques reduced to the most undignified of roles, hawking his truth on the streets − or rather trying to give it away in the form of his hand-written letter 'A tout Français aimant encore la justice et la vérité'. And as he recounts it, the reaction of passers-by is just that of people shying away from an unwanted salesman. There was no sale, and this, according to Rousseau's final work, the *Rêveries*, marked the end of any commerce between self and other. In this swan-song there is no longer any question of bargaining, communication or even of a *dépôt*. Rousseau is alone. With words like those of his hero Alceste, he explicitly rejects 'le commerce des hommes': 'avec le dédain qu'ils m'ont inspiré, leur commerce me serait insipide ou même à charge' (I, 998). The *Rêveries* (which is of course an unfinished work) contains no preface. There is no overt presentation of the self to others, or at any rate Rousseau deliberately avoids openly addressing the reader at any point in his text (quite unlike the *Confessions* in this respect). What we have instead is simply (simply?) an examination of the self, a self that is discovered, created, and presented − to whom? To himself, would be Rousseau's answer. The commerce has become a self-contained circle.

Few readers will take these final protestations at face value, as they find themselves reading this elaborate and eloquent presentation of the self. The reader may be formally excluded from the text, but he or she is a constantly present spectre. Even so, one may be reminded of Montaigne's *De trois commerces* (Montaigne being of course a great if insufficiently acknowledged inspiration for Rousseau's autobiographical writings). After friendship and sexual love, the last and most secure of Montaigne's 'commerces' was that of books. Books will not betray you. To write for writing's sake, to write for oneself may free you, if such a thing is possible, from the pains of negotiation and the problems of self-presentation which are visible even in Adam Smith's optimistic account of socialization. No doubt Jean-Jacques would have preferred the *doux commerce*, but failing that he turns inward, and this turn is a key moment in the modern development of a literary representation of the self.

7

THE WRITER AS PERFORMER

The word 'performance' has shifted its meaning over the last two hundred years. Today, if it is not used to describe the qualities of a machine, it usually means an act of display, intended to win applause. In the England of Johnson and Gibbon it was a normal word for a composition, a painting or a piece of writing. Thus Johnson's dictionary gives as its meanings: (1) completion of something designed (2) composition, work; (3) action, something done. ('Performer', however, is 'generally applied to one that makes a public exhibition of his skill'.) Johnson is reported as judging books by Warburton and Whitehead as 'poor performances' (*Tour*, pp. 66, 84), Gibbon refers to Oldys's *Life of Sir Walter Raleigh* as 'a very poor performance' (p. 119), Boswell applies the word frequently to any kind of writing.[1]

None of this necessarily implies that these writers had a particularly histrionic view of their act. Nevertheless, reading Gibbon's *Autobiography* and Boswell's accounts of Johnson, one is often struck by the suitability of the word 'performance' in its modern connotation to the literary attitudes of these two dedicated men of letters. Johnson we see as the man who makes his way in the world by pen and tongue, a man deeply attached to the affirmation of moral, religious and political standards in writing, yet at the same time very much a professional writer. Although he is well known for his assertion of independence against Lord Chesterfield's would-be patronage, he was also skilled in the art of writing prefaces and dedications, usually for the books of others; he told Boswell 'he believed he had dedicated to all the Royal Family round' and 'in writing dedications for others, he considered himself as by no means speaking his own sentiments' (*Life*, p. 353).[2] The real man of letters can perform on any subject, and 'a man may write at any time, if he will set himself doggedly to it' (*Life*, p. 144).

The consciousness of universal literary ability went with an eye for fame and the ways his contemporaries sought it. The idea occurs many times in Boswell's *Life* from the early account of his schooling – 'he discovered a great ambition to excel, which roused him to counteract his indolence' (*Life*, p. 35) – to Johnson's mature awareness that 'it is difficult to get literary fame, and it is every day growing more difficult' (*Life*, p. 623). In such a situation writers may be tempted to adopt paradoxical opinions so as to win attention, and Johnson is quick to criticize Hume or Rousseau for doing just this. Yet in conversation at least the desire for 'colloquial fame' was strong enough to lead Johnson to his notorious 'talking for victory'; he attacked this in the name of frankness and sincerity, but it often led him into the wilful defence of exposed positions, as Boswell recognized: 'He could, when he chose it, be the greatest sophist that ever wielded a weapon in the schools of declamation'. We must note however that Boswell is quick to qualify this image of the rhetorician: 'But he indulged this only in conversation [...] he was too conscientious to make error permanent and pernicious by deliberately writing it.' (*Tour*, p. 7). There is a lot more to Johnson than performance – and he always showed great contempt for actors, whose profession is to please an immediate audience.

Gibbon did not graduate from Grub Street, but a similar note is to be heard in his autobiography, for instance when he shows himself casting about for a suitable subject for a historical essay – the word still seems to have some of its early flavour of a trial of skill – or when he describes his first publication. This work, *Essai sur l'étude de la littérature*, is the production of a young man fresh from study and anxious, like a good rhetorician, to turn his reading into a performance of his own: 'his hopes and fears are multiplied by the idea of self-importance, and he believes for a while that the eyes of mankind are fixed on his person and performance' (p. 100).

In both these examples there is a 'commerce' between writer and public (wit for fame) which is rather different from the commerce I considered in the previous two chapters. In this chapter, I shall be exploring ways in which the polite French audience can be seen as transforming its writers into performers, and the reactions of two *philosophes* to this process. Let us start with the *ancien régime* colleges which were so often criticized by the champions of Enlightenment, and which so many of them attended. These schools, above all those run by the Jesuit order, set out to prepare their pupils to play a part well. In doing so, they used emulation and public exercises extensively. Here is a highly coloured picture of the process:

Les 'Exercices publics' permettent aux élèves de faire montre de leur talent, cette fois-ci devant des spectateurs adultes: chaque classe expose ses 'productions', c'est-à-dire ses compositions les plus réussies brillamment décorées; les meilleurs élèves, postés auprès de leurs œuvres, en font les honneurs non seulement à leurs parents et amis, mais aussi aux notabilités invitées (autorités du collège, personnes 'en vue' dans la ville); certains élèves prononcent des plaidoyers, des dialogues, développent des commentaires d'auteurs, ou expliquent les règles des différentes pièces de poésie et donnent des exemples de leur propre cru; ou encore ils répondent à des questions portant sur la Blason ou la Fable, résolvent des énigmes et charades.[3]

Dainville has shown that we should not accept too quickly an Encyclopedist's *image d'Epinal* of the Jesuit colleges,[4] but the textbooks of the time show the cultivation of performing skill to have been an important matter. So it seemed to Rollin of the University of Paris, who writes in his *Traité des études* of the exercises and interrogations which his pupils underwent in public, and also of the need for eloquent teachers 'qui se distinguent par beaucoup d'érudition, qui brillent au dehors par des compositions et par des actions publiques' (IV, 425).[5] One is reminded of Julien Sorel's recitation of the Bible before the *notables* of Verrières. In the classroom too competitive display was the rule; Rollin writes of his method, 'Par là je tenais toujours la classe en haleine: toutes les compositions étaient travaillées comme celles où il s'agissait des places: et les écoliers étaient comme des soldats qui attendent à chaque instant le signal du combat, et qui s'y tiennent toujours prêts' (II, 25). The same ideal is to be seen in his image of the practical application of these skills: 'Lorsque dans de certaines occasions d'éclat, et dans les places distinguées, on voit un jeune magistrat cultivé par les belles-lettres s'attirer les applaudissements du public, qui est le père qui ne désirât pas un tel fils?' (I, xxix—xxx).

The lawyer with the golden tongue was one model; the man of letters might be another, though it did not usually carry quite as much prestige. Even though there is no reason to suppose that students at the various colleges were not curious to find out about things, it was probably words that took most of their time, particularly in their early years. Performance gave power; eloquence could bring success. Let us follow this process in one well-known career, fully if not reliably documented, that of the star performer Jean-François Marmontel.[6] His *Mémoires*, even though like all such works they are not an entirely authentic record of his life, do at least give us a reflection of the attitudes of their author — admittedly towards the end of his life — and his estimate of what was valuable for social success. The set speeches which he invents for his younger self at high points in his career may not be what he actually said, but they show us what he would have liked to have said.

Marmontel's way to the top started from low down; he came from a peasant family, and for much of his life his urge to shine and succeed was fuelled by the need to provide for his widowed mother and his brothers and sisters. Having learnt to read in his village, he put his foot on the first rung of the ladder when he was accepted at a nearby Jesuit school. His account of his education shows how it encouraged him to become a performer. Coming from a poor background, he has to put on a good front, playing a trick on a new *préfet* so as to have a chance to show off his abilities: 'je me hâtai de me produire, et ne négligeai rien pour être remarqué' (*M*, I, 26), he says, rather like Julien Sorel in the seminary. In various episodes which follow one sees the same tactics; the most picturesque of these occurs at Toulouse, where the young Marmontel is put in charge of a philosophy class in which 'presque toute l'école avait de la barbe et le maître n'en avait point'. To impress and subdue his audience (for pupils in this system are an audience) he learns his first lecture by heart and delivers it as if he were talking spontaneously; this piece of acting is entirely successful and he repeats it for the rest of the course – 'ainsi, chez les Gascons, je débutai par une gasconnade; mais elle m'était nécessaire' (*M*, I, 47–8).

The final scene from Marmontel's education will complete the picture: the description of his culminating *soutenance*. His teacher was anxious to show off his pupil in public, 'et comme il était membre de l'Académie des Sciences de Toulouse, il voulut que ce fût à cette compagnie que ma thèse fût dédiée; spectacle assez nouveau et assez frappant, disait-il, qu'une thèse ainsi présidée. Ce fut par là qu'il voulut terminer sa carrière philosophique; et il imagina d'ajouter à la pompe de ce spectacle un coup de théâtre honorable pour moi, mais dont je fus étonné moi-même.' This 'coup de théâtre' involves Marmontel himself taking the place of his teacher; such an honour throws him off balance, and his memory nearly deserts him, but at the last moment his head clears:

Mes idées renaissent, je ressaisis le fil de mon discours, et bien fatigué, mais tranquille et rassuré, je le prononce. Je ne parle pas du succès qu'il eut; il est rare que les louanges soient mal reçues. J'avais assaisonné celles-ci de mon mieux. Je ne me vante pas non plus de la faveur qui me soutint dans tout cet exercice. En me faisant passer par les plus belles questions de la physique, ceux des académiciens qui daignèrent me provoquer ne s'occupèrent que du soin de faire briller mes réponses.

In this ceremony of mutual gratification, Marmontel, by his own account, did so well that he was offered a vacant place of *adjoint* in the Academy: 'Je l'acceptai avec une humble reconnaissance, et au bruit de l'approbation publique, je reçus le prix du combat' (*M*, I, 51–2). Here we see not only the place of public performance in the educational system, but something of the attitudes fostered by a provincial academy. These places, which flourished so vigorously in the eighteenth century, combined a concern for serious learning and technical progress with a taste for epideictic oratory, *éloges*, public orations and the like. Later on, Marmontel was to become a successful member (and indeed the secretary) of the Académie Française; in that institution, while representing the *philosophe* party, he was able to indulge his outstanding gifts as reader (mentioned by both Grimm and Diderot) and to try out in public some of the pieces which now make up his *Eléments de littérature*. Schools, universities and academies together made up a framework in which it is small wonder that eloquence was a major value.

Encouraged by Voltaire, the young Marmontel decided to seek his fortune in Paris. Like a good pupil, he immediately set about displaying his gifts and making a name for himself (the verb which he used of his school life, 'se produire', still fits the case exactly). His first interview with the master is an entertaining one. Voltaire praises his determination to use his talents, and asks him what he is going to write. Alas, says Marmontel, I have no idea, please tell me. The theatre, says Voltaire, that's the place to win fame and fortune. '"Ce n'est pas l'ardeur qui me manque, lui répondis-je; mais au théâtre que ferai-je? – Une bonne comédie, me dit-il d'un ton résolu. – Hélas! Monsieur, comment ferais-je des portraits? Je ne connais pas les visages." Il sourit à cette réponse. "Hé bien! faites des tragédies." Je répondis que les personnages m'en étaient un peu moins inconnus, et que je voulais bien m'essayer dans ce genre-là' (*M*, I, 63–4). This is the way to begin, and Marmontel goes off dutifully, studies the approved books on the theatre, Aristotle, Corneille, etc., goes to the theatre and, skimming through ancient history, quickly lights on a subject, *Denys le Tyran*. And, wonder of wonders for the diligent student, it is a winner. For a time at least Marmontel is hailed as the new hope of French tragedy. At this time, as Voltaire told him, the theatre dominated French literary life, took the lion's share of the periodical press, and with its quick successes and conventional eloquence set the tone for literary production. From what Marmontel tells us about himself we can imagine that this public art suited him very well indeed, though he never justified the early hopes he had aroused.

And now we see the hero of the memoirs promoted to literary lion, swept into the 'tourbillon de Paris'. He gets to know salon life, of which the memoirs give interesting accounts. As more than one commentator has pointed out,[7] the good salon for Marmontel is like a concert or a well-regulated spectacle; conversation is an art, and the expression that comes naturally to Marmontel's pen is 'jouer son rôle'. Mademoiselle de Lespinasse's circle is the ideal, a place of harmony where the hostess, like a theatrical producer, blends many different talents in a perfect composition. The good performer here is one who fits in, not seeking to distinguish himself but playing the part laid down for him.[8] Indeed Marmontel, for all his readiness to shine in the approved manner, is critical of solo performers: thus his first experience at Madame de Tencin's is that 'on y arrivait préparé à jouer son rôle' and that 'l'envie d'entrer en scène n'y laissait pas toujours à la conversation la liberté de suivre son cours facile et naturel' (*M*, I, 100). How much more will he disapprove of the outlandish and apparently ostentatious Rousseau, who deliberately flouts the conventions of polite talk. Perhaps because of his own interest in success, he suspects Jean-Jacques, as he will later suspect the orators of the Revolution, of adopting extreme positions simply in order to win fame and gratify vanity.

At this early stage in his Parisian life, Marmontel lived above all in the entourage of the rich tax-farmer La Popelinière. Writing about it in his old age, he presents this episode as favourably as possible, but it is clear that his talents allowed him to lead a parasitic life not very far removed from that of Rameau's nephew. In his house at Passy, full of actors, artists and musicians, La Popelinière had his own plays performed at a private theatre, and these pieces, says Marmontel, 'quoique médiocres, étaient d'assez bon goût et assez bien écrites, pour qu'il n'y eût pas une complaisance excessive à les applaudir' (*M*, I, 105). The memorialist remains discreet about the services rendered in exchange for this life of luxury, but looking back from his retirement he deplores 'le mal qu'il [La Popelinière] me fit en me voulant du bien' and 'les attrayantes et nuisibles douceurs qu'eut pour moi sa société' (*M*, I, 94). Rather like the Diderot of *Le Neveu*, he sees in the life of the performing parasite the grave of real achievement.

A few years later we find Marmontel hobnobbing with another figure out of Diderot's dialogue, the famous Bouret, presented by Rameau as king of the art of flattery. This is at a time when Marmontel, realizing that his early theatrical success was a flash in the pan, is trying to make his way in the court world at Versailles.

Madame de Pompadour has replaced La Popelinière as his protector, and here too a willing eloquence is his great standby. Although a sinecure enables him to write for himself (i.e. his *Eléments de littérature*), his pen is called on in a number of different causes, whether to rewrite Rotrou's *Venceslas* for a Versailles performance, to compose a dedicatory epistle for a book on agriculture, or to correct the 'français tudesque' of a Viennese diplomatic document. This last task is performed for Bernis and the Comte de Staremberg, who 'me marquèrent tous les deux combien ils étaient affligés d'avoir à publier un manifeste si mal écrit dans notre langue, et me dirent que je ferais une chose très agréable pour les deux cours de Versailles et de Vienne, si je voulais le corriger et le faire imprimer à la hâte, pour être présenté et publié dans quatre jours' (*M*, I, 146). Marmontel, always a quick worker, did what was required. Bernis was for him a tantalizing example of the possibilities open to the writer of talent; he describes him as 'un poète galant, bien frais, bien poupin, et qui, avec le gentil Bernard, amusait de ses jolis vers les joyeux soupers de Paris'. But 'c'est de là, sans autre mérite, qu'il est parti pour être cardinal et ambassadeur de France à la cour de Rome' (*M*, I, 145). So he cultivates Bernis, singing his praises in an epistle to the King; but nothing comes of it, and Marmontel abandons his court career and returns to Paris, journalism and writing.

A final example of the place of performance in Marmontel's life is afforded by his *Contes moraux*, perhaps his most celebrated work. His first moral tale was written overnight to help out a friend with copy for the *Mercure de France*. The genre proved popular, it came easily to Marmontel, and he continued to turn out stories with ever-increasing success. Because these *contes* have lost most of their appeal for modern readers, commentators have assumed, not entirely justifiably, that their author was simply pandering to the passing taste of an audience.[9] What is more interesting, from our present point of view, is to read Marmontel's description of their first 'performance':

Les nouveaux contes que je faisais alors, et dont ces dames avaient la primeur, étaient, avant ou après le souper, une lecture amusante pour elles. [...] J'avoue que jamais succès ne m'a plus sensiblement flatté que celui qu'avaient mes lectures dans ce petit cercle où l'esprit, le goût, la beauté, toutes les grâces étaient mes juges ou plutôt mes applaudisseurs. Il n'y avait, ni dans mes peintures, ni dans mon dialogue, pas un trait tant soit peu délicat ou fin, qui ne fût vivement senti; et le plaisir que je causais avait l'air du ravissement. [...] Mais, malgré les ménagements d'une politesse excessive, je m'apercevais bien aussi des endroits froids ou faibles qu'on passait sous silence, et de ceux où j'avais manqué le mot, le ton de la nature, la juste nuance du vrai; et c'était là ce que je notais, pour le corriger à loisir.   (*M*, I, 170)

We have here the closeness to a specific well-bred audience which is so characteristic of much literature of the *ancien régime*. Writing and conversation blend together; the writer is not a solitary, but one who plays his part, and wins immediate applause. He is an actor, using his voice, his face and his body to make his own text as persuasive as possible. And he responds quickly to the public in front of him. This would appear to be one of Marmontel's particular characteristics, though we find the same thing in other and greater writers of the time (e.g. Montesquieu). At the beginning of his career, soon after *Denys le Tyran*, Raynal remarked of him: 'Ce qu'il y a de plus admirable en lui, c'est cette docilité parfaite qui le plie au sentiment de ceux qui le critiquent par goût et par raison.'[10] It would be wrong, however, to paint too simple a picture of a supple careerist. Marmontel was associated with the *philosophe* party at a time when the *Encyclopédie* was in trouble, he spent a few honourable days in the Bastille, and Diderot congratulated him on his forthright articles 'Grand' and 'Grandeur'. He was also by no means such an adaptable creature as I may have suggested; he himself in his memoirs speaks rather complacently of a certain stubbornness in his nature, his friend Morellet mentions his 'très grande irritabilité'[11] and Diderot refers to him as a noisy, opinionated and long-winded talker.[12] He was apparently not so good at harmonizing as he would have wished. In writing, too, he seemed to some contemporaries to lack that perfect ease which he so appreciated. Grimm, whose opinion of him is like Diderot's but even less favourable, sees him as 'un homme de bois, mais qui a vécu avec des philosophes, avec des enthousiastes de la belle poésie, et qui a appris à parler leur langage sans le sentir'.[13] The good pupil is not the same as the good performer.

Again, though we can see Marmontel winning an increasingly solid economic position for himself by his successes with tongue and pen, we cannot assume (as Grimm does here) that he did not mean what he wrote. I have used him as an example of the role of performance in a literary man's life, but in doing so I have given a distorted image of the whole man. *Bélisaire* in particular, as John Renwick has shown,[14] sprang from a desire to be useful and achieve a sort of posthumous greatness which his earlier works, for all their success, could hardly guarantee him. And even if here posterity has ratified Grimm's and Diderot's judgement that he was no genius ('débitant des lieux communs méthodiquement et sans mesure'),[15] Marmontel knew quite well that talent is not genius. In the piece on genius in his *Eléments*, he puts forward the distinction that was becoming familiar by the end of the eighteenth century: the attribute of the genius is 'le don de créer', whereas 'l'homme de talent pense et dit les choses qu'une foule d'hommes aurait pensées et dites'; 'le mérite de l'une est dans l'industrie, le mérite de l'autre est dans l'invention'. He had (or at least expressed) a high idea of the lyric poet, a 'vertueux enthousiaste', and affirmed that 'le sentiment et le génie ont des mouvements qui ne s'imitent pas' (IV, 765). In the article 'Mœurs', he declares that the artist who wants to paint the human heart must live among uncultivated people, since 'le grand monde est un bal masqué' (IV, 707); and in 'Usage', which he read out to the Academy, he talks like d'Alembert in his *Essai sur la société des gens de lettres avec les grands*, of the debilitating effect of polite society on literary language:

Lorsque le goût du temps a paru aux hommes de génie dans les arts ou trop timide ou trop frivole, qu'ont fait ces grands artistes? Ils se sont recueillis, retirés de leur siècle, et se sont mis devant les yeux les grands exemples du passé, pour être dignes, en les imitant, des suffrages de l'avenir.

(*O*, V, 258)

A statement like this is hedged around with caution and qualifications in Marmontel's writing. This ideal of the 'écrivain solitaire et indépendant' was not one for his own use, and it is possible, as Grimm says, that these were only notions that Marmontel had picked up from Diderot and the *philosophes*. They do show, however, that a careerist could have qualms about the pitfalls of talent.

Marmontel was no exception. His enemy, the uncivilized Rousseau, knew only too well the perils of rhetoric. Both Johnson (in conversation) and Marmontel (in his memoirs) accused him of harnessing his great eloquence to wilful paradoxes in order to distinguish himself. Others said as much openly, and he had to fight hard to avoid the taint of performance, to maintain the distinction between sincere orator and flexible actor, and to separate himself from those philosophers who were spurred on by a thirst for applause rather than the pursuit of a truth to live by.[16] Here is his classic statement of the problem, which is thrown into fuller relief when seen against the career of a Marmontel:

J'en ai beaucoup vu qui philosophaient bien plus doctement que moi, mais leur philosophie leur était pour ainsi dire étrangère. [...] Plusieurs d'entre eux ne voulaient que faire un livre, n'importe quel, pourvu qu'il fût accueilli.

[...] Pour moi, quand j'ai désiré d'apprendre, c'était pour savoir moi-même et non pas pour enseigner.[17]

Perhaps Rousseau protests too much. One cannot expect any writer's motives to be as simple as he suggests, but his case does shed light on the ease with which a person's work could be reduced to a prize essay or a bid for applause.

We do not know which particular philosophers Rousseau had in mind when he wrote these lines, but to judge from contemporary comment, the author of *De l'esprit* could well have been among them. Several readers whose comments have come down to us thought of Helvétius as an eager performer, more anxious to make a lasting name for himself than to tell the truth. Thus Marmontel, whose suspicion of unfamiliar ideas we have noted:

> Pour faire un livre distingué dans son siècle, son premier soin avait été de chercher ou quelque vérité nouvelle à mettre au jour, ou quelque pensée hardie et neuve à produire et à soutenir. [...] Rien ne ressemble moins à l'ingénuité de son caractère et de sa vie habituelle que la singularité préméditée et factice de ses récits; et cette dissemblance se trouvera toujours entre les mœurs et les opinions de ceux qui se fatiguent à penser des choses étranges.   (*M*, I, 164)

In the memoirs of another *philosophe*, Morellet, Helvétius is again described as straining after glory, but this time the emphasis is on the form of the work; Morellet recalls seeing Helvétius sweat blood 'pour échauffer ses idées ou leur donner une forme qui ne fût pas commune'.[18] A similar note comes from the ever-critical Grimm, who remarks that Helvétius 'n'avait cherché qu'à s'écarter des routes battues', but that the writing of paradoxes did not make him a genius.[19]

Even among those who were more or less on the same side of the philosophical battle as Helvétius, there was then a tendency to write him off as a performer. It should be noted, however, that this was a different sort of performance from that illustrated by Marmontel. We may see the author of the *Contes moraux* as one who learns all his lessons well and becomes adept at jumping through all the approved hoops. But even if Helvétius's contemporaries were right about his motives, his performance was not destined to win immediate applause by flattering the taste of his readers, but rather to cut out a new place for himself and impose his name on posterity − or as Grimm puts it, 's'élever une colonne à côté de celle de Montesquieu'. He wanted to show that he was a genius.

And of course he does not describe himself as a performer. In what he says about *De l'esprit*, and even more so *De l'homme*, he stresses usefulness as his main concern. After the bitter lesson of *De l'esprit*, according to Saint-Lambert, 'la violence de la persécution avait beaucoup diminué de son amour de la gloire' (I, 163),[20] and his second book opens with a strongly worded preface on the need for posthumous publication. 'Ce n'est plus maintenant que dans les livres défendus qu'on trouve la vérité', he writes, 'on ment dans les autres. La plupart des auteurs sont dans leurs écrits ce que les gens du monde sont dans la conversation: uniquement occupés de plaire' (VII, ix). The great books are original and fearless – and greatness was still a goal, even if he had abandoned notions of immediate reputation.

For *gloire* was Helvétius's driving force; 'il a aimé la gloire avec passion, et c'est la seule passion qu'il ait éprouvée' (I, 176), writes Saint-Lambert. Early in life he was apparently stung into excellence by emulation. Brought up by the Jesuits, he had to perform in public and 'comblé d'éloges dans les exercices publics de son collège, voulut réussir dans tout ce qui pouvait être loué' (I, 6–7). Later in life, having decided to follow the example of Montesquieu, he was interested in the reasons for conversational or literary success and the definition of such words as *esprit, bon sens, sottise* and *folie*. Many of his 'Réflexions', like the maxims of La Rochefoucauld or the jottings of Montesquieu, dwell on these questions in a way that suggests that Helvétius is pondering his own case:

> Il ne faut pas avoir trop de petitesse ni trop d'étendue d'esprit pour paraître avoir du bon sens; car on n'appelle bon sens parmi presque tous les hommes que l'acquiescement aux choses reçues par les sots; et un homme qui n'a en but que la vérité, et qui par conséquent s'éloigne ordinairement des vérités reçues, passe pour fou. (XIV, 137–8)

> L'envie dit souvent qu'un tel livre ne fait du bruit que par sa hardiesse, pour dire hautement: 'Je passerais pour avoir autant d'esprit que cet homme-là si j'étais aussi imprudent.' Vérité hardie est une vérité importante au grand nombre, et peut-être nuisible à des hommes ou à des corps puissants. Celles qui ne font point de bruit n'ont donc nulle importance; les auteurs de ces vérités devraient donc moins s'applaudir de leur prudence que rougir de l'inutilité de leur esprit. (XIV, 122–3)

In *De l'esprit* too, one of the author's main concerns is to define as clearly as possible the qualities (originality, usefulness, appropriateness, etc.) which win praise for one mind rather than another and to explain the reasons for these preferences.

As with Montesquieu, there is here both a disdain for quick success and a considerable interest in the achievement of it. But this thirst for *gloire* does not mean that one can do what his contemporaries did and dismiss Helvétius's work as simply the product of literary vanity. He himself asserts that the desire for reputation, like the desire for physical pleasure (to which he claims it is ultimately reducible), provides the necessary impetus for the performance of any great deed. Fame is the spur; the Jesuit rhetoric teachers may have been right to believe that competition and public display rather than spontaneity were the best way to valuable achievement. Helvétius's various epistles, which won the praise and encouragement of Voltaire, give the impression of being exercises on set themes, deliberate first steps on the road to fame – and no doubt the same desire for reputation impelled him in the writing of the work for which he is in fact famous.

If we read the early chapters of *De l'esprit*, we may be impressed by the philosopher's plain writing. Are we to say that this is simply what contemporaries would have called 'le ton de la chose', the natural style of a serious man, or should we detect here the deliberate playing of a part by the former tax-farmer, the universal charmer, whose early poem 'Le Bonheur' had been criticized by an enthusiastic Voltaire as too full of beauties? We could say either; it depends whether we want to praise or denigrate. It is the same with the use of entertaining example and anecdotes, the same too with the purple passages in which Helvétius seems to be imitating another of his models, the 'grand phrasier' Buffon. Within the book's methodical framework we find not only the endless tales and titbits which irritated Voltaire, but also frequent pieces of fine writing which recall the grandiloquence of 'Le Bonheur', pages such as this one:

Il en est du moral comme du physique. Lorsque les peuples croient les mers constamment enchaînées dans leur lit, le sage les voit successivement découvrir et submerger de vastes contrées, et le vaisseau sillonner les plaines que naguère sillonnait la charrue. Lorsque les peuples voient les montagnes porter dans les nues une tête également élévée, le sage voit leurs cimes orgueilleuses, perpétuellement démolies par les siècles, s'ébouler dans les vallons et les combler de leurs ruines; mais ce ne sont jamais que des hommes accoutumés à méditer qui, voyant l'univers moral, ainsi que l'univers physique, dans une destruction et une reproduction successives et perpétuelles, peuvent apercevoir les causes éloignées du renversement des états. C'est l'œil d'aigle des passions qui perce l'abîme ténébreux de l'avenir: l'indifférence est née aveugle et stupide. (V, 16–17)

What is the function of these grandiose sentences, these repetitions, effects of symmetry, personifications and traditional metaphors? Is this the style appropriate to an important subject, or perhaps the style that is needed to persuade the average reader? Or is it simply the grand style which had been acquired by the pupil of the Jesuits and the youthful member of the Academy of Caen and which was intended to win him an enduring reputation for fine writing? Our answer is bound to include all of these, and it may be more or less indulgent to a rhetoric which makes posterity smile. Certainly, in writing this sort of prose, Helvétius was giving a hostage to fortune and laying himself open to all the customary criticisms of ostentatious display.

We have seen that for personal reasons he was very conscious of the distinction between the mind of genius and the ordinary mind. In his discussion of this question, it is interesting to see what Helvétius has to say about the corrupting power of society on the writer. In a passage from the 'Réflexions' quoted above he asserted that the truly original man or idea will seem stupid or mad to the mediocre majority. They may even persecute him – and presumably Helvétius, like Diderot, could take comfort in adversity from the example of Socrates. The same ideas are to be found in *De l'esprit*, but also, more insistently, the notion that society drags down the superior man to its own level, forcing him to perform the parts it dictates. He sounds a note which is familiar among the *philosophes* when he denounces French frivolity and 'la préférence que nous donnons à l'ésprit d'agrément sur tout autre genre d'esprit; préférence qui nous accoutume à regarder l'homme d'esprit comme divertissant, à l'avilir en le confondant avec le pantomime' (III, 66) (Diderot to Rameau: 'Vous dansez, vous avez dansé et vous continuerez de danser la vile pantomime').[21] In particular he attacks the claims of polite society to set the tone and make conversation the standard for writing. Chapter 9 of the second *discours* of *De l'esprit* analyses the supposed superiority of fashionable wits, and notes:

Ce qui fait le plus d'illusion en faveur des gens du monde, c'est l'air aisé, le geste dont ils accompagnent leurs discours, et qu'on doit regarder comme l'effet de la confiance que donne nécessairement l'avantage du rang; ils sont à cet égard ordinairement fort supérieurs aux gens de lettres. Or la déclamation, comme le dit Aristote, est la première partie de l'éloquence. Ils peuvent donc, par cette raison, avoir, dans les conversations frivoles, l'avantage sur les gens de lettres: avantage qu'ils perdent lorsqu'ils écrivent; non seulement parce qu'ils ne sont plus alors soutenus du prestige de la déclamation, mais parce que leurs écrits n'ont jamais que le style de leurs conversations', et qu'on écrit presque toujours mal lorsqu'on écrit comme on parle. (II, 127–8)

At the time when Helvétius wrote this, writing and speech were still equally valued by many members of the public, but he at least had no doubt that writing a book is a different matter from talking in a salon.

Not of course that he is totally hostile to the demands of what he calls 'des sociétés particulières' – as opposed to mankind in general. As he says, 'il est si difficile [...] de vivre dans les sociétés du grand monde sans adopter quelques-unes de leurs erreurs, que les gens d'esprit les plus en garde à cet égard ne sont pas toujours sûrs de s'en défendre' (II, 138–9). With his eye for success, Helvétius has a strong rhetorical awareness, and several chapters of his fourth *discours* are concerned with style, literary effectiveness and so on.[22] And although obviously the philosopher's first concern must be with what he is saying rather than how he says it (Helvétius makes the typical eighteenth-century assumption that the two are separable, and that you can hang garlands of flowers over the thorns of thought), he does warn the serious writer against an unjustified contempt for *bel-esprit* (V, 222). Society life can accustom the philosopher to an ease and clarity of expression which will enable him to communicate more successfully. It is important however to distinguish *bel-esprit* from the mere *esprit du siècle*, the tittle-tattle which the serious person will avoid at all costs. Even stronger is the condemnation of yet another variety of *esprit*, the *esprit de conduite*; here (in Chapter 13 of the fourth *discours*) Helvétius is talking about action rather than writing, but the sort of self-abasement he has in mind could be that of the writer just as much as the courtier. His diatribe reads yet again like a comment on *Le Neveu de Rameau*:

Que de gens d'esprit, en conséquence, ont joué la folie, se sont donné des ridicules, ont affecté la plus grande médiocrité devant des supérieurs, hélas! trop faciles à tromper par les gens vils dont le caractère se prête à cette bassesse!
(VI, 86)

Or later, with a curious appearance of the word 'rameau':

L'esprit élevé ne peut s'abaisser jusque-là: il aime mieux être la digue qui s'oppose au torrent, dût-il en être renversé, que le rameau léger qui flotte au gré des eaux.
(VI, 91)

For in theory at least, the rich ex-financier maintained the call to independence and solitude:

On sent que, trop heureux d'échapper au mépris des sociétés particulières, le grand homme, surtout s'il est modeste, doit renoncer à l'estime sentie de la plupart d'entre elles. Aussi n'est-il que faiblement animé du désir de leur plaire. Il sent confusément que l'estime de ces sociétés ne prouverait que l'analogie de ses idées avec les leurs, que cette analogie serait souvent peu flatteuse, et que l'estime publique est la seule digne d'envie, la seule désirable, puisqu'elle est toujours un don de la reconnaissance publique, et par conséquent la preuve d'un mérite réel.
(I, 144)

If the great man performs, it is not for an immediate audience, but before the eyes of humanity past, present and to come.

On their own terms, we may have doubts, as their contemporaries did, as to whether Marmontel or even Helvétius were writers of genius. But there is one work of genius in which the threads of my present discussion are woven together, the work I have already quoted more than once, *Le Neveu de Rameau*. Here we find Helvétius's concern to define the genius and his role in society. Here too above all we have a meditation on performance. Rameau has the *esprit de conduite* which Helvétius condemns; he is the courtier, accepting humiliation and devoting his talent to self-advancement, but arguably unworthy of admiration because the skill is not matched by the value of the results. Talking, acting, miming and singing, he does what he can to vindicate his existence, praising his superior skills as a parasite and flatterer and seeking – unsuccessfully I think – to share by mimesis the evil sublimity of the renegade of Avignon. This voluntary self-abasement he attributes partly to his own (biological) nature, but more insistently to the pinch of poverty and the unjust order of the world: 'Que diable d'économie, des hommes qui regorgent de tout, tandis que d'autres qui ont un estomac importun comme eux, une faim renaissante comme eux, et pas de quoi mettre sous la dent. Le pis, c'est la posture contrainte où nous tient le besoin' (p. 189). Even so, the probing philosopher exposes the raw nerve of dignity which will not let him rest on his petty laurels and forces him to envy the creative genius of his boorish uncle.

In MOI we see an increasingly desperate attempt to define a non-performing role for the artist or the philosopher. He is not to be a buffoon, as Rameau would have it, or one who can use his talent to write flattering dedicatory epistles. But in order to escape the universal 'vile pantomime' he is driven in a final paroxysm to a Rousseauist retreat from society, eating roots rather than submit to servile performance – 'je veux mourir, si cela ne vaudrait mieux que de ramper, de s'avilir, et se prostituer' (p. 193). There is, however, something absurd in these noble words as they come from the mouth of the serene paterfamilias who dreams on the bench in the Allée d'Argenson. It is earlier in the dialogue that we find a compromise solution; instead of allowing himself to be drawn into the role of society clown, Diderot tells Rameau, 'il fallait d'abord se faire une ressource indépendante de la servitude' (p. 118). And if, assuming with Roland Desné[23] that this dialogue is indeed about Diderot, we ask what this 'ressource' actually is, we must answer that it is the income of the pen, the payment for the *Encyclopédie*.

The liberation is incomplete of course. As the writer comes to appeal more to a book-buying public and depends less on face-to-face contact with a polite audience, he may come to feel less a buffoon and more a leader, but a readership is still an audience with its desire to be flattered and its power to turn the anti-performer into a performer. Nor is the bookseller necessarily a better task-master than the patron, as Diderot found out with Le Breton. Even so, MOI is a freer and more creative man than LUI because he does not have to flatter Bertin and can compose a work which will change the course of future thinking. So is Helvétius, who follows the example of Buffon and Montesquieu and does what Marmontel recommends to the would-be genius, going off to the country to create his great work — none of these rich men had to worry about their next meal. The Helvétius of *De l'homme* is even freer because he has decided to publish his work posthumously and claims to be no longer interested in immediate reputation. And of course Diderot himself kept the *Neveu* and most of his other important works from the eyes of publishers and the vast majority of his contemporaries, preferring to please a tiny audience, or even just himself, and gambling on the praise of posterity. There is still an audience here, a very limited or an unknown one, but the image of writing is no longer one of performing tricks for the satisfaction of hunger or vanity. The inescapable compulsion to perform for applause is in the best cases transformed into the pursuit of lasting fame, which Helvétius saw as one of the sharpest spurs to any great achievement.

8

BEYOND POLITENESS? SPEAKERS AND AUDIENCE AT THE CONVENTION NATIONALE

What is the politeness of a revolutionary? What indeed have revolutions to do with politeness? The last three chapters have been concerned with the codes regulating behaviour, speech and writing in a confined world, that of the *honnêtes gens*, of fashionable or at least respectable society. In Chapter 4, however, I considered the possibility of a politeness that would go beyond this narrow world. As the social hierarchy was overturned in the months and years following the fall of the Bastille, the social norms of the *ancien régime* – involving for instance dress, modes of address, meeting places, relations between the sexes – were all called in question. But all societies, however turbulent, need rules or conventions to prevent conflict getting out of hand and promote the common happiness. Whether such rules and conventions could still go by the name of politeness in 1792 is another matter. The subject is a large and fascinating one; I shall approach it here by discussing one limited (though still enormous) subject, the eloquence of the revolutionary assemblies.

French writers of the *ancien régime* often lamented the decline of high political eloquence, whose distant echo they heard in the literature of ancient Greece or Rome. There are periods, however, when persuasive speech recovers some of its old powers. May 1968 was perhaps such a period in France; another, on a much vaster scale, was the French Revolution. Between 1789 and 1794 in particular, the French people, and above all the Parisians, witnessed a flood tide of the spoken word, and a series of verbal battles in which the very survival of the speaker and his party might be at stake. They also saw attempts to inaugurate a new French language capable of uniting the new nation. For a few years oral persuasion regained its former prestige – and this is doubtless one reason for the virtual eclipse of this period in the standard histories of French literature, since speech offers less resistance than writing to the wear and tear of time.

Until recently the eloquence of the revolutionary period, like its literature, was a neglected subject.[1] Even the rhetorics and histories of rhetoric allotted far less space to it than to the sermons and funeral orations of a Bossuet. Domairon, in his *Rhétorique française* of 1804, when he comes to deal with political eloquence, says nothing at all about the preceding fifteen years and concentrates on Condé, Henri IV and the Roman generals. If Aulard composed his vast tableaux of revolutionary eloquence,[2] it was precisely to restore to their rightful place the orators who did not even figure in the histories of rhetoric in 1880.

Deep-rooted prejudice stood in the way of the serious study of the subject. In the first place there was what one might call the school of Taine. Not that Hippolyte Taine was the first person to denigrate the oratory of the revolutionary assemblies; in his *Les Origines de la France contemporaine* (which appeared at the same time as Aulard's volumes), he was in fact following the example of such predecessors as La Harpe, author of *Du fanatisme dans la langue révolutionnaire* (1797), even if his voice is far more strident than La Harpe's.[3] Taine's example was widely followed, and he is still regarded as an authority in some quarters. In his view the great debates of the Assemblée Constituante were nothing but 'parades de foire' – 'verbiage et clameurs, à cela se réduisent la plupart de ces scènes fameuses'.[4] The Assemblée Législative is described as 'une école d'extravagances et un théâtre de déclamations' (II, 99), and the Convention Nationale, dominated as it was by its vulgar audience, was even worse. What is more, this eloquence is the last gasp of an outdated way of speaking, the eloquence of pedants and lawyers of the *ancien régime*. Robespierre is 'le suprême avorton et le fruit sec de l'esprit classique' (III, 190). There is nothing new about this rhetoric except a kind of crazy overblown enthusiasm, which is easily mocked by the good sense and good taste of the Third Republic. So Ferdinand Brunot, whose *Histoire de la langue française* remains an essential starting point for the study of revolutionary language, clearly finds amusement in collecting examples of revolutionary bombast, such as the sentence with which Danton ended his famous anti-Girondin peroration on 1 April 1793: 'Je me suis retranché dans la citadelle de la raison, j'en sortirai avec le canon de la vérité, et je pulvériserai les scélérats qui ont voulu m'accuser' – a sentence that was not at all funny in the context of a declaration of war on his political adversaries.[5] It is all too easy to be ironic at a distance.

If for some historians the eloquence of the revolutionary orators was a caricature of ancient eloquence, the grotesque declamation of pedants playing bloodthirsty games under the mask of a Brutus or a

Cicero, for others, as one can easily imagine, it was the harbinger of a new world, a new way of writing and speaking. This is a mirror-image of the Tainean myth. One might cite as examples not only the Michelets and the Aulards (or even the Garaudys),[6] but nearer our own time Béatrice Didier writing in 1976 that 'notre prose romantique est née dans la bouche des orateurs de la Révolution'.[7] This idea was already current in the 1790s. Mercier, for instance, declares that 'comme il s'est fait un changement prodigieux dans les circonstances actuelles, notre éloquence a pris un nouveau caractère'.[8] Good taste and purity of style have given way to a new impetuous freedom. Charles Nodier, who was thirteen in 1793, was perhaps the person who did most to propagate this idea. In his *Recherches sur l'éloquence révolutionnaire*, he affirms: 'De cette prétendue exception [the Revolution], il est sorti une forme nouvelle de société, et par conséquent [...] une forme nouvelle de littérature'.[9] In other words, this was a cultural revolution.

Do we have to make a choice between these diametrically opposed views?[10] Is it not possible to view this phenomenon more dispassionately? I do not wish to judge the eloquence of the Revolution in either political or literary terms. The point is not to evaluate, but to analyse. Having, in the previous chapters, considered the performances of writers, and sometimes of speakers, in the more or less orderly, civilized world of polite society and literature, the world of the academy, the salon, the theatre and the journal, I shall examine here what happens to speaking (and the same would largely hold true for writing) in a dramatically different context, a world of violence, excess and freedom, in which the old constraints no longer apply.

Those who have written about this eloquence have usually concentrated on the speeches of the great orators, Mirabeau, Danton, Vergniaud, Robespierre. The reason is simple: their speeches have been better preserved and edited. But such an approach misses a great deal of what is most living in the subject, and fails to recognize the great diversity of revolutionary speech. Ideally, one should look at speech outside the national assemblies, in contexts such as the street, the revolutionary clubs and sections, the *fêtes*, the theatre or indeed such catechisms as Léonard Bourdon's *Recueil des actions héroiques*, published in 200,000 copies for reading aloud in all the villages of France. But even if one remains within the walls of the Assemblée Nationale, for which the evidence is most plentiful, one must stress the great diversity of styles of speaking. At the Convention one might hear dry reports, clumsy letters from popular or provincial sections, rapid and sometimes familiar exchanges as well as the great set speeches. How can one study this diversity? Arguably the right way is to attempt to encompass the totality of parliamentary proceedings over a limited time-span, even though no sample can claim to be fully representative. In a previous article, I studied in some detail the unfolding of the events of one particular day (10 April 1793) at the Convention Nationale.[11] Here, taking a rather different angle, and concentrating on a small number of questions, I shall extend my range to cover a period of five days, the first five days in the existence of the Convention, from 21 September to 25 September 1792.

The problem of sources for the study of speech is well known. In the case of the French Revolution, once one goes beyond the major speeches, many of which were published separately from the authors' manuscripts and have in some cases been properly edited in recent times,[12] one is essentially dealing with records of debates in the *procès-verbaux* of the assemblies or in the newspapers. None is entirely satisfactory. The *Archives parlementaires*, compiled at the end of the last century, bring together material from several sources, but for the period concerning me in this chapter these sources are not generally identified. The *Moniteur* is usually reckoned to be the best of the newspaper accounts, though it is often incomplete (stenographic techniques were rudimentary) and may be biased (towards the Gironde in September 1792). Notwithstanding their defects, I shall rely principally on these two sources.[13] It has to be said, however, that even if one had a verbatim account of all that was said, one would still be far removed from the reality of the thing. Gesture, voice and all other aspects of what the rhetoricians called *actio* – for Demosthenes the be-all and end-all of eloquence – can only be guessed at, sometimes with the help of contemporary accounts. Likewise the atmosphere of the assembly, even in the quite literal sense of the term, was obviously crucial in these debates. The records give sparse 'stage directions' such as 'double salve d'applaudissements', 'murmures' or 'Plusieurs députés s'élancent à la tribune', and these can be supplemented with pictures or eye-witness accounts such as those of Chateaubriand. This last example will serve to remind us that eye-witness accounts are as reliable as the eye-witness. The present-day scholar is bound therefore to feel rather as the Russian critic Kazansky did when analysing Lenin's oratory: 'The text of the speech confronts him like a text written in a barely comprehensible language'.[14]

Contemporaries were conscious that the development of political oratory – like that of political journalism – was a remarkable new development of the revolutionary years. The sudden explosive expansion of the political scene confronted speakers with the need to work out new forms of speech for the new − often disturbingly new − situation. The *procès-verbaux* of the Comités d'Instruction Publique of the different assemblies contain interesting arguments about the appropriate rhetoric for revolutionaries, as do such works as Saint-Just's *Institutions républicaines* or Vergniaud's *Eloge de Mirabeau*.[15] There were precedents of course. Not a few deputies had cut their teeth in the law-courts of the *ancien régime*, and models could also be sought in the eloquent discourses of the eighteenth-century *philosophes*, in the written records of ancient Greece or Rome and in the actual experience of parliamentary proceedings in England and America. Nevertheless the rapid and often violent development of events both inside and outside the national assemblies threw down a formidable challenge to the deputies, who could feel, without too much exaggeration, that not only their own fate, but the fate of the nation (or indeed of the whole world) hung on the way they spoke.[16]

Of the five principal parts of rhetoric, two (*memoria* and *actio*) cannot be used for the analysis of speech that has long since fallen silent. Of the other three, *dispositio* only really concerns the shape given to set speeches of some length, and *elocutio*, while clearly essential, is of dubious usefulness when one is not certain of the precise words spoken. I shall not therefore be aiming at a stylistic analysis, but shall use rather two concepts belonging to the domain of *inventio*, which concerns the material of persuasion. These are *ethos*, whereby the speaker contrives to present himself in such a way as to win trust and carry conviction, and *pathos*, which involves the appeal to the passions of the audience. The third member of this triad, *logos*, or the forms and figures of proof, will figure here less, since it is more complex and variable, less amenable to generalization. I shall begin, however, with a category belonging less to rhetoric than to poetics, and indeed to that debate about politeness explored in the preceding chapters, *decorum*, since it seems to me that one of the crucial problems facing the assembly and its speakers was the elaboration of a code of propriety suitable to the revolutionary situation.

Before coming to this, let me say a few words about the moment and the place. There is no need to go into any detail about the political situation on 21 September 1792. It is the immediate aftermath of the popular, Parisian insurrection of 10 August and the September massacres. This is a period of national danger, which is halted, for the time being, by the French victories culminating in Valmy (20 September). Danton is very much the man of the moment. The Convention, rapidly elected by a much broader suffrage than the previous assemblies (though with lower participation), assembles in Paris on 21 September, some of the new deputies arriving late. Hostile observers may describe it as 'collected principally from the dregs of France',[17] but in fact its members are neither plebeian nor inexperienced in politics − if two thirds are new to the national assembly, almost all have been involved in regional and local administration.

A great deal of business awaits the new *conventionnels*. They formally abolish the monarchy on day 1, proclaiming the Republic almost as an afterthought. Thereafter they are concerned equally to deal with current disorder, assuring some continuity in law enforcement, taxation and so on, and overseeing the national war effort, and to plan the future, which means above all working out a new constitution to be submitted (or such is the theory) to the people. In fact, however, the essential business is the coming to terms with the new developments of August and September. For the Girondins this means dealing with the threat to law and order, security and property which they see in the actions of the Paris Commune, and heading off the danger of a revolutionary dictatorship (that of Robespierre). For the Montagne, the threat is rather the Girondin conspiracy to defraud the people of their revolution. From the outset, in fact, there is a battle for power between the two groups (even if the demarcation between them is uncertain). The Girondins appear to be in control, their majority giving them key positions such as that of president of the assembly, but the Montagnard minority can appeal to their popular Parisian support, which is physically present in the *tribunes* or public galleries.

It is important to have a clear idea of the actual physical setting when considering these debates. Until May 1793 the Convention continued to sit, like the Législative, in the Salle du Manège of the Tuileries. This was a totally unsuitable hall. It was a very elongated rectangle, with the President sitting in the middle of one of the long sides and the speaker's *tribune*, together with the *barre* to which endless deputations were admitted, exactly opposite him. The deputies sat to the left and right of the speaker, many of them far to one side, so that they could not hear or see, and were naturally inclined to talk among themselves or interrupt the speaker. At the far ends of the rectangle, above the level of the deputies, were the popular galleries, which were to prove such an uncontrollable and powerful element in the debates. The poor audibility, visibility and ventilation had a considerable impact on the conduct of debates, as many contemporary statements indicate in graphic terms. Here for instance is Quatremère de Quincy, speaking to the Législative in October 1791: 'la forme

actuelle de la salle a bien d'autres inconvénients; elle est très sourde
[...] on n'y parle pas, on y crie; l'homme qui crie est dans un état forcé,
et par cela même il est prêt à entrer en violence; cette disposition où
il est, il la communique à ceux qui l'écoutent.'[18]

Decorum

It may be helpful at the outset to recall Grégoire's famous statement,
made to the Convention on 20 Prairial, An II:

Sous le despotisme, le langage avait le caractère de la bassesse; c'était le jargon
de ceux qu'on nommait gens de bon ton, et qui étaient presque toujours
l'opprobre des mœurs et la lie de l'humanité. Le langage des républicains
doit être signalé par une franchise, une dignité également éloignée de
l'abjection et de la rudesse.[19]

These words were spoken many months later, and of course Grégoire
is not mainly concerned with the language to be used in the Assemblée
Nationale. Even so, he does give an idea of the standard Jacobin
line on modes of address. Manly and noble simplicity, including
tutoiement, is welcomed, but, contrary to the views of a Hébert,
vulgarity is rejected as unworthy of the new Republic.

One of the stock images of the revolutionary assemblies, as of many
other aspects of revolutionary culture, is of a world in which the old
norms of decorum no longer hold and vulgarity runs riot. It is
therefore worth noting that one of the features of the first debates
of the Convention is the concern to maintain dignity and orderly
procedures, to keep the level of debate at a proper height. This had
of course been a problem from 1789 onwards, and the successive
assemblies had worked hard at it. One of the first motions on 21
September comes from the deputy Manuel, who speaks as follows:

Il faut voir ici une assemblée de philosophes occupés à préparer le bonheur
du monde. Il faut que tout ici respire un caractère de dignité et de grandeur
qui impose à l'univers. Je demande que le Président de la France soit logé
dans le palais national des Tuileries, que les attributs de la loi et de la force
soient toujours à ses côtés, et que toutes les fois qu'il ouvrira la séance, tous
les citoyens se lèvent.   (*AP*, 69)

The use of the word 'univers' takes one back to classical tragedy,
where Racine's Titus had felt himself to be acting in a 'plus noble
théâtre'.

Quite apart from the unfortunate reference to a 'President
of France', Manuel's proposal is greeted with hostility. Gravely
underestimating the importance of the symbolic, Mathieu ridicules

135

the proposal, noting that 'nos prédécesseurs ont perdu beaucoup de temps à régler des dimensions du fauteuil du ci-devant roi'. More to the point, Chabot asserts: 'Vous ne pouvez rechercher d'autre dignité que de vous mêler avec les Sans-Culottes qui composent la majorité de la nation'. True dignity is to be sought in simplicity. Manuel's motion is set aside then, but the assembly returns constantly to the question of dignity. The first session had opened with a very formal speech by François de Neufchâteau on behalf of the Législative and an equally solemn reply by Pétion, the President, who proclaims: 'Nous allons nous occuper de cette mission auguste avec le recueillement profond qu'elle inspire' (*AP*, 68).

What does this mean in practice? In the first place a certain formality of address. The *conventionnels* call one another 'représentants du peuple souverain', 'législateurs', 'citoyens' and so forth – and still, occasionally, 'Monsieur', though this is on its way out. *Tutoiement* is very rare. In the second place, a vocabulary that belongs to the noble register, free of all trivial and vulgar words. And thirdly, a high seriousness; there are, to judge from the records, few jokes at the Convention Nationale. An interesting exception proves the rule, and it is worth noting that here again it is a question of symbolism, that essential but vulnerable part of the new revolutionary culture. Immediately after the adoption of the new seal for the revolutionary archives (the birth of Marianne), there are proposals to eliminate the white from the tricolore and to do away with the *fleur de lys*. An unnamed member, no doubt wanting to get on with 'real business', shouts: 'Je réclame le renvoi de ces propositions à un comité de marchands de mode', upon which 'Le Président improuve cette saillie comme peu séante à la dignité des représentants du peuple' (*AP*, 81). The motions are set aside none the less.

Laughter is a powerful, but unseemly weapon. Another threat to decorum comes from interruptions. From the beginning of the first sessions, members are protesting at these and insisting that all speakers should obtain the permission of the President. (It is significant that from early on the Constituante had decided not to follow the British example of requiring members to address their remarks to the President.) Naturally enough, interruption persists, though of course it is hard to tell from the written accounts just how frequent and rude it was. At one point on 25 September we read: 'Un grand nombre de membres s'élancent à la tribune et veulent parler en même temps' (*AP*, 130) – but this disorder is apparently far from reaching the heights of the following April, or indeed of the recent events of 10 August.

It is noticeable that the speakers most often interrupted are Robespierre and Marat. In other words, most interruptions come from the benches of the Gironde. Accused of aiming at dictatorship, Robespierre launches into a long self-justification which visibly riles his opponents. At one point the debate reads like this:

(*Nouveaux murmures*)
ROBESPIERRE: Quand l'Assemblée ne voudra plus m'entendre, elle me fera connaître sa volonté [through the President presumably]. Je sens qu'il est fâcheux pour moi d'être toujours interrompu.
PLUSIEURS MEMBRES: Abrégez.
ROBESPIERRE: Je n'abrégerai point. Eh bien, je m'en vais vous forcer à m'écouter. (*AP*, 133)

The other main source of interruptions is the public galleries, whose noisy behaviour dogged all the assemblies until Thermidor, when they were suppressed. By the time of the Convention, the social composition of the *tribunes* had changed considerably, with women of the people playing an increasingly important role. They usually favour the Montagne, and on 25 September, when they are clearly giving vociferous support to Marat against a hostile assembly, a Girondin member makes the often repeated appeal: 'Je demande que le Président rappelle à l'ordre les tribunes, qui se permettent des murmures. Elles ont trop longtemps tyrannisé l'Assemblée' (*AP*, 139). To no avail.

Orderly procedure was disrupted by interruptions, but the greatest threat to decorum was probably the use of 'personnalités', in other words personal abuse. This surfaces regularly – and no doubt the *Moniteur* only tells a part of the story. One example occurs on 22 September, when Danton is arguing for having judges elected by popular vote. Addressing Danton, the deputy Chasset says:

Avec ces flagorneries continuelles envers le peuple, on remettrait son sort à l'arbitraire d'un homme qui aurait usurpé sa confiance; ce sont des flagorneries, je le répète.
DANTON: Vous ne flagorniez pas le peuple lors de la révision. (*Murmures prolongés*)
MASUYER: Je demande que M. Danton soit rappelé à l'ordre, et à ce qu'il doit à lui-même, à la majesté du peuple, et à la Convention nationale.
LE PRESIDENT: Je conçois que l'Assemblée, pénétrée de la dignité qui doit présider à ses délibérations, voie avec douleur qu'on les avilit par des débats scandaleux. Faisons-nous une loi impérieuse de ne jamais nous permettre aucune personnalité. (*AP*, 85)

'Flagornerie' does not seem particularly scandalous, and there are no recorded examples in these five days of really vulgar abuse. It is not really surprising then that one person's abuse was another person's plain speaking. An interesting episode, again involving Danton, occurs on the following day. Billaud-Varenne has been causing a storm by accusing a fellow deputy of being a partisan of La Fayette – 'plusieurs membres crient à la calomnie: une agitation violente se manifeste'. But Danton defends such forthrightness with a reference to one of the great heroes of the age: 'Dans le Sénat romain, Brutus disait hautement des vérités que dans nos mœurs pusillanimes nous appellerions des personnalités' (*AP*, 112). Such brutal frankness is demanded of the honest republican, who should be above the delicateness of aristocratic politeness.

Decorum collapses most notably in relation to Marat, who is the target of exceptionally violent abuse from many members. When he gets up to give what appears to be his 'maiden speech' at the Assembly, he comments on his unpopularity: 'J'ai donc dans cette Assemblée un grand nombre d'ennemis personnels', and the reporter notes: '"Tous, tous", s'écrie l'Assemblée entière, en se levant avec indignation' (*AP*, 138). He is referred to crudely as 'le plus scélérat des hommes et le plus fou' or simply 'cet homme'. He is directly addressed by other deputies (this is relatively unusual), and what is more, they call him *tu*. This is not a sign of manly frankness, as in Grégoire's ideal, it is simply abuse. Apart from Marat, *tutoiement* is only recorded as being used for Robespierre during these five days. And whereas he replies with aggrieved dignity, Marat, who is quite capable of a calm and reasonable posture, does himself flout parliamentary decorum quite deliberately. A famous – and it must be said, unusual – example occurs on 25 September. Marat has been speaking in favour of a temporary dictatorship on the Roman model. Greeted by jeers, he declares dramatically: 'Je ne crains rien sous le soleil, et je dois déclarer que si le décret d'accusation eût été lancé contre moi, je me brûlais la cervelle au pied de cette tribune', whereupon he pulls out a pistol and puts it to his forehead (*AP*, 142). Not surprisingly, such a flagrant breach of decorum scandalizes. It should be remembered, however, that the ancient rhetorical tradition (as well as Rousseau's *Emile*) spoke of an eloquence of things or of deeds which spoke louder than mere words, associated often with a decadent civilization. It is two new members of the Assemblée Nationale, Danton and Marat, who appear willing to challenge decorum in the name of democracy or republicanism.

It is not by any means easy to gauge the extent to which dignity is actually undermined in the proceedings of the Convention Nationale on these days. What are we to understand by 'murmures'? A gentle ripple or a violent storm? Nor should one, by way of comparison, have too exalted an idea of the decorum of such a model as the English House of Commons, where interruption and general noise were endemic.[20] Even so, the overall impression created by a study of these days – and others like them – is of an attempt, in some quarters at least, to hang on to a fragile dignity in the face of potential violence, and even barbarism, both within and without. Against such forces, the deputies try to play a proper part in a great drama, preserving classical decorum against increasing odds.

Ethos[21]

Many of the essential recommendations in the *inventio* section of classical rhetorics concern the way in which the orator conveys to his public, if possible unobtrusively, an idea of his own qualities. This is normally thought to be particularly important in the opening section of a speech, in which the speaker will attempt, for instance, to appear honest, trustworthy, public-spirited, or modest. In this way the orator's role comes close to the actor's. The two professions had long been linked (Cicero learns from Roscius), and the comparison takes on a new life in the French Revolution, where the protagonists are often seen, by themselves as well as by their enemies, as the actors in a tragic, or sometimes comic, drama.

Sincerity and emotion are probably the dominant values, at any rate at the period we are concerned with. Eloquence presents itself as the language of the heart. Again and again we hear the tones of eighteenth-century *sensibilité*, the tones of Jean-Jacques above all. Marat is only one of the dozens of deputies who protests 'la pureté de mon cœur' (*AP*, 142). A characteristic emotional stance is that of *chaleur*, an ardent zeal for the public good, and horror or indignation ('je frémis') at all that threatens it. So much is virtually universal, and there is no need to dwell on it.

One specific form taken by this shared civic ardour is the oath, the *serment*. La Harpe wrote of the 'incurable manie des serments', and in the records of debates we can easily find notations such as this: 'L'Assemblée entière est levée, dans l'attitude du serment' (1 April 1793), re-enacting the founding gesture of the Jeu de Paume. Indeed the *serment* is one of the first subjects of discussion on 21 September. One member 'propose que l'Assemblée prête le serment de maintenir

139

la liberté et l'egalité, ou de mourir en les défendant' (*AP*, 67). There is an immediate objection, but later in the same day Tallien returns to the charge, calling on the *conventionnels* to commit themselves with a solemn oath in the presence of the people (the people being of course the spectators in the *tribunes*). But again there are sceptical objections to what could be seen as empty play-acting – 'tant de serments ont été violés depuis quatre ans' (*AP*, 70), remarks Basire, who prefers the greater security of penal laws.

Eventually, in this debate about law and order, the proposed *serment* is superseded by a decree. But on an individual level, many deputies continue to proclaim the same type of commitment in an extreme, often theatrical form. In the proposal just quoted, the deputies were to swear to preserve liberty and equality or die in their defence. In this manner, again and again, speakers proclaim, with greater or lesser sincerity, their willingness to die as martyrs to the cause – a willingness that was all too often to be put to the test. Jean-Claude Bonnet remarks pertinently: 'Ils acquièrent cette certitude de mourir dans l'exercice même de leur parole dont Mirabeau étonné découvre le péril le 28 février aux Jacobins: "Je viens de prononcer mon arrêt de mort, c'en est fait de moi, ils me tueront".'[22] When Marat threatens in a moment of exaltation (or play-acting) to blow his brains out, one may doubt whether he has attained quite the same level of tragic awareness.

Stopping short of self-immolation, many deputies are willing enough to speak of their suffering. This is notably the case with Robespierre. Accused by his numerous enemies of seeking to become a dictator, he is virtually forced to speak of himself and his past behaviour. In doing so, he stresses not only his zeal for the popular cause, but the persecution it has brought on him: 'un homme qui lutta si longtemps contre tous les partis avec un courage âpre et inflexible, sans se ménager aucun parti, celui-là devait être en butte à la haine et aux persécutions de tous les ambitieux, de tous les intrigants' (*AP*, 133). This display of self-sacrifice seems like hypocrisy to his opponents, who react with 'rires et murmures', but Robespierre turns this to advantage, since it enables him to appear as a Christ, or an Alceste,[23] alone against the laughing Pharisees: 'Je demande que ceux qui me répondent par des rires, par des murmures, se réunissent contre moi, que ce petit tribunal prononce ma condamnation, ce sera le jour le plus glorieux de ma vie'. Notice however the words 'petit tribunal', suggesting that Robespierre, unlike Alceste, is not really alone and that the greater tribunal of the people will avenge him.

Robespierre's stance, perhaps too blatantly adopted, is one of incorruptible courage. Courage, 'manly' courage, does indeed seem to be an indispensable virtue, deployed in attack as well as in defence. Citing yet again one of the great models against whom some at least of the *conventionnels* measure themselves, Gorsas declares that every deputy is a Brutus (Marcus Brutus on this occasion), and Merlin picks up the hint to present himself as an intrepid patriot: 'je déclare que je suis prêt à poignarder le premier qui voudrait s'arroger un pouvoir de dictateur' (*AP*, 130). Soon after which Danton seems to be measuring himself implicitly against the fortitude of the other Brutus (Voltaire's and David's Lucius Junius), when he declares that he would sacrifice his best friend if he were guilty of unpatriotic designs.

A related ethical topos is that of reluctant, but intrepid truth-telling. Here the speaker is not so much pouring out the fulness of his heart as doing his duty, against his humane inclinations (since sensibility and civic virtue should be equally part of the good man's make-up). So various deputies speak of the duty to speak the truth against the opinions of the majority. So Roland, reporting as Minister of the Interior on the lawless state of the nation, says: 'il me serait inutile de m'étendre davantage sur un sujet qui répugne à mon cœur. Mais j'ai cru devoir dire de grandes vérités. Elles intéressent le salut de mon pays; et jamais la crainte ne m'a arrêté quand j'ai cru mes discours capables de servir' (*AP*, 109).

There is an interesting variant on this on 25 September, in a maiden speech from Maure, who tells his audience how intimidating it is to speak to the Assemblée Nationale (as indeed it must have been in the Manège):

Citoyens, je monte à la tribune pour la première fois et je vous assure que ce n'est pas sans émotion que je parais devant les représentants d'un peuple libre et souverain. Cependant, investi de la confiance de mes concitoyens, portion moi-même du souverain, je ne pourrais sans crime vous taire la vérité. Je vous dirai ce que Laocoon disait aux Troyens [...]   (*AP*, 129)

If Marat was Cassandra, here is another figure of the tragic prophet, but combined with that familiar topos of the unaccustomed orator. If we leave Laocoon on one side, this is a less dramatic role than that of Brutus. Here the speaker presents himself as the simple, honest fellow who will not, like his opponents, seek to mislead his audience with the tricks of rhetoric. Now some of the *conventionnels* were undoubtedly not particularly skilled at public speaking (and many of them hardly spoke), but even the most experienced will not disdain this oldest of rhetorical ploys, to which the new situation adds the added attraction of republican virtue and dignity. 'Nos mandataires', says Maure, 'ne nous ont point envoyés pour étaler de grandes phrases et faire parade d'un esprit orné' (*AP*, 129). Such vanity and frivolity belong to the old regime.

An interesting example of the 'simple soul' topos is to be found in an orator of the opposite camp from Maure, the Girondin Buzot. He had been a deputy at the Constituante, and now voices his Candide-like surprise (not an infrequent rhetorical device) at what he finds on returning to Paris:

Etranger aux révolutions de Paris, je suis arrivé dans la confiance que je retrouverais ici mon âme indépendante, et que rien ne me ferait sortir de la voie que je m'étais tracée. [...]

Je n'appartiens pas à Paris, je n'appartiens à aucun d'eux [the departments], j'appartiens à la République entière. Voilà mon vœu fortement exprimé, malgré les déclamations de ceux qui parlent des Prussiens, de je ne sais quels hommes que je ne connais pas, moi qui vivais paisiblement dans ma province, en cultivant mon âme forte contre toute espèce d'événement.

(*AP*, 126)[24]

Cincinnatus rather than Laocoon. Speaking at the Club des Jacobins the same night, Fabre d'Eglantine was to mock Buzot's show of provincial innocence.[25] We notice, of course, that he associates honest virtue with the provinces, such declarations being common coin among the anti-Commune speakers – and Danton too does not miss the chance to speak of his provincial origins. Naturally Buzot also proclaims his independence. He belongs to no faction – not Paris, not any particular *département*, but 'la République entière'. It has to be said that this is a dubious claim, but it is one that is routinely made by the majority of speakers. As has often been remarked, it is very difficult for the revolutionaries to admit that they represent a specific group rather than France or the Republic or the people as a whole. The Rousseauist ideology of the general will makes it hard to accept the reality of political division, which is regularly branded as factionalism.

In all that I have so far said about *ethos*, whether it is a question of zeal or of modesty, the stress has been on sincerity, the heart, the emotions. It would be surprising, however, if this were not sometimes countered by a stress on cool reason, the head against the heart. In a setting of extravagance and passion, the role of calm statesman can be an attractive one, and some deputies do indeed make a show of setting logic and philosophical principles against the easy emotions of their opponents. In the five days I have studied, I would not say that this is the dominant mode – though one should not under-estimate the amount of plain, down-to-earth, unemotive speaking that did go on during the long days of the Convention. The individual who most clearly wishes to present this image of cool reason is probably Danton. He was of course capable of great 'warmth' – his 'de l'audace, encore de l'audace, toujours de l'audace' of 2 September was still ringing in many ears. But when the deputies are plunged in a heated debate about whether judges should be freely elected (which was indeed an incendiary issue), we see him deliberately trying to rise above the fray, avoiding as far as possible any accusation of demagogy: 'Je répondrai froidement et sans flagorneries pour le peuple' (*AP*, 86; he is referring to the accusation by Chasset quoted above). And indeed this is what he does, at any rate to judge from the reports, adopting a reasoning tone, analysing his opponents' speeches, seeking to base his arguments on acceptable philosophical principles. This is a frequent stance with Danton, and it is to be found too in some of the speeches of Marat – contrary to the legendary images.

It seems however that the place was not conducive to this type of *ethos*. As Quatremère de Quincy put it, the orator who has to shout is 'prêt à entrer en violence'. This auto-intoxication no doubt leads to what seems to a distant reader the excessive and theatrical display of passion, the great and imprudent gestures of tragic self-sacrifice. The *conventionnels* are playing to a large audience, including as it does the popular galleries, and in this heightened context, there is nothing surprising in their self-projection on the models of Brutus or the Cornelian hero. But one should not forget the tension between heart and head, which we find reflected in the arguments about oratorical *pathos*.

Pathos

In a well-known section of his project for public education of 1792, Condorcet, not himself an impressive speaker, had warned of the dangers of passionate oratory. (In doing so, incidentally, he is following in an ancient tradition, as old as rhetoric itself.) He deplores the imitation of models such as Demosthenes, whose primitive emotionalism is not suitable for the present age of reason: 'il était alors permis, utile peut-être, d'émouvoir le peuple, mais nous lui devons de l'instruire. [...] Hâtons-nous donc de substituer le raisonne-ment à l'éloquence, les livres aux parleurs'.[26] In a similar vein, Lequinio, an interesting and little-known figure, exposed all the ways in which the Assembly and the tribunes were in fact manoeuvred by unscrupulous speakers.[27] Whether Condorcet liked it or not, however, the appeal to the passions remained an integral part of persuasive oratory in the revolutionary assemblies.

Whose passions? What precisely is the audience the orator seeks to sway? The 'vous' (and less frequently the 'nous) which figures so often in the speeches refers in the first instance to the 'législateurs', the 'représentants du peuple souverain'. But no doubt the speakers were conscious of a wider public – though less so than in the days of television. They are appealing often to 'la France', for many French people will shortly afterwards be able to read at least a part of the debates in published form. And, most important, they are speaking to the visible representatives of the people, the men and women (but mainly women, it seems) in the *tribunes*. These could be vitally important allies. They could also, it is true, be a nuisance and a danger, but in spite of some deputies' complaints about their conduct, the general view was that they had to be there, that the representatives of the people had to do their business in the presence of the people. As Volney put it in 1789, 'nous sommes dans les conjonctures les plus difficiles; que nos concitoyens nous entourent de toutes parts, qu'ils nous pressent, que leur présence nous inspire et nous anime'.[28] And press they certainly did.

It is hard from the written record to tell when deputies are playing to the gallery – certainly, to judge from the applause, this was Marat's constant tactic. There were many exhortations to the deputies, usually from Montagnards, to trust the people. This would please the *tribunes*; it may also be calculated to inspire fear in the deputies, as when Collot d'Herbois presses his case with a veiled threat:

Non, vous ne la prononcerez pas, cette loi; nous avons trop de confiance dans le peuple; et la preuve que les lois sont toujours en vigueur, c'est que le peuple se ferait justice lui-même, si les lois ne la lui faisaient pas.   (*AP*, 125)[29]

A mere two weeks after the September massacres, the mention of the 'glaive du peuple' hanging over the Assemblée Nationale could be relied on to produce an effect.

At the same time, there is another type of appeal to fear, this time used mainly by the Girondins. This is the evocation of the spectre of anarchy. The state of France, and particularly of Paris, is repeatedly painted in a frightening light, calculated to push the law-abiding, property-owning deputies and their electors to approve punitive laws. So Lasource, on the first day of the Convention, exclaims: 'Si les propriétés de chacun n'étaient pas sous la protection des lois, la

144

société ne serait qu'un théâtre de brigandage où il n'y aurait d'autre droit que celui de la force' (*AP*, 71).

In a situation of real violence, the appeal to fear is natural. It is coupled with what one might cynically call the appeal to vanity, or at least self-respect. Deputies, who may well have felt intimidated by the dramatic theatre in which they found themselves, are constantly being reminded of the grandeur of their mission in hyperbolic language which resembles that of a Cornelian or Racinian confidant trying to bring his vacillating master up to the mark. In his welcoming speech on behalf of the outgoing assembly, François de Neufchâteau had set the tone: 'Remplissez, Représentants, vos grandes destinées' and Pétion, the President of the new assembly, replies in kind (*AP*, 68). Others will call the Convention an 'assemblée de philosophes', and Danton will more than once urge his listeners to rise 'à la hauteur des grandes considérations' (*AP*, 84).[30] Alternatively, speakers attempt to shame their audience. Robespierre, trying to gain a hearing, appeals to an elementary sense of justice, and Marat taunts provocatively: 'Si vous n'êtes pas à la hauteur, tant pis pour vous' (*AP*, 139). The point is to persuade the *conventionnels* that the eyes of the world ('l'univers') are upon them as they set about their task. As Danton puts it, 'il faut que l'ennemi sache que la Convention nationale existe' (*AP*, 119).

The object of such exhortations varies, but one of the commonest is to show strength. The orator shows himself to be manly (the word 'mâle' is ubiquitous) and the deputies are urged to follow his example, to dare to act, to be worthy of their station. So Danton, with Valmy fresh in the minds of his hearers, declares: 'Il faut nous montrer terribles' (*AP*, 112). A less well-known *conventionnel*, Osselin, speaks in similar tonès against feeble hesitation (the issue being the way to treat an apparently treacherous general): 'Cette marche incertaine ne convient point à une Assemblée nationale. Cette conduite marquerait une faiblesse et une pusillanimité indigne d'elle' (*AP*, 116).

Now this praiseworthy decisive action is often supposed to be based on unanimous feeling, and it is this feeling which orators seek to generate and use. The deputies should be unanimous among themselves, and at one with the whole of the French people, sharing with them emotions of horror, indignation, faith and so on. The deputy Mathieu, pressing for an oath of fidelity early on 21 September, urges: 'Oui, Citoyens, je demande que, sans délibération, uniquement par la force du sentiment [...]vous juriez d'être fidèles à la nation' (*AP*, 71). The words 'sans délibération' are essential here. Discussion is replaced by a common impulse.

A fine example of this is provided by the abolition of the monarchy (*AP*, 73–4). This is proposed without much of a preamble by Collot d'Herbois, whose words are greeted by 'applaudissements unanimes'. Some doubts are expressed however, and Grégoire returns to the charge with some vehement eloquence, appealing to the audience's passions of hate and indignation against 'des races dévorantes qui ne vivaient que de chair humaine'. Whereupon 'l'Assemblée entière se lève par un mouvement spontané, et décrète par acclamation la proposition de M. Grégoire'. Even then, Basire, deputy of the Côte d'Or, attempts to cool things:

On ne peut qu'applaudir à ce sentiment si concordant avec celui de l'universalité du peuple français. Mais il serait d'un exemple effrayant pour le peuple de voir une Assemblée de philosophes,[31] chargée de ses plus chers intérêts, delibérer dans un moment d'enthousiasme.

While welcoming the fictitious universality of feeling, he feels that this is not enough for an assembly of law-givers. But he loses. There is no discussion; as Grégoire says, 'qu'est-il besoin de discuter quand tout le monde est d'accord?'

Exhilarating as this is, it is a dangerous precedent for parliamentary debate, as certain deputies point out on the days following. Attempting to stem the tide, they (and in particular the more 'moderate' members) urge rational discussion as a check on the rapidity of feeling. Thus on 22 September, as Danton is pressing the Convention for a quick decision on the question of the election of judges, Kersaint proposes that this be referred to the Committees, where it can be properly considered. He puts it in this way:

Il est de toute nécessité que nous ne nous engagions pas dans la discussion d'un objet aussi important que celui qui vous est soumis, avant d'avoir une règle sûre de délibération. Nous devons nous prémunir contre l'éloquence, si nous ne voulons pas être conduits par les orateurs qui auraient le talent de nous entraîner. Nous devons nous prémunir contre nos propres passions, et donner au peuple une caution de notre prudence.   (*AP*, 86)

The 'règle sûre de délibération' is proposed as a much-needed brake on a machine that can easily run out of control. In vain. Sergent, one of the Parisian deputies, denies the need for caution 'quand il s'agit de déclarer des vérités gravées dans tous les cœurs' − and it is such a truth that judges should be elected by popular vote.

Again we see the power of the Rousseauist model of unanimity. The deputies desire to be seen to speak for the whole nation, for the general will as popularly understood. A great deal of the oratorical *pathos* of their speeches is devoted to creating this unanimity.

146

The perorations, in particular, seek to transcend debate in the kind of unity of feeling that the great *fêtes* were meant to embody and to create. As a model for the proceedings of a parliament, the *fête* is more than dubious. It may work for the almost festive abolition of the monarchy, but thereafter it can only partially mask the real divisions in the house.

The Convention Nationale is a place of excess. No doubt all oratory involves some degree of self-projection and self-aggrandizement; the forum is not the place for polite understatement. In the revolutionary assemblies, however, even though many voices were raised to call for the maintenance of a decorum and dignity suited to the greatness of the occasion, there was a constant tendency to flout the norms of civilized debate. In their vast barn of a hall, orators shout and gesticulate, interrupt and abuse one another, while attempting to deal with the barracking of the public galleries. They present themselves in hyperboles, and make violent appeals to the passions of their audience.

All this is true – and it explains the mockery of the revolutionary orators both by polite contemporaries and by historians who apply to these debates the standards of civilized good taste. Such a judgement may seem irrelevant here. What we see in the Convention Nationale, as in the assemblies that preceded it, is a struggle for power in which vehement oratory is used as a weapon which may decide the fate of individuals, groups or the whole nation. In such a situation, politeness was not enough. What was needed was 'de l'audace, encore de l'audace, toujours de l'audace'. And if we look at the spectacle of the Revolution, two hundred years later, from an aesthetic vantage point, these debates offer a drama more gripping than the fine speeches of the *ancien régime*. Whether France would have been better served by more decorum and less drama, more politeness and less *pathos*, is another question.

Part III
CONFRONTING THE OTHER

9

TRANSLATING THE BRITISH

In the last chapter a polite tradition of speaking was seen struggling to maintain itself in unpropitious circumstances. Where earlier practitioners of the oratorical art, in France at least, had generally assumed a consensus about what could or could not be said, many of the revolutionary orators found themselves face to face with a more disquieting audience. In the public galleries of the Convention were men and women for whom the time-honoured decorum of rhetoric meant little. This seems to me an emblematic case of the confrontation with an alien world which will be the theme of the following chapters. For polite culture, this alien world could take the form of the common people. Or it could be, quite literally, the culture, and in particular the writing, of a foreign country.

Translation is a particularly revealing phenomenon in this respect, for it implies the assimilation of foreign bodies. To translate is to carry across, to invade a foreign territory and bring back a prize which is then made available to enrich the native store, to infuse new blood into the traditional culture. In certain historical cases the new import is the literature of a politer society. So, in the French Renaissance, the learning and urbanity of the Greek and Roman classics were set against a native tradition that had come to seem barbarous or rustic. The aim was to 'illustrate' the French language. Over the following two centuries, however, a gradual change took place. While the classics retained their schoolroom prestige, it became at least possible to see in them not so much the representatives of a virtually un-attainable model of politeness as relics of the infancy of the world. At the same time, as new, unfamiliar cultures swam into the ken of Europeans, offering them strange worlds to contemplate, reject or absorb, the classics began to appear in all their strangeness. For Père Lafitau, the religious system of the ancient Greeks displayed fascinating similarities with the religions of the newly discovered peoples of North America.[1] Homer, in particular, came to seem less familiar than he had to earlier generations, and it is not surprising that the 'querelle d'Homere' involved not only the acceptability of the ancient epics to a polite modern audience, but also the problem of making the Homeric text a constituent part of modern French literature.[2]

George Steiner has written with polymathic learning, and at great length, about the dilemmas facing all translators.[3] The fundamental choice is between assimilation and respect for foreignness. While Dryden, in typical seventeenth-century fashion, wrote: 'I have endeavoured to make Virgil speak such English as he would himself have spoken, if he had been born in England, and in this present age', others see the translator's task rather as being to create something new in the 'target language', a something which corresponds to the felt otherness of the original. At its extreme, this latter position can result in such eccentricities as Littré's remaking of Dante's *Inferno* in 'vieux langage françois' (1879) or Nabokov's wilfully over-faithful *Eugene Onegin*. But almost all literary translators feel the need, which Steiner endorses, to create a text which whether through archaism, use of foreign words, or other such means, is emphatically not what the translated author would have written had he or she been a native speaker of French, English or whatever.

Translation flourished in eighteenth-century France. New versions continued to appear of the time-honoured classics. But different sources were increasingly important, and some of these were perceived as more remote from polite modern French. One of the most important is Galland's *Les Mille et une nuits*, which immediately assimilated into the French tradition, with all the necessary accommodation to current taste, a vast body of writing which was in some respects far removed from any literature familiar to its first readers. Later in the century, probably equally important for the development of European literature, came the Gaelic bard Ossian, who had already been tricked out in appropriately tasteful garb by James Macpherson. Nearer at hand, though still intriguingly different, was the prose and poetry of modern Britain, which was increasingly providing models of life and thought for its European neighbours in the eighteenth century. Britain was both near and far, similar and different. As Steiner remarks, the preservation of otherness is more difficult for the person translating from a nearby culture, since 'the innocence of great distance, the conventionally negotiated immediacy of exoticism are unavailable' (p. 361). It is all the more interesting therefore to see what the French, conscious of their position of cultural hegemony, made of the writings of their newly ascendant neighbours. How far are these 'foreign bodies' allowed to continue their own life? How far are they assimilated into the patterns of French politeness? I shall discuss this by way of two separate but overlapping examples, the translating practice of Diderot and the French fortunes of Alexander Pope.

Diderot's English translations

As Jean Starobinski puts it, 'la parole des autres' plays an essential part in Diderot's writing.[4] Whether he is dealing with Brücker's *Historia critica*, Helvétius's *De l'homme*, Bougainville's travels, or *Tristram Shandy*, he carries to an extreme the normal tendency of writers to create their own work by assimilating, transforming or attacking the texts that surround them. One might ask what this typically Diderotian approach means. He is often seen as the 'man of dialogue', open to the thought of others, always available for new thoughts or sensations, even to the point of inconsequentiality, like the famous weathercock of Langres. But one could equally well claim that if Diderot embraces the other it is, as Néron says in *Britannicus*, 'pour l'étouffer'. Seen in this light, the appearance of dialogic openness is really a mask for Diderot's characteristic 'discours éternel'.[5] And Jacques Proust has rightly reminded us of the limits of Diderot's availability, since he remains, for all his immense curiosity, a prisoner of classical humanism.[6] It seems worthwhile, then, to scrutinize his theory and practice of translation, since this is one area in which the openness to the other is most sharply tested. In what follows I shall not be concerned with his bread-and-butter translations (Stanyan, James), but with his versions of Shaftesbury, Ossian and Moore, all of which seem to correspond to some personal commitment on his part.[7]

It is no doubt an exaggeration to talk of Diderot's 'theory of translation', when all we have is his youthful commentary on Silhouette's translation of the *Essay on Man*, a number of fascinating remarks in the *Lettre sur les sourds et muets*, and a revealing comparison between the engraving of a painting and the translation of a poem in the *Salon* of 1765. To these should be added the article 'Encyclopédie', the first part of which shows a keen interest in the problems of linguistic communication, including translation.[8] In these pages Diderot shows himself to be very conscious of the post-Babel diversity of tongues, not only from country to country, but from person to person. It is a diversity which appears to the Encyclopedist more as a defect than as a virtue, and the ideal remedy for it would be a common language, the universal language which would correspond to the reality of the world as it is perceived by humanity at large; 'Supposé cet idiome admis et fixé, aussitôt les notions deviennent permanentes; la distance des temps disparaît; les lieux se touchent; il se forme des liaisons entre tous les points habités de l'espace et de la durée, et tous les êtres vivants et pensants s'entretiennent' (VII, 189). To which one would have to add that the poor translator would be out of a job. But of course this is only a dream. Until it comes true, translation will continue to be necessary as a bridge between peoples separated by language.

In the *Lettre sur les sourds et muets*, to be sure, Diderot proclaims the impossibility of translation, or at any rate of poetic translation, since poetic language is full of 'hieroglyphs' in which the meaning is embodied in the physical form of the words: 'plus un poète est chargé de ces hiéroglyphes, plus il est difficile à rendre'; 'Je croyais avec tout le monde, qu'un poète pouvait être traduit par un autre: c'est une erreur, et me voici désabusé' (IV, 170–2). His examples of hieroglyphs are all taken from Greek or Latin poetry, but earlier in the *Lettre* he had included English and Italian with Greek and Latin as 'langues [...] plus avantageuses pour les lettres' because of their 'tours' and their 'inversions' (IV, 165). Translating English poetry is thus a challenge. Even so, when he annotated Silhouette's translation of the *Essay on Man*, Diderot had not yet reached the position that poetry is untranslatable. On the contrary, he thinks that Pope could be translated much better than in Silhouette's version, and is very critical of a translator who has weakened Pope's text: 'Voilà le corps du poète', he says, 'mais son esprit est perdu' (I, 251). He reproaches Silhouette with failing to catch the metaphorical force of the poem and with watering down its laconic vigour. Often he thinks it would have been preferable to translate more literally, to keep Pope's image or turn of phrase.

This doesn't mean of course, that Diderot is a champion of word-for-word literalism. When he is writing of poetry, he seems to belong rather to the camp of the scholarly Madame Dacier than to that of her adversary La Motte, who wanted Homer to speak to eighteenth-century readers like a contemporary. But in prose the translator enjoys more freedom. His first priority is to transform his original into a living French text. The 'Discours préliminaire' to his own translation of Shaftesbury's *Inquiry concerning Virtue, or Merit* declares: 'Je l'ai lu et relu; je me suis rempli de son esprit, et j'ai, pour ainsi dire, fermé son livre, lorsque j'ai pris la plume. On n'a jamais usé du bien d'autrui avec autant de liberté. J'ai resserré ce qui m'a paru trop diffus; étendu ce qui m'a paru trop serré; rectifié ce qui n'était pensé qu'avec hardiesse' (I, 300). This means that he has improved Shaftesbury's text so as to allow it to exist and find readers in another language. What is more, this other language is superior to English, for Diderot explains in the article 'Encyclopédie' that 'notre langue est faite' whereas the English 'ne songent pas encore à former la leur' (VII, 197). All of this seems to imply that any statement is the expression of a basic thought which can take on various forms, just as the great variety of existing languages can be measured against a common and unchanging general grammar. Cicero, we read in the *Lettre sur les sourds et muets*, 'a pour ainsi dire suivi la syntaxe française avant d'obéir à la syntaxe latine' (IV, 165). When we translate Cicero into French, therefore, we are restoring the fundamental syntax, even if this means losing the eloquence of Latin inversions.

The dangers of such an attitude are obvious, especially when one is translating a foreign text which possesses a certain originality. By attempting to make it talk French, one risks forcing it into the Procrustean bed of French eloquence. Diderot is aware of this when in the *Supplément au Voyage de Bougainville* he notes ironically that the not particularly 'Tahitian' style of the old man's speech bears the marks of a twofold translation, from Tahitian into Spanish and from Spanish into French. In this case, of course, we are dealing with a hoax rather than a genuine translation, but we shall see that when he translates Shaftesbury or Moore, or indeed the primitive Ossian, Diderot has a tendency to turn his British authors into French orators.

Let us then consider his practice as a translator. He never went to England, and his knowledge of the language was essentially bookish – he explains in the article 'Encyclopédie' that he learnt it by means of a Latin–English dictionary. Inevitably, therefore, he makes some mistakes, as for instance when he reads 'wainscot' as 'waistcoat' in Act IV of *The Gamester*. Even so, one is struck, for instance in his notes on the *Essay on Man*, by his rather impressive understanding of the meanings and connotations of English expressions. This does not mean that he is always a faithful translator. He exaggerates when he says of his translation of Shaftesbury: 'on n'a jamais usé du bien d'autrui avec autant de liberté', but it is true that he does often rework the English text, pushing it in the direction of his own anticlericalism, or laying particular emphasis on the defence of the passions. The Shaftesbury we read in the first volume of Diderot's works is already almost Diderot, a French *philosophe* who is no longer writing for a British audience.

Shaftesbury's tone has changed. The English text shows something of the careless ease of the English gentleman; in spite of its systematic plan, the *Inquiry* is often disjointed and familiar in its rhetoric. The English lord seems to write as he would speak, without paying too much attention to the shape of his sentences. His thought is sinuous, and not always too easy to follow. Diderot's text is more carefully constructed; he has made Shaftesbury speak like an orator, write like a professor. Even for a British reader, the French text is easier to read, because the translator has reworked the sentences in accordance with oratorical syntax. Consider for instance the last page of the work. Shaftesbury writes as follows:

> Thus the wisdom of what rules, and is first and chief in Nature, has made it to be according to the private interest and good of everyone to work towards the general good, which if a creature ceases to promote, he is actually so far wanting to himself, and ceases to promote his own happiness and welfare. He is on this account directly his own enemy, nor can he any otherwise be good or useful to himself, than as he continues good to society, and to that whole of which he is himself a part. So that virtue, which of all excellences and beauties is the chief and most amiable; that which is the prop and ornament of human affairs; which upholds communities, maintains union, friendship, and correspondence amongst men; that by which countries, as well as private families, flourish and are happy; and for want of which, everything comely, conspicuous, great and worthy, must perish and go to ruin; that single quality, thus beneficial to all society, and to mankind in general, is found equally a happiness and good to each creature in particular, and is that by which alone man can be happy, and without which he must be miserable.
>
> And thus virtue is the good and vice the ill of every one.[9]

Diderot submits this rather idiosyncratic English to a degree of French discipline. His text reads:

> C'est ainsi que la sagesse éternelle qui gouverne cet univers, a lié l'intérêt particulier de la créature au bien général de son système; de sorte qu'elle ne peut croiser l'un sans s'écarter de l'autre, ni manquer à ses semblables sans se nuire à elle-même. C'est en ce sens qu'on peut dire de l'homme qu'il est son plus grand ennemi, puisque son bonheur est en sa main, et qu'il n'en peut être frustré qu'en perdant de vue celui de la société et du tout dont il est partie. La vertu, la plus attrayante de toutes les beautés, la beauté par excellence, l'ornement et la base des affaires humaines, le soutien des communautés, le lien du commerce et des amitiés, la félicité des familles, l'honneur des contrées; la vertu, sans laquelle tout ce qu'il y a de doux, d'agréable, de grand, d'éclatant et de beau, tombe et s'évanouit; la vertu, cette qualité avantageuse à toute société, et plus généralement officieuse à tout le genre humain, fait donc aussi l'intérët réel et le bonheur présent de chaque créature en particulier.
>
> L'homme ne peut donc être heureux que par la vertu, et que malheureux sans elle. La vertu est donc le bien; le vice est donc le mal de la société et de chaque membre qui la compose.   (I, 428)

Translating the British

Shaftesbury's first sentence is not obscure, but it does not flow at all smoothly. Diderot simplifies the periphrastic reference to God, he introduces a neat balance between 'l'intérêt particulier de la créature' and the 'bien général de son système' (this very Diderotian 'system' does not figure in the original), and uses the conjunction 'de sorte que' to smooth out the transition to the second part of the sentence, which once again is much more clearly symmetrical than in Shaftesbury. In the second sentence the expressions 'en ce sens' and 'puisque' make more explicit a logic which is implicit in the English text. 'Son plus grand ennemi' strengthens 'his own enemy', while 'son bonheur est en sa main' adds a new element, stressing the free will of the agent. The long sentence which occupies all the second half of the paragraph brings out very clearly the way in which Diderot replaces Shaftesbury's abrupt construction by an elegant oratorical development, in which a succession of noun phrases leads to a double repetition of the essential word, 'vertu'. And to finish, where Shaftesbury had used a laconic formulation isolated from what precedes in a new paragraph, Diderot rounds off and emphasizes his conclusion by turning the final clause of the original penultimate sentence into a separate sentence, which is echoed in the last sentence of all. The word 'donc', repeated three times in two sentences, aims to make the final assertions appear like the logical conclusion of a rigorous argument, and Shaftesbury's familiar sounding 'everyone' becomes 'chaque membre qui la compose', a heavy, professorial expression.

One may prefer the freedom of the English or the more regular eloquence of the French, but in any case the two texts speak with different voices. However, if Diderot pours Shaftesbury's thought into the rhetorical mould of the Jesuit colleges which he had frequented, he shows himself freer and more vehement in the personal notes he added to the text. These owe a good deal to Shaftesbury, but they are interesting in that they show the next stage in the assimilation of the thought of another person. After more or less free translation, we have here the re-use of a text for the author's own purposes, which can in its turn lead to what we call original creation. If for instance we take the note where the atheist is compared to a man who has never seen a ship, we can see not only the syntactical transformation of a text from Shaftesbury's *Moralists* but also the way in which Diderot makes of this ignorant man a Mexican, thus paving the way to the fable of the Mexican in the *Entretien d'un philosophe avec la Maréchale de* ***.

The tendency to amplification which one sees at work in the

157

Shaftesbury translation is also visible in the 'Erse song', which
Diderot translated in 1761, and which has already been amply
discussed by Paul Van Tieghem and Jacques Chouillet.[10] In translating Ossian, Diderot was of course translating a text that proclaimed
itself a translation from the Gaelic. Quite apart from the authenticity
of *Fingal* and the other texts presented by Macpherson, the highly
rhythmical prose in which he chose to present them to the English-
speaking public is a fascinating subject in its own right. Clearly,
the language of the King James Bible provided a model, and helped
Macpherson find a halfway house between the unfamiliar manner
of genuine Gaelic poetry and the polite language of eighteenth-
century English literature. Indeed it seems probable that the enormous
success of Ossian in continental Europe was largely due to the
fact that Macpherson had done the essential work already with
his adroit mixture of the exotic and the civilized.[11] One is not surprised that Diderot was struck by 'le goût qui règne là'. The energy
and simplicity which he so admired in Macpherson's text fitted
exactly into his conception of heroic and primitive poetry without
shocking it.

Even so, Diderot does dress up Macpherson (like Shaftesbury)
in a somewhat French way. In particular he extends and rounds
out the strongly rhythmical sentences of the Scottish poet. Take
these few lines from 'Shilric and Vinvela':

My love is a son of the hill. He pursues the flying deer. His grey dogs
are panting around him; his bow-string sounds in the wind. Whether by
the fount of the rock, or by the stream of the mountain thou liest; when
the rushes are nodding with the wind, and the mist is flying over thee,
let me approach my love unperceived, and see him from the rock. Lovely
I saw thee first by the aged oak; thou wert returning tall from the chase;
the fairest among thy friends.[12]

Macpherson uses here a 'Biblical' prosody in which each 'verse'
is divided into two more or less equal halves. I do not know whether
Diderot noticed this mannerism. Perhaps because he did not have
that almost instinctive knowledge of the Bible on which Macpherson
could count, he eliminates the monotonous symmetries of the original
in favour of a more prosaic (or more oratorical) rhythm:

Celui que j'aime est fils de la montagne; il poursuit le chevreuil léger.
La corde de son arc a résonné dans l'air, et ses chiens noirs sont haletants
autour de lui ... Soit que tu reposes à la fontaine du rocher, ou sur les
bords du ruisseau de la montagne, lorsque le vent courbe la cime des bruyères
et que le nuage passe au-dessus de ta tête, que ne puis-je approcher de

toi sans être aperçue! que ne puis-je voir celui que j'aime, du sommet
de la colline! ... Que tu me parus beau, la première fois que je te vis!
C'était sous le vieux chêne de Branno. Tu revenais de la chasse; tu étais
grand, tu étais plus beau que tous tes amis.   (XIII, 279)

The final case, Moore's *The Gamester*, shows a similar pattern.
The British dramatist explains in his preface that he would have
found it easier to write his tragedy in verse than in prose, and one
can easily detect in it the influence of a poetic prosody which goes
back to the great English playwrights of the preceding century.
Lines such as these are almost verse:

For me it is enough. And for your generous love, I thank you from my
soul. If you'd oblige me more, give me a little time.[13]

As one might expect, Diderot is not interested in preserving the
rhythms of the English (quite rightly so, one might add); his translation is longer, more polite, more prosaic:

Le reste m'importe peu. Leuson, vous devez être content de lui et de
vous. Vous vous êtes montré assez généreux, et je ne saurais trop vous
marquer combien je suis sensible à votre procédé; mais voudriez-vous
encore ajouter à ma reconnaissance, rendez-moi ma parole pour un moment.
                                                                (XI, 394)

The other omnipresent tendency in Diderot's *Le Joueur* is amplification. Moore is often eloquent, Diderot doubly so. Examples are
legion. Here is a passage where Moore's desperate gambler, Beverley,
is lamenting his enslavement to the habit:

O this infernal vice! how has it sunk me! A vice, whose highest joy was poor
to my domestic happiness. Yet how have I pursued it! Turned all my comforts
to bitterest pangs! and all thy smiles to tears. Damned, damned infatuation!
                                                                 (p. 449)

Diderot turns this into a full-blown tirade which would not be out
of place in a melodrama of the turn of the century:

Vice infernal! Que je suis malheureux! Que je suis vil! Qu'as-tu fait de moi,
jeu, manie terrible du jeu? Cependant quelle comparaison de la plus faible
de mes joies innocentes et domestiques, et des transports les plus violents d'un
jour de fortune! Avec quelle fureur ne les ai-je pas recherchés? Aussi, tout
est anéanti. Plus de bonheur. Des transes mortelles ont succédé aux con-
solations les plus délicieuses de la vie; les larmes de l'amertume, à celles de
la tendresse. La tristesse sombre et morne s'est établie au fond de ce cœur
pour tant qu'il battra. Je pleurerai sans cesse. Je ne sourirai plus. Jeu
détestable! Ivresse détestable. Voilà tes suites.   (XI, 378)

The whole range of rhetorical figures is used here to produce a violent effect. One could not say that Moore is being softened down to suit polite French taste; it is rather that he has been put through the mill of an eloquence which hardly serves him very well.

And indeed, what strikes the reader of all of Diderot's translations is that he does not really seek to *serve* his authors. In 1760 he is not looking to Britain for the same thing as in 1745; now it is sentimental literature rather than moral philosophy. But being himself a strong writer, he goes abroad to seek what suits him, rather to learn something new. Perhaps he already knows what he is going to find – such seems to be the case with *The Gamester*. With Shaftesbury, it is not so clear; is it the English author who opens new horizons to the young Frenchman, or is it not rather that Diderot finds in Shaftesbury the ideal pretext for putting before the public ideas which had been germinating in his mind for some time? However it may be, Diderot is too much himself to be the ideal translator.

How much, one may ask, was Diderot in a position to understand what came to him from across the Channel (since he did not make the journey himself)? 'Homo sum' – he liked to quote the old adage from Terence, and as a good humanist he saw everything in a universalizing perspective. Experience was filtered through the Latin and Greek education of the Jesuit college. When he sings the praises of Richardson, he seems relatively unaware of the specifically British aspects of *Pamela* or *Clarissa*; Richardson, he says, paints the world in which *we* live, and he takes his place among the great world classics: 'tu me resteras sur le même rayon avec Moïse, Homère, Euripide et Sophocle' (XIII, 196).[14] Diderot's savages, like those of other Enlightenment writers, are French *philosophes* in disguise, and his English and Scottish authors undergo a similar transformation. This is not to deny Diderot's merits as a translator, for he is only following the normal habits of his century. Only later did national specificity begin to worry translators, and this may have been a mixed blessing. The translator who annexes the other may be denying his or her otherness, but such translations often give to the original text a new life which one does not find in many would-be authentic simulacra.

We have seen that Diderot's translations owe a good deal to a certain type of French eloquence, the eloquence of the colleges, the preachers, the barristers, which was subsequently to become that of the republican orator.[15] Sometimes this eloquence bears the individual stamp of the *philosophe* of Langres, but it belongs also to the good pupil of the Jesuit college. I believe this is an essential voice, often a dominant one, in the polyphony that we call Diderot. It tends to embarrass us, with our taste for the ironical, the understated (I am thinking of *Le Joueur*, but equally of some of his original texts, or even of his letters to Sophie Volland), and we attempt to neutralize it by invoking irony or dialogism. We should be wrong however to underestimate its intrinsic importance in Diderot's writings. And I speak from experience when I say that this eloquence is the 'foreign body' that poses the trickiest problems for a twentieth-century British translator.[16]

The French Pope

In the age of Louis XIV, English literature had been of little interest to the French. Shakespeare and Milton were virtually unknown. *Paradise Lost*, for instance, was not translated into French until 1729 – and few French people were capable of reading it in the original. The first English poet to become widely known across the Channel was Alexander Pope. If Britain provided first and foremost models of philosophy (Bacon, Newton, Locke), Pope inaugurated the line of British literary figures, including Richardson and Ossian, who were capable of generating enthusiasm and imitation among the French. His reputation, from about 1735 onwards, was immense. The most tangible sign of this is to be found in the numerous editions of his works in French translations. Audra, in his invaluable bibliography, *Les Traductions françaises de Pope (1717–1825)*,[17] lists a total of 240 editions, including not only versions by several hands of the more popular poems, but also numerous multi-volume selections and indeed complete collections.

Before discussing the Frenching of Pope, it may be worth saying a little about the way in which he acquired his French popularity. The key figure was Voltaire.[18] It is true that even before Voltaire took refuge in England in 1726, Pope's name had reached France; his *Essay on Criticism* was first translated in 1717, and his preface to the *Iliad* had been taken up in the final phase of the *Querelle des Anciens et des Modernes*.[19] But it was Voltaire who raised the stakes by declaring him one of the great poets and encouraging the French to translate him. He did this first in private letters and then in his *Lettres philosophiques* of 1734. Chapter 22, 'Sur M. Pope et quelques autres poètes fameux' is the *locus classicus*, and is worth citing as an indication of the way the English poet was to be received:

C'est, je crois, le poète le plus élégant, le plus correct et, ce qui est encore beaucoup, le plus harmonieux qu'ait eu l'Angleterre. Il a réduit les sifflements aigres de la trompette anglaise aux sons doux de la flûte. On peut le traduire, parce qu'il est extrêmement clair, et que ses sujets, pour la plupart, sont généraux et du ressort de toutes les nations.[20]

The adjectives suggest a Pope who will fit well into a polite French tradition, while the final sentence stresses the translatability of universally valid ideas; the whole passage tends therefore to underplay the concise force and imaginative richness which several translators emphasized. It may indeed seem that Voltaire's is somewhat faint praise, implying that Pope's virtue is to have shaken off the barbarity of the English and come nearer to the norms of French classicism. In a subsequent edition, however, we find the much more unequivocal praise of the *Essay on Man* as 'le plus beau poème didactique, le plus utile, le plus sublime qu'on ait jamais fait en aucune langue' (p. 139) – and this in spite of the hostility to 'Whatever is, is right', which is so memorably expressed in *Candide*.

Influenced (and probably aided) by Voltaire, Abbé du Resnel published a new translation of the *Essay on Criticism* in 1730, but it was the *Essay on Man* that really established Pope's reputation.[21] Three different translations followed in quick succession between 1736 and 1739; two of these, by Du Resnel and Silhouette, went into many editions. The reason for this popularity is largely to be found in the polemic the work generated. Since its supposed unorthodoxy provoked refutations by French Roman Catholics and Protestants alike, the poem became a rallying point for 'philosophical' readers. This was presumably what attracted the young Diderot to write a long commentary on Silhouette's first translation.

The *Essay on Man* retained its popularity throughout the century, and several new translations were done over the next fifty years. In its wake, all of Pope's poetry was gradually made available to French readers. To judge from Audra's bibliography, five texts led the field (not counting the brief 'Universal Prayer', which shared some of the notoriety of the *Essay on Man*).[22] Although less popular than its sister, the *Essay on Criticism* was often printed with the *Essay on Man*; it was easily assimilated into the French classical tradition alongside Boileau's *Art poétique*. In the same way, the *Rape of the Lock* owed some of its favour to the possibility of comparing it with Boileau's *Lutrin*; it attracted eight translators, including Marmontel. The fourth text, *Eloisa to Abelard*, is a different case; it remained untranslated until 1751, but thereafter was probably Pope's most popular poem, being translated or adapted by some fifteen writers, imitated by many more, and included in a composite publication entitled *Les Lettres et épîtres amoureuses d'Héloïse avec les réponses d'Abeilard*, which went into many editions between 1776 and 1825. And finally, the later years of the century saw many versions of the *Pastorals* at a time when descriptive or seasonal poetry was in vogue in France. The Pope of the translations is therefore above all the thinker and the poet of feeling and imagination. The satirist is less in evidence, and indeed French opinion was rather dismayed by the vicious personal abuse contained in such works as the *Epistle to Arbuthnot*, which in any case was too full of local allusion to translate easily.[23]

The best single place to study French translations of Pope is the eight-volume *Œuvres complètes* of 1779, reprinted in 1780.[24] This uses with slight modifications the text of the *Œuvres diverses* produced by Arkstée and Merkus in Amsterdam and Leipzig in 1767. It differs from the *Œuvres diverses*, however, in printing the English text for the most important works – an indication, one presumes, of a growing interest in learning English. Like its predecessor, it includes alternative translations for the most popular poems. The most striking thing, though, is that the greater part of this edition is in prose. Indeed almost all the poems apart from the most famous are given in prose only. Nor should it be thought that where prose and verse translations existed, the former was regarded simply as a crib. The translation of poetry into prose was quite normal in eighteenth-century France, and the example of Pope allows one to consider some of the theoretical disputes this involved.

In 1743 Abbé Desfontaines, who had been responsible for the first (prose) version of the *Rape of the Lock*, published the first volume of a French translation of Virgil. He notes in his preface that there are six such translations, five of them in prose. A new one is needed, however, and in a 'Discours sur la traduction des poètes', Desfontaines outlines his own theory of translation. Uttering familiar warnings against the Scylla of excessive literalism and the Charybdis of paraphrase, he declares himself in favour of prose versions which remain as faithful as possible to the figures of the original. Metre is less essential, since poetry resides above all 'dans les images hardiment dessinées, dans les couleurs vives, dans les expressions vigoureuses, dans les tours serrés et expressifs, dans un langage doux, coulant et mélodieux, sans faiblesse, sans langueur, sans prolixité'.[25] Verse poetry may be superior to prose poetry since it has an additional 'ornament', but in translation it inevitably leads to infidelity. What is more, long translations in verse (like most long poems) are wearing.

In writing all this, Desfontaines knows he will meet formidable opposition. He notes, interestingly, that the English always translate verse with verse, and tells us that he has argued with English people about the excessive freedom of Dryden's Virgil. Roscommon, in his versified *Essay on Translated Verse*,[26] had made a vigorous defence of the English tradition. In France, prose translation of poetry was the norm, and it had been advocated most notably by Madame Dacier in her famous quarrel with La Motte about Homer, but this practice had been attacked by Bouhier (among others) in the preface to his verse translation of *Aeneid IV*. And it was the Bouhier line that was consistently defended by Voltaire. In his 'Essai sur la poésie épique' (which Desfontaines attempts to refute in his 'Discours'), Voltaire compares translations of poetry to engravings of paintings, which preserve the line, but lose the colour: 'les traductions augmentent les fautes d'un ouvrage, et en gâtent les beautés'.[27] These are sadly familiar notes for the poor translator. However, Voltaire does not conclude that poetry should not be translated, but simply that it must be translated in verse, by a great poet, and freely. This was how he himself had worked when in the *Lettres philosophiques* he rendered into French some fragments of Shakespeare, Rochester, Waller and indeed Pope.

Abbé du Resnel, who made verse translations of Pope's two *Essays*, and whom Voltaire claimed to have helped with the *Essay on Criticism*,[28] is the leading exponent of free poetic translation in the Pope *Œuvres complètes*. His twin versions, appearing respectively in 1730 and 1737, were often issued together as *Les Principes de la morale et du goût*. To judge from the periodical press of the time they were much admired, although by 1782 his *Essay on Man* was sufficiently outmoded for Fontanes to feel that another verse translation was needed. Du Resnel is a great amplifier; Pope's first eight ten-syllable lines become twelve twelve-syllable lines in his version:

> Awake, my St John! leave all meaner things
> To low ambition, and the pride of kings.
> Let us (since life can little more supply
> Than just to look about us and to die)
> Expatiate free o'er all this scene of man;
> A mighty maze! but not without a plan;
> A wild, where weeds and flowers promiscuous shoot;
> Or garden, tempting with forbidden fruit.

> Sors de l'enchantement, Milord; laisse au vulgaire
> Le séduisant espoir d'un bien imaginaire:
> Fuis le faste des cours, les honneurs, les plaisirs;
> Ils ne méritent pas de fixer tes désirs.
> Est-ce à toi de grandir cette foule importune,
> Qui court auprès des rois encenser la fortune?

Viens; un plus grand objet, des soins plus importants,
Doivent de notre vie occuper les instants.
Ce grand objet, c'est l'homme, étonnant labyrinthe
Où d'un plan régulier l'œil reconnaît l'empreinte;
Champ fécond, mais sauvage, où par de sages lois
La rose et le chardon fleurissent à la fois.   (*Œuvres*, III, 167–8)

The main addition here is the dilation of Pope's 'all meaner things'.
Du Resnel's phrases ('bien imaginaire', 'faste des cours', 'foule
importune', 'encenser la fortune') are the stock-in-trade of French
moralizing verse, and they totally obscure Pope's brutal dismissal of
the 'pride of kings'. The English poet's urgency has been lost. Look
for instance at what has happened to the 'wild, where weeds and
flowers promiscuous shoot' – Du Resnel's 'sages lois' preside over
a reassuring balance (rather than a puzzling 'promiscuity') of fertility
and wildness, rose and thistle, and the violent verb 'shoot' has given
way to the decorative 'fleurissent'. Pope throws a challenge to his
readers, Du Resnel soothes them with the bland discourse of the
comfortable moralist. What is more, he completely omits line 8 with
its allusion to the Garden of Eden.

Such fairly obvious criticisms were made in 1737 by Du Resnel's
rival Etienne de Silhouette, who was later to become more famous
as the French finance minister. Silhouette, who was living in England,
had produced his own (prose) translation of the work in 1736. In a
new edition of 1737 he published his 'Réflexions préliminaires du
traducteur sur le goût des traductions', in which he remarks of Du
Resnel's version that 'le sublime ainsi que le sens et la concision de
l'original me paraissent noyés dans la paraphrase'.[29] The three nouns
are important: the word 'sens' reflects Silhouette's belief that translation must be accurate, whereas 'sublime' and 'concision' refer to
the poetic qualities which he admires in Pope and hopes to render
in his own text. It is worth looking in a little more detail at what he
has to say on this subject.

Silhouette defends prose translation of poetry for the same sort
of reasons as Desfontaines – that too much of the original is lost
and diluted in verse. He too favours a faithful and figurative poetic
prose. Indeed he goes further, and criticizes Desfontaines's translation
of *Gulliver's Travels* as excessively prettified. Desfontaines believed
that foreign authors could be improved, and in his review in the
Observations sur les écrits modernes, he, like others, criticized
Silhouette's *Essay on Man* for being unnecessarily obscure. Silhouette
for his part is full of respect for his original. He repeatedly stresses
the English poet's power and richness, admitting that he cannot match

165

Pope's expressive harmonies, but hoping that an accurate translation will convey something of the vigour of the original. Pope's concision is such, he says, that 'la moindre paraphrase énerve sa vigueur, lâche et dissout pour ainsi dire un corps entièrement solide et serré' (*Essai*, p. 13).

This emphasis on strength and density is some way removed from Voltaire's praise of Pope's elegance and clarity. It appears to indicate a greater willingness to admire English poetry in its own right, rather than as a worthy copy of the French. In his 1736 preface Silhouette declares that the greater freedom, force and subtlety of English verse makes it far more suitable than French verse as a medium of translation. Indeed he goes further, saying 'C'est ce qui fait que leurs poésies sont fort supérieures aux nôtres' – something Voltaire could never have allowed. He adopts in fact the position so memorably expressed in the often-quoted lines of Roscommon:

> But who did ever in French authors see
> The comprehensive English energy?
> The weighty bullion of one sterling line
> Drawn to French wire would through whole pages shine.

Interestingly, these lines are also quoted by Du Resnel in his 'Discours préliminaire du traducteur' (written in 1737, partly in answer to Silhouette's criticisms). He too notes the general 'hardiesse' of English poetry and Pope's incomparable brevity, imaginative richness and intellectual sublimity. He concludes, however, firstly that only a verse translation can 'répondre en quelque sorte à cette brièveté', and secondly that French taste cannot accept a literal rendering of Pope's highly original way of writing: 'il faut avouer que l'air étranger, loin de nous plaire, est souvent un fâcheux préjugé contre tout ce qui en porte le caractère' (*Œuvres*, I, 186). He has therefore felt obliged to introduce some order into the poems and to eliminate whatever might seem vulgar, obscure, or excessively figurative. Silhouette, on the contrary, holds that the translator's task is precisely to preserve the otherness of the foreign author; if Pope is obscure, this is a pregnant obscurity.

Such disputes about assimilation and faithfulness surface in all discussions of translation. What is interesting is to see the extent to which Pope was perceived by French readers as a difficult, dense, challenging poet. When we turn to Silhouette's practice, however, we are likely to be disappointed, for it displays little of the force he had praised, and is not even very accurate. Here is his 1736 version of the opening of the *Essay on Man*:

Réveillons-nous, Milord: laissons les petits objets à la basse ambition et à l'orgueil des rois. Puisque la vie ne s'étend et ne se termine guère qu'à regarder ce qui nous environne et à mourir, parcourons donc au moins cette scène de l'homme: prodigieux labyrinthe, mais qui a pourtant sa régularité, campagne où la fleur croît confondue avec le chardon; jardin qui tente par des fruits défendus. (*Œuvres*, III, 23–5)

One might prefer this to Du Resnel's bland paraphrase, but it is still very inadequate. Perhaps the most striking weakness is the virtual disappearance of Pope's extended hunting metaphor. It is not surprising that Silhouette's work should have been so severely criticized by Diderot in the commentary referred to earlier in this chapter. We do not know why Diderot should have written this commentary – perhaps to help himself learn English better. At all events, it looks as if Silhouette may have made use of his comments in the revisions he made for later editions. The text of the 1736 London edition (quoted above) was considerably modified in 1737, and further changes were incorporated in the collections of Pope published by Arkstée and Merkus, though unfortunately the 1736 text is still used in the 1779/80 *Œuvres complètes*. Thus he followed Diderot's advice by changing 'regarder ce qui nous environne' to the more accurate and vigorous 'regarder autour de nous'. And in particular, he changes the opening invocation along the lines suggested by Diderot: 'Réveillons-nous, Milord' becomes the more energetic and familiar 'Réveillez-vous, mon cher Bolingbroke'. Even so, his revised text does not go far towards meeting Diderot's basic objection: 'Voilà le corps du poète, mais son esprit est perdu'.

There were several other versions of the *Essay on Man*, for instance a prose version by the Marquis de Saint-Simon (1771) which claims to be an 'essai de traduction littérale et énergique', but those of Du Resnel and Silhouette remained the essential ones. Their merits were differently judged by contemporaries, who were by no means as critical as Diderot – at least in public. Abbé Goujet includes a comparison of the two in Volume 8 of his *Bibliothèque française*; in an informative but not very illuminating overview of the whole range of translations of Pope from the point of view of a reader who knows no English,[30] he praises Du Resnel's taste, purity of style and talent for versification, but is less happy with Silhouette's version. This, in his view, is more obscure than the same translator's successful rendering of the *Essay on Criticism*, 'parce qu'il a voulu être trop littéral, au lieu que M. du Resnel s'est prêté davantage au génie de notre langue et au goût de notre siècle' (p. 247). Assimilation wins again.

For the *Essay on Criticism* contemporaries had a similar choice between a very free verse adaptation and a rather limited prose version which was improved by revision. It is not entirely clear how much Voltaire helped Du Resnel, but he certainly approved of the Abbé's efforts, and the latter offered a token of gratitude by including in Pope's poem four lines of Denham which Voltaire had translated. As well as making such additions and writing lengthy notes, Du Resnel sought to win acceptance for his English author by turning his rambling piece into something more like a treatise in verse, with proper subdivisions and correct rhetorical progression. His success in doing so was applauded by critics such as Goujet. He also felt the need to eliminate the type of coarseness which the English enjoyed, but the French repudiated. Like many others, he expresses a kind of regret for the polite taboos on low language, but sees them as a fact of literary life. His example is Pope's comparison of bad critics with apothecaries:

> So modern 'pothecaries, taught the art
> By doctor's bills to play the doctor's part,
> Bold in the practice of mistaken rules,
> Prescribe, apply, and call their masters fools.

Du Resnel comments: 'Cette image plaît aux Anglais; tous les Français que j'ai consultés la trouvent choquante' (*Œuvres*, I, 195). So what does he do? Naturally he omits the image altogether, substituting a quite different and much longer development in which jealous hornets are to be found stinging active bees. Silhouette is less inhibited, though he too feels the pressure of French decorum. His first version of 1736 is quite literal ('les apothicaires de nos jours'); by 1737, however, the offending apothecaries have become the periphrastic 'suppôts modernes de la pharmacie', but with a note explaining that the original contained 'le terme d'apothicaire auquel on n'attache point en anglais une idée aussi ignoble qu'en français' (*Œuvres*, I, 93).

One of the greatest challenges of the *Essay* was provided by the passages on 'numbers' and imitative harmony. Here it does seem that Du Resnel has the advantage over his rival. In the satire on 'equal syllables', 'expected rhymes' and the like, Silhouette's version is long-winded and plodding, giving little idea of the sharpness of the original, though he does improve things in later editions by introducing metric equivalents for 'And ten low words oft creep in one dull line' or 'That like a wounded snake drags its slow length along'. Du Resnel makes no such attempts, but his adaptation, while less pointed than Pope's original, does at least convey amusingly his general tone and sense, as in these lines:

Jamais de tours nouveaux, jamais de traits sublimes,
Mêmes expressions, et toujours mêmes rimes.
Partout où vous voyez couler de clairs ruisseaux,
Il vous faut préparer au doux chant des oiseaux.
On aperçoit toujours une belle bergère
Assise mollement sur la tendre fougère.
Entendez-vous des eaux murmurer et frémir,
Vous n'êtes pas en vain menacé de dormir. (*Œuvres*, I, 244–5)

Typically, Du Resnel has added a shepherdess in the bracken, and his opening couplet is dogmatic rather than witty, but he does quite successfully acclimatize Pope in the French tradition.

As for imitative harmony, Silhouette notes in his 1736 preface that the English poet here practises what he preaches 'avec un art inimitable'. As a 'disciple' he has tried to do the same in French prose, but in vain. Again Du Resnel has the advantage, and his translation of the passage in question was still being praised in 1761,[31] for instance his rendering of the couplet about Ajax:

Qu'Ajax soulève et lance un énorme rocher,
Le vers appesanti tombe avec cette masse.

The arrangement of the lines means that this is no longer a rhyming couplet, but the second line, with the heavy stress on 'tombe' coming after the slight pause at the caesura, does come close to Diderot's 'hieroglyph', in which sound and sense are fused together. The specific effect (a falling rock) is not in Pope, but the spirit of the poem survives the change.

These last examples suggest that it was not merely Pope the thinker who was presented by his translators to the French public. What then of the *Rape of the Lock*, where the poetry is all? It was by translating a passage from this poem that Voltaire sought to illustrate Pope's quality in the *Lettres philosophiques*. Audra records eight translations of the *Rape*, most of them in verse. The first was in prose, however, and was the work of Abbé Desfontaines, whose ideas about translation we considered earlier. According to Goujet, who knew no English, it was Desfontaines's version that helped dispel the prejudice that the English were incapable of wit. His text was used moreover by some of the subsequent translators. Let us take just six lines from the passage cited by Voltaire (Canto IV, lines 17–34) and see how Pope's poetry fared in the hands of his interpreters:

Two handmaids wait the throne: alike in place,
But differing far in figure and in face.

> Here stood Ill-nature like an ancient maid,
> Her wrinkled form in black and white arrayed;
> With store of prayers, for mornings, nights and noons,
> Her hand is filled; her bosom with lampoons.

Desfontaines's supposedly literal version gets off to a bad start when 'handmaids' becomes for some reason 'chœurs de filles' (later corrected to 'filles') and 'in black and white arrayed' is taken to refer to the ancient maid's skin. These mistakes find their way into later translations. Otherwise one can only be amazed that this prose rendering convinced anyone that the English could be witty. For instance, all the force of the chiasmus in the late two lines is lost:

> Deux [chœurs de] filles égales en dignité, mais différentes par leurs figures, environnent son trône; la Méchanceté y paraît sous la forme d'une vierge antique; elle a la peau rude, noire et ridée, les mains pleines de prières et le sein rempli de satires.   (*Œuvres*, II, 59)

It is not worth wasting time on the translations offered by Despreaux in 1742 and by Costard des Ifs in 1744. Both use Desfontaines, and Costard, who knew no English, waxes eloquent about his elegance, precision, 'feu poétique' and harmony. Despreaux's version is unusual in using a ten-syllable line, which is presumably a concession to literalism, but otherwise he feels free to alter and add, so that his text is twice the length of the original.

Both of these versions were soon ousted by that of Jean-François Marmontel, which was to be the standard one used in the collected editions. Later in his life, in his *Eléments de littérature*, Marmontel wrote about the theory of translation, attempting to steer a middle course between the schools represented by Du Resnel and Silhouette. His *Boucle de cheveux enlevée* is an early work, published in 1746 at the age of twenty-two, when he was still Voltaire's young protégé. For the passage that concerns us, however, he does not try to use his master's version, but produces his own free translation. It was based on Desfontaines, for Marmontel had no English to speak of. When compared with the original, its most noticeable characteristic is its length:

> Aux côtés de son lit paraissent deux Vestales:
> Leurs traits fort différents, leurs dignités égales,
> L'une, vieille Sibylle, au teint noir et plombé,
> Y traîne un corps mourant sous cent lustres courbé;
> C'est la Malignité. Sur ses membres arides
> S'étend un cuir tanné que sillonnent les rides.

Les yeux pleins de douceur, le cœur rempli de fiel,
Déchirant les humains, elle bénit le Ciel,
Et flattant avec art le mérite modeste,
A ses embrassements mêle un poison funeste. (*Œuvres*, II, 120)

One presumes Desfontaines is responsible for the misreading of 'in black and white arrayed'. Generally, Marmontel's translation is free rather than inaccurate. It is not without energy (e.g. the syntax and choice of words in the fifth and sixth lines), but the amplification of the portrait of Ill-nature tends to reduce its immediacy. The physicality of the hand filled with 'store of prayers' and of the bosom stuffed with lampoons has given way to the conventionally metaphorical 'fiel', 'déchirer' and 'poison', and once again Pope's asymmetrical chiasmus has been lost. French commentators tended to assimilate the *Rape of the Lock* to Boileau's *Lutrin*, but Marmontel's language here is more akin to the French satirist's moral epistles than to his mock-heroic poem, which shares some of the unexpected trans-formational powers we associate with Pope.[32]

Not surprisingly, it is Voltaire, the advocate of free poetic trans-lation, who came closest to the feel of the *Rape of the Lock*. Unlike Marmontel, Voltaire knew English and knew it well. For some of the extract he too expands and embroiders on his original, but he also allows himself to cut. Thus in the six lines we are looking at, he omits the first two (which are less interesting than what surrounds them), while altering the rest to suit his own preoccupations:

La médisante Envie est assise auprès d'elle,
Vieux spectre féminin, décrépite pucelle,
Avec un air dévot déchirant le prochain,
Et chansonnant les gens l'Evangile à la main.[33]

With his 'air dévot' and his 'Evangile', Voltaire has seized the chance of satirizing religious hypocrisy in the manner of *Tartuffe*, but the 'black and white' and the 'prayers' of the original fully justify this. The heavily loaded second line catches the grotesque quality of Pope's picture, and above all the final line echoes his down-to-earth brutality with its unexpectedly familiar verb and the precise image of the hand clutching the Bible. Here, for once, Pope has not been doctored to suit French decorum. One can only regret that there were so few translations of this quality.

The interlocking examples of Pope and Diderot suggest something of the difficulties encountered by the French classical tradition in coming to terms with English literature, a near neighbour which was regarded as less polished but in some respects more innovative. Pope, far from seeming blandly 'Augustan', struck French readers as jagged, dense and obscure. Translators such as Du Resnel and Silhouette acknowledged the freedom and richness of English poetry, which, as Roscommon suggests, could hardly be matched in the French literary language of the day. Translation was therefore, as it must always be in all cultures, an area of compromise. Here the native tradition faced alien worlds, from the Arabic popular culture of the *Thousand and one Nights* to the ancient Scandinavian poetry translated in 1755 by Abbé Mallet, from Homer (now perceived in a more exotic light) to his supposed Caledonian peer, Ossian. The hegemony of polite culture was still too powerful to be much upset by these foreign bodies; with few exceptions, it assimilated them triumphantly, finding a modest renewal of its forces by bringing them into the fold of polite French literature.

10

JACQUES OR HIS MASTER?
DIDEROT AND THE PEASANTS

In Chapter 2, I asked how Charles Perrault adapted for the use of polite society material which had its origin in 'les moindres familles', those who lived in 'des huttes et des cabanes'. The world of these families, the French peasantry of the *ancien régime*, has been massively studied over the last thirty years. In such investigations, it must be said, the historian has received little help from the polite literature of the day, for this largely ignored the life of the majority of the population.[1] Only in the nineteenth century did French novelists begin to take peasant life seriously. Even then, moreover, the representation of the peasant world for middle-class readers had its difficulties – as is witnessed, for instance, by an interesting discussion of problems of linguistic decorum in rustic fiction in the introduction to George Sand's *François le champi*.[2]

With such thoughts in mind, I want now to look at the practice of one enlightened representative of French elite culture of the eighteenth century, Denis Diderot. I shall ask how he saw peasant life from outside and above – or, to generalize, how a member of the polite minority saw the not-so-polite majority. What ways did he find of depicting them, and how much was his presentation determined by literary models? How true is it that for him the peasant, like the savage or the child, remained the Other?

First, a few reminders about peasant existence in eighteenth-century France, as modern historians have reconstructed it. In the first place, we must bear in mind Goubert's warning: 'Le paysan français n'a jamais existé'.[3] By this, Goubert means that it is impossible to generalize, when the regions of France differed so widely from one another in (for instance) the place of grain in their economy or the relative weight of seigneurial dues, taxes, tithes, rents and debts. And we should add to this the changes that took place over the century. It is only in mythical views that the peasant world is immobile (as opposed to the dynamic towns).

Even so, there are a few simple remarks that can be made, and that bear repeating when we are thinking about eighteenth-century French society. The peasants constituted the vast majority of the French population – at least four-fifths, however we define the word 'peasant'. It was their work that fed the towns; or as Saint-Lambert puts it more grandly at the beginning of *Les Saisons*, referring to the sun:

> Il prodigue au Printemps la grâce et la beauté,
> Du trésor des moissons il enrichit l'Eté;
> L'Automne les enlève aux campagnes fertiles,
> Et l'Hiver en tribut les reçoit dans les villes.[4]

In dues, taxes, tithes, rents and debts, both in money and in kind, the produce of the peasants' labour was appropriated by the more privileged groups of society, most of whom lived and spent their money in the towns. Robert Mandrou, drawing together the findings of such historians as E. Labrousse, J. Meuvret, P. Goubert and P. de Saint-Jacob, wrote as follows: 'La ponction seigneuriale et ecclésiastique sur la production paysanne est énorme – de l'ordre de 30 à 40%'.[5] And this says nothing of what went to the tax-gatherer, the landlord or the debt-collector.

There was therefore an enormous gap in income between, for instance, the well-off bourgeois and the poor *métayer*. Of course there were intermediate stages, and there was both rural opulence and urban poverty – we are not talking of a simple town–country contrast. But one can illustrate the disparities in income by pointing out that the first edition of *Emile* cost eighteen *livres* (in 1762) or that a British traveller in Paris in 1776 paid twelve *livres* a day for the hire of a carriage, when at roughly the same period Turgot estimated that the average annual consumption among peasants in a backward region was the equivalent of some thirty-five *livres* per head.

It is not surprising then that there was a great difference in styles of living, particularly if we add the opposition between town and country to that between rich and poor. Certain kinds of evidence might lead one to overestimate this, but one indication of the problem – for a problem it was in the revolutionary years – is to be found in the answers to the questionnaire sent out to country *notables* in 1790 by Abbé Grégoire concerning the possibility of eliminating the *patois*. Quite apart from other differences in wealth or life-style, the peasants in many areas spoke what seemed a foreign language to the people of the towns. A correspondent from the Mâcon region wrote to Grégoire that the *patois* 'fait des gens de la campagne une caste isolée qui ne communique point avec la ville'.[6] Michel de

Certeau, who with two colleagues analysed Grégoire's *enquête*,[7] argued that this town–country polarity is central to it, and that the *notables* of the provincial towns looked at the peasants who surrounded them with the eyes of ethnographers. To them the peasant world was a savage world, provoking what De Certeau calls an 'exotisme de l'intérieur'.

The difference between *patois* and standard French may stand as an example of other cultural divides. Writing on Restif's villagers, Le Roy Ladurie notes that they had almost no contact with the Enlightenment or with high culture – only the priest provided a tenuous link. There was a traditional rural culture of song, story, proverb, joke, dance, festival and above all religious or 'superstitious' belief and observance, which was an object of contempt for the educated elite of the towns. There were points of contact of course: what we might call the 'mass culture' of chapbooks (the Bibliothèque Bleue) and popular engravings echoes at a distance the forms and themes of upper-class urban art and literature, while at the same time many members of the educated minority took notice of the culture of the majority.[8] Not only did the late eighteenth century in Europe witness a great increase of interest in folklore and popular song, but in France members of the elite took pleasure in fairground theatre and had popular chapbooks bound up in fine bindings. It was possible therefore for the privileged to share, or at least to know, the culture of the unprivileged – the seigneur at the fair. But the converse was not true.

Almost without exception writers at this time belonged to the town world, whatever their place of origin. Few in any case had origins that could be described as peasant, though some had experience of country life. There were no poets in eighteenth-century France whom one could set alongside the famous English 'thresher-poet' Stephen Duck, or even alongside Robert Burns.[9] So writers naturally articulated the well-off urban view of the peasants, a view which was often contradictory or ambiguous.

In eighteenth-century literature the peasants (and indeed the common people in general) rarely have an important role, though there are exceptions in genres such as the *conte moral* and certain types of poetry. In so far as they do appear, the image they present is normally shaped by literary convention. The most obvious convention is that of a pastoral idyll with its decorative shepherds and shepherdesses. One may also cite, for instance, the image of the honest uncorrupted countryman, the grotesque world of country clowns, the *paysan parvenu* (or *perverti*), and the declamation on the theme of peasant as victim.

The last of these is represented in classic form by La Bruyère's famous tableau of the 'animaux farouches' in *Les Caractères*, which was echoed in milder form by many humanitarian *philosophes* (and indeed non-*philosophes*) of the following century. It is also common knowledge, however, that certain *philosophes*, whatever their progressive ideals, displayed considerable scorn for the unwashed many. Voltaire, for instance, wrote: 'A l'égard du peuple, il sera toujours sot et barbare, témoin ce qui est arrivé à la canaille de Lyon. Ce sont des bœufs auxquels il faut un joug, un aiguillon et du foin'.[10] Such remarks shock modern readers (and rightly so). H. C. Payne, in his book *The Philosophes and the People* (1976) makes an attempt to set them in perspective, claiming that for all the difficulty the *philosophes* had in seeing the common people as fully human, they also showed an increasingly serious concern for popular welfare. In general terms I think Payne is right; it is too easy to make a lot of certain 'revealing' remarks. So what does the example of Diderot show?[11]

He was a commoner, the son of a cutler. In a sense then, he belonged to *le peuple*. But this word was elastic in its meaning;[12] it could be used of the whole of the third estate, it could be reserved for the more respectable members of it (as opposed to the *canaille* or *populace*), or conversely it could designate the poorer commoners, the manual labourers for instance, as opposed to relatively privileged people such as master cutlers. At one point in his life, Diderot wrote: 'se dépopulariser et se rendre meilleur, c'est la même chose' (*AT*, III, 263),[13] and this in a sense is what he did. He rose in the world by traditional channels (Jesuit college, literature, theatre, etc.), so that by the end of his life he could slap the knees of the Empress of Russia. However, even his starting point was some way up the ladder; his father owned land and houses and appears in the *Entretien d'un père avec ses enfants* as a Langres *notable*. Diderot's *Apologie de l'abbé Galiani* (1770), a discussion of the grain trade, reveals a clear consciousness of his status as landowner; he taunts his opponent Morellet with the remark: 'Je gage que l'abbé Morellet n'a pas un pouce de terre' (*POL*, 96). And indeed after his father's death the *philosophe* had become part-owner of the family estate, from which he received a *rente* of 1,500 *livres* a year (partly in cash, partly in kind) in typically bourgeois fashion.

At the same time, the *Apologie* shows that Langres gave him a real knowledge of the problems of the peasants. He was not one of them, but he saw their hard conditions, particularly during the journey he made to Langres and Bourbonne in the harvest time of 1770, a journey which gave him cause to respond to Morellet:

Je vais lui en apprendre les effets [of the freedom of the grain trade] parce qu'ils ont eu lieu sous mes yeux. [...] Le petit peuple a souffert des maux infinis, et [...] il y aurait eu un soulèvement dans presque toutes les villes de ma province sans les remontrances très violentes des officiers municipaux et l'attention des intendants.   (*POL*, 101)

Naturally this experience had an impact on Diderot's writing, including his fiction. However, for most of his writing life, he lived either in Paris or nearby, in the country houses of friends. As he writes in 1759 to Sophie Volland from Le Grandval for instance, his view of the peasants is that from the château window:

Dès le matin j'entends sous ma fenêtre des ouvriers. A peine le jour commence-t-il à poindre qu'ils ont la bêche à la main, qu'ils coupent la terre et roulent la brouette. Ils mangent un morceau de pain noir; ils se désaltèrent au ruisseau qui coule; à midi, ils prennent une heure de sommeil sur la terre; bientôt ils se remettent à leur ouvrage. Ils sont gais; ils chantent; ils se font entr'eux de bonnes grosses plaisanteries qui les égayent; ils rient. Sur le soir, ils vont retrouver des enfants tout nus, autour d'un âtre enfumé, une paysanne hideuse et malpropre, et un lit de feuilles sèches; et leur sort n'est ni plus mauvais ni meilleur que le mien.   (*CORR*, I, 319)

For the Parisian intellectual, provincial life is distant, and peasant life even more so.

At the same time, Diderot was brought by his professional work to write about the peasants, particularly in the *Encyclopédie*. He was influenced by the economic theories of the Physiocrats, Quesnay and his colleagues, several of whom were among his contributors. For them, the land was the essential source of human wealth, and agriculture was therefore the basic economic activity. Not that this view was peculiar to this group; Diderot was in a venerable tradition when he wrote in his article 'Agriculture' (published in 1751, before he had come under the influence of the Physiocrats): 'cet art est le premier, le plus utile, le plus étendu, et peut-être le plus essentiel des arts' (*OC*, V, 290). In 'Homme' he argues the case for decent agricultural incomes in terms which are both compassionate and utilitarian: 'Si les agriculteurs, qui sont les hommes de l'Etat qui fatiguent le plus, sont les moins bien nourris, il faut qu'ils se dégoûtent de leur état, ou périssent. Dire que l'aisance les en ferait sortir, c'est être un ignorant et un homme atroce' (*OC*, VII, 424).

In general, in his later years, Diderot became more democratic in his outlook, proclaiming the sovereign rights of the people and stressing the dangers of autocracy, however benevolent. In the *Mémoires pour Catherine II* and the *Observations sur le Nakaz*, he

underlines the need to increase the prosperity of the peasants, mainly
by a more equitable taxation system, and again his arguments are
both humanitarian and economic. But this does not imply a high
estimate of peasant life as such. Rather he seems to see the peasants
as victims of Marx's 'rural idiocy': 'les dix-neuf vingtièmes d'une
nation sont condamnés à l'ignorance par leur état et leur imbécillité'
(*POL*, 358). In order to become fully human, therefore, the peasant
needs to raise himself above this primitive level, and Physiocracy,
by laying too much stress on agriculture, 'tend à tenir l'homme
dans une sorte d'abrutissement, et dans une médiocrité de jouissances
et de félicité tout à fait contraire à sa nature' (*POL*, 404). For the
Diderot of the *Observations*, if not for the primitivist of the *Supplément au Voyage de Bougainville*, human nature only finds its true
expression in advanced urban society. Consequently he advocates a
system of popular education and *concours*, a meritocratic system
which would allow at least the gifted to escape the fate of 'mute
inglorious Miltons'.

Nor should it be forgotten that the concern for peasant welfare,
in Diderot as in others, sprang partly from fear. He knew something
about the brutality of peasant rebellions, and in the *Apologie de l'abbé
Galiani*, the work which proclaims his break with the Physiocrats,
he writes: 'L'abbé Galiani craint le peuple; et quand il s'agit de pain,
il n'y a qu'un homme ivre qui n'en ait pas peur' (*POL*, 117). Fear
and contempt mix with his distant but genuine sympathy for the
majority of the population. So much, in brief, for his attitude as
a *philosophe*. But what of his activity in the narrower field of
imaginative literature?

A good starting-point is the review of Saint-Lambert's *Les Saisons*
which Diderot contributed to the *Correspondance littéraire* in 1769.
Imitated in part from the Scottish poet Thomson's *Seasons*, but also
from the *Georgics*, Saint-Lambert's poem paints a picture of rural
life which was meant to encourage an active interest in agriculture
on the part of wealthy town-dwellers. The author presents the work
as 'des Géorgiques pour les hommes chargés de protéger les campagnes, et non pour ceux qui les cultivent' (p. xxxix). He could not
expect to be read by the peasants he wrote about. Nor indeed does
he conceal the fact that he has concentrated on the more attractive
side of peasant life; as he puts it, 'il y a dans les campagnes de riches
laboureurs, des paysans aisés; ceux-là ont des mœurs' (p. xxv), and
these will be his subject, rather than the poor. Village life is not seen
through uniformly rose-tinted spectacles, and there is an outspoken

section showing the suffering brought by the feudal *corvée*, but the poem still belongs essentially to the idyllic pastoral tradition.

In his notes on the poem, as well as criticizing Saint-Lambert's general lack of verve, Diderot expresses doubt about the possibility of writing an equivalent of the *Georgics* in eighteenth-century France. The problem is essentially one of language; it turns on the great divide between the poetry-reading public and the people of the country. There are plenty of French agricultural terms, but

cette langue technique ne se parle point hors de nos villages; les mots n'en ont point été prononcés dans nos villes. Un poème donc, où toutes ces expressions rustiques seraient employées, aurait souvent le défaut ou de n'être point entendu ou de manquer d'harmonie, d'élégance et de dignité, ces expressions n'ayant point été maniées par le goût, travaillées, adoucies par le commerce journalier, présentées à nos oreilles apprivoisées, ennoblies par des applications figurées, dépouillées des idées accessoires ignobles de la misère, de l'avilissement et de la grossièreté des habitants de la campagne.

(*OC*, XVIII, 18)

Saint-Lambert, who timidly mixes a few *realia* with the allegories, classical allusions and periphrases of elevated poetry, is bound to produce an insipid text. This was not the case in the simpler days of the Greeks and Romans when 'la langue du laboureur ne fut point étrangère à l'homme consulaire'. In modern France, however, it would need a genius to reconcile the two, and in general 'les poètes modernes ont été ou bas ou raboteux, ou vagues ou louches'. Diderot (like George Sand in the following century) is thus a prisoner of literary decorum; as a Parisian man of letters — and by no means a conservative one — he has to go by the rules of the game, which makes realistic country poetry a fairly hopeless undertaking.

All this may seem unadventurous from the author of *La Religieuse* and the man who wrote that 'la poésie veut quelque chose d'énorme, de barbare et de sauvage' (*OC*, X, 402). But there is an important distinction between the barbaric or horrific, which might qualify as sublime, and the mundane or low, which was harder to accommodate in serious writing. This was Diderot's problem when he came to write his own serious tale of low life, *Les Deux Amis de Bourbonne*, which is also a reaction to the writing of Saint-Lambert.[14] The author of *Les Saisons* had written a story called 'Les Deux Amis', a touching tale of friendship set among the Iroquois. Rather than a critique, Diderot this time wrote a story of his own, in which his aim, at least in part, is to show that there is no need to go to North America for sublime qualities worthy of the story-teller's art. His own tale is set in the French countryside, in the forests round the watering-place of

Bourbonne north of his native Langres, where he spent several weeks in the summer of 1770, in the company of Madame de Maux and her daughter. *Les Deux Amis de Bourbonne* is intriguing in its attempt to solve the artistic and linguistic problems of depicting peasant life for a sophisticated audience.

The hero of the story is a smuggler, Félix, whose friend, Olivier, is killed while rescuing him from execution. He takes refuge with a charcoal-burner, who is killed by the *maréchaussée* on his account. Félix is left with the two widows and their children; he marries off the children to each other and disappears, turning up again as a game-keeper, becoming involved in his master's disputes and finally going abroad as a soldier. As we read this very brief story, we are given quite a clear image of some aspects of French rural life, though perhaps with a liberal *philosophe* tinge. We see (but without any picturesque detail) the drawing of lots for military service, the ferocious enforce-ment of the laws against smuggling, the social relations between rich and poor, master and servant. There are also a certain number of small physical details − nothing like what we shall find in Balzac, but when Félix learns of Olivier's death, he faints and cracks his head on a kneading trough. This is the kind of detail which, according to Diderot's concluding remarks on realism (*OC*, XII, 454−7), are the warts added to a portrait to make it seem life-like. But in these same remarks he also stresses the need to grip the audience's attention, and it is here that the *sublime* comes in.

From the outset the two heroes are cast in the antique mould, 'les Oreste et Pylade de Bourbonne'. The final glimpse of Félix is equally heroic: 'son nom de guerre est le Triste'. The whole story is one of noble passion and devotion, and it is told in the language which Diderot thought appropriate for this. Take the following passage:

C'est là que Félix va apprendre la mort d'Olivier et se trouver entre les veuves de deux hommes massacrés à son sujet. Il entre et dit brusquement à la femme Olivier: 'Où est Olivier?' Au silence de cette femme, à son vêtement, à ses pleurs, il comprit qu'Olivier n'était plus. Il se trouva mal; il tomba et se fendit la tête contre la huche à pétrir le pain. Les deux veuves le relèvent; son sang coulait sur elles; et tandis qu'elle s'occupaient à l'étancher avec leurs tabliers, il leur disait: 'Et vous êtes leurs femmes, et vous me secourez'.

(*OC*, XII, 447)

The tableau here might be transferred directly to one of the great history paintings which Diderot describes in his *Salons* − or perhaps to their modern equivalent in Greuze. The narrative, with its kneading trough and its aprons, has the sublime simplicity he admired in Homer

('Patrocle n'est plus. On combat pour son cadavre. Hector a ses armes').[15] And the dialogue, entirely free of any trace of rusticity, reminds one of certain high points of Racinian tragedy ('Vous êtes empereur, Seigneur, et vous pleurez'). All this lends the characters an exotic grandeur. They are like figures from Ancient Greece or the poems of Ossian (of which Diderot had translated a *sublime* fragment some ten years earlier).[16]

And of course these heroes are not ordinary peasants. They may be of peasant origin (the story has little to say about this), but when we see them they are forest people, smugglers, outlaws, charcoal-burners – and Félix finishes as a soldier. So they belong to a glamorous line which includes folk heroes such as Mandrin, or Robin Hood, Schiller's noble bandits, the Testalunga whom Diderot actually cites in his story, and a whole host of Romantic outlaws.

In reading *Les Deux Amis de Bourbonne*, one is conscious, perhaps uncomfortably so, of the gap between the principal characters and the various narrators (or indeed the author and the probable reader). The very setting, a watering-place in a wild part of France, intensifies this. At the beginning of the tale, the confrontation of two alien worlds is made vividly present to us: 'Un soir que nous allions à la promenade, selon notre usage, nous vîmes au devant d'une chaumière une grande femme debout, avec quatre petits enfants à ses pieds; sa contenance triste et ferme attira notre attention, et notre attention fixa la sienne. Après un moment de silence, elles nous dit: "Voilà quatre petits enfants; je suis leur mère, et je n'ai plus de mari"' (*CC*, XII, 442). The sublimity is all on the side of the widow. One may be reminded of the contrast between the different figures in the *Supplément*. The rustic characters here seem both greater and lesser than the narrators: they are given 'grandeur d'âme', but the first narrator speaks of their 'amitiés animales et domestiques', which if not derogatory is at least condescending. They are the appropriate object of alms-giving and protection.

Moreover, again as in the *Supplément au Voyage de Bougainville*, Diderot presents the action through several screens. The opening pages are supposedly a letter written by the tourists to Naigeon, but the central section, in which linguistic sublimity is most apparent, is a report from the 'subdélégué Aubert', and this in turn is based on the words of the charcoal-burner's widow. As with the eloquent 'Adieux du vieillard' in the *Supplément*, the language here is robbed of a direct source and appears as the result of a complex process of transposition and thence stylization. Diderot can no more approach Félix directly than he can the Tahitians. It is true that this sort of distance can also be found when he writes of members of his own social group (Madame de La Pommeraye for instance), but there is a degree of stylization in this story which recalls De Certeau's 'exotisme de l'intérieur'.

Stylization of a different kind can be seen in the other fictional work in which peasants play an important part, *Jacques le fataliste*. Here again scenes and stories are presented to us at two removes. The reader learns of them from a narrator who is reporting a conversation in which Jacques tells stories to his master (and vice versa). Jacques is a peasant; indeed his name makes of him *the* peasant, and the novel can be read as the triumph of peasant over seigneur, for Jacques has all the vigour which his master so clearly lacks. But there is more to it than that. Jacques is no ordinary peasant. For one thing, he is Diderot, and his perplexities about freedom echo in a mocking form those of his creator. For another, he is a kind of *paysan parvenu*; he started life as a peasant, but he is no longer what he was. Like a true *philosophe* he sees in his master's horse 'le symbole de Jacques que voilà et de tant d'autres lâches coquins comme lui, qui ont quitté les campagnes pour venir porter la livrée dans la capitale, et qui aimeraient mieux mendier leur pain dans les rues ou mourir de faim que de retourner à l'agriculture, le plus utile et le plus honorable des métiers' (*OC*, XXIII, 272). One recognizes the themes and tone of Diderot's *Encyclopédie* articles and his writings for Catherine.

So when Jacques tells of his experiences (whether first-hand or second-hand) of peasant life, he speaks across a gap of some years, from the standpoint of one who has changed his place in society. Time separates him from the youth about which he tells his merry tales; the peasant world is an archaic world of old stories and customs. And in the other scenes which are set somewhat nearer to the time when the novel is set, Jacques is an onlooker — a *voyeur* even — rather than someone directly involved in peasant life. As a wounded soldier, he is an involuntary eavesdropper on a conjugal scene which he recounts with knowing superiority, acquiescing in his master's comment that 'rien ne peuple comme les gueux'.

But even if Diderot's hero is not the voice of the peasantry, the novel gives a most interesting set of representations of peasant life. Broadly one can divide these into two groups, Jacques's experiences after Fontenoy, and the stories of his youth. The first group is largely concerned with poverty and its attendant problems. It can be considered in part as the fictional equivalent of the *Apologie de l'abbé Galiani*, a satire on the economic mismanagement of France. We see the day-to-day business of making ends meet, paying rents, taxes and debts and feeding a family: 'L'année est mauvaise, à peine pouvons-nous suffire à nos besoins et aux besoins de nos enfants. Le grain est d'une cherté! Point de vin! Encore si l'on trouvait à travailler; mais les riches se retranchent, les pauvres gens ne font rien, pour une journée qu'on emploie, on en perd quatre. Personne ne paye ce qu'il doit, les créanciers sont d'une âpreté qui désespère' (*OC*, XXIII, 40). This is worth setting against the picture painted by historians such as Goubert. It is supposedly set back in 1745 (the date of Fontenoy), but it seems probable that as he wrote it Diderot was thinking of what he had seen more recently in France. Indeed a similar note is struck in the 'bourru bienfaisant' episode between the host and his *compère*, and this is set at the time of the supposed voyage of Jacques and his master, nearer to the time of writing.

In these scenes after Fontenoy, Diderot (or rather Jacques, since he is the narrator) strikes a balance between the sublime simplicity of *Les Deux Amis de Bourbonne* and the traditional comic treatment of the peasant. If the latter is more obvious in the scene of the itching ear, we can observe a shift to tearful pathos in the passage where the poor woman spills the oil. This is something like a Greuze set piece, with Jacques in the role of Good Samaritan: 'Dans ce moment survinrent les petits enfants de cette femme, ils étaient presque nus, et les mauvais vêtements de leur mère montraient toute la misère de la famille, et la mère et les enfants se mirent à crier. Tel que vous me voyez, il en fallait dix fois moins pour me toucher; mes entrailles s'émurent de compassion, les larmes me vinrent aux yeux' (*OC*, XXIII, 98). In this scene, as in the rest of this group, there is little attempt to reproduce real peasant speech. Even if the characters are not given the Homeric sublimity of Félix and Olivier, they are figures from a *drame* and they all speak standard French.[17] No doubt, as Diderot's comments on Saint-Lambert suggest, peasant speech would have seemed grotesque and unintelligible. One looks in vain in *Jacques* (and indeed in most eighteenth-century French fiction) for the imitation of popular language which Smollett gives – for laughs – in *Humphrey Clinker* and which Walter Scott some forty years later was to establish firmly in the serious novel.[18] In Diderot's novel there are at most a few conventional signals that this is lower-class or peasant speech: the very simplicity of the peasant woman may act this way, and there is a sprinkling of forms of address ('ma bonne', 'compère', 'filleul') which locate the speakers in particular social groups.

Diderot was aware of this language problem, particularly in the more grotesquely rustic episodes from Jacques's youth. He mocks the expression 'une mortelle heure' which he (or Jacques) puts into

Dame Marguerite's mouth. Nevertheless, Dames Marguerite and Suzon, Bigre *fils* and *père* and the rest of the cast of yokels all speak 'pure' French, not at all like the equivalent of Mummerset that Molière gave to his peasants in *Dom Juan*. One might perhaps read this linguistic decorum as a sign that Diderot wants us to react to his peasants as human beings, not mere figures of fun. Be that as it may, they are certainly comic characters, and the episodes in which they figure are stylized to the point of caricature. Jacques is looking back from some distance at the world he has left, and holding it up as a fit object of amusement for his master, who responds appropriately ('Scélérat! double scélérat!'). The story of Bigre and Justine, for instance, has every appearance of coming from an old stock of country tales, far removed from the dramatic world of Madame de La Pommeraye.

Bigre, with his euphonious name, gives Diderot the chance for a piece of wonderfully ambiguous word-play (*OC*, XXIII, 217–19). A peasant with such a name, even more than a Lubin, is fair game for mockery, and Diderot makes the most of this. He scolds his supposedly squeamish reader (for example, himself reading *Les Saisons*) for not wanting to admit such low names into fiction,[19] and then launches into a 'what's-in-a-name' routine. Why should the reader regard Bigre as any more comic in itself than Boule (the cabinet-maker) or indeed Pompey, Caesar or Condé? 'C'est qu'il y a Bigre et Bigre comme Guillaume et Guillaume. Si je dis Guillaume tout court, ce ne sera ni le conquérant de la Grande-Bretagne, ni le marchand de drap de l'*Avocat Patelin*, le nom de Guillaume tout court ne sera ni héroïque ni bourgeois. Ainsi de Bigre.' All well and good, but Bigre is a euphemism for Bougre, and Diderot has chosen it deliberately as the name for his rustic character. Of course it is possible that there was, as the author assures us, a real-life Bigre: 'C'est le vrai nom de famille de mon charron; les extraits baptistaires, extraits mortuaires, contrats de mariage en sont signés Bigre. Les descendants de Bigre qui occupent aujourd'hui sa boutique s'appellent Bigre. Quand leurs enfants, qui sont jolis, passent dans la rue, on dit: Voilà les petits Bigres.' If so, what a windfall for Diderot, who is able to amuse himself and cock a snook at decorum as he concludes his digression with a whole litany of Bigres: 'Et moi, je vous dirai: Bigre, Bigre, Bigre; pourquoi ne s'appellerait-on pas Bigre? C'est, comme le disait à un officier son général le grand Condé, qu'il y a un fier Bigre, comme Bigre le charron, un bon Bigre, comme vous et moi, de plats Bigres comme une infinité d'autres.'

This page seems to me to show an ambiguity characteristic of

Diderot's attitude to the peasant world in his novel. On the one hand, it is seen as the world of nature, where funny names are of no importance, a world of happy sexuality which we can compare with the Tahiti of the *Supplément* (in which the *grivois* tone of Jacques is not absent). To look at this world is like looking back in time, and it is significant that this part of the book is set under the twin patronage of those writers of the good old days, Rabelais and Montaigne. If we compare these country people, with their simple joys and sorrows (Jacques's Justine is not Sade's), with the members of the privileged social groups who appear in the novel, we see again the contrast between the world of Tahiti and the mixed-up Parisian world of *Ceci n'est pas un conte* and *Madame de la Carlière* (this trilogy was written not long before *Jacques*, as indeed was *Les Deux Amis*). Madame de La Pommeraye is only the most prominent example among many of a person who suffers because of the codes imposed on behaviour by civilized society and its members. Monogamy, unjust laws, religious vows, private property and military honour take their toll of the various nobles, bourgeois, soldiers and clerics, and indeed of Jacques's master, whose noble affair involves him in a sordid world of blackmail and prostitution.

Similarly Diderot, who was not always a great admirer of popular culture, has Jacques quote with approval the wisdom of the people embodied in the Fable of the Knife and the Sheaf — 'une vieille fable des écraignes de mon village', says Jacques. Or again, Jacques has words of praise for the warmheartedness of the common people (perhaps not the peasants here) at public executions. We seem to hear the same populist (or Rousseauist) message as in *Les Deux Amis*: simple and poor people are more likely than their social superiors to display the natural virtues of love, generosity and solidarity.

However, all this takes us some way from Dame Suzon and the little curate perched on the pitchfork. It has to be said that whatever nostalgia Diderot felt for a happier rustic state, his treatment of the peasants, in the later part of *Jacques* at least, tends to reduce them (as they were so often reduced) to the role of charming but unreflecting children. The Fable of the Knife and the Sheath is described as 'gaie', and Jacques's amours are funny stories. *Les Deux Amis* is different, but none of the peasant figures in the novel can be given the status of a Madame de La Pommeraye, who struck Schiller as sublime. If Jacques is more than a match for his master, it is because he has risen in the world. 'Se dépopulariser et se rendre meilleur, c'est la même chose'.

I have indicated some of the different ways in which Diderot reacted as a writer to one aspect (but a dominant one) of the French society of his day. It is not surprising that this reaction is a divided one. He is pulled in opposite directions. One can see how certain literary topoi (moral declamation, sublime simplicity, rustic comedy) guide his writing; one can see too how at different times, whether in his work as Encyclopedist, his visits to Langres or his talks with Catherine of Russia, he was brought to reflect more seriously on the condition of the peasants. It is not a criticism of the *philosophe* to say that one is aware above all of the distance that separates even this well-intentioned and intelligent commoner from the majority of the French population. The character of Jacques – peasant, valet, story-teller and philosopher – allows him to bridge the gap a little, to fill in some of the space between the sublime and the grotesque. In the end though, Diderot is like Grégoire's *notables*, interested and sympathetic, but living in another world. He retains a rather abstract solidarity with the peasants, but seems irremediably different from them – as most writers have been ever since.

11

ENLIGHTENED PRIMITIVISM

The Enlightenment is usually taken to be a progressive movement, devoted to the values of modern commercial society, turning its back on an obscurantist and primitive past in the search for a new era of material well-being and rational social organization. Yet it is notorious that the same period is also one in which a new esteem is accorded to more primitive forms of society and art: the noble savage, the folk bard, the Spartan citizen. Nor is this simply a reaction on the part of the enemies of enlightenment. We saw the modern Perrault giving new life to the ancient, irrational world of the folk-tale; by the same token, it is often the same people who are attracted both by the advanced values of the *Encyclopédie* and by the myths of ancient simplicity. Primitivism seems paradoxically to be a constituent part of the Enlightenment. The aim of this chapter is to discuss the significance of this enlightened primitivism in the writings of a small number of philosophers and moralists on either side of the Channel.[1]

To do this I should like to concentrate on two small countries, Geneva and Scotland. In 1750 Geneva was independent, though much influenced by France; Scotland, on the other hand, was governed from London, but was actively defending or re-creating its cultural identity, partly perhaps as an alternative to the political autonomy lost with the Union of 1707.[2] If the eighteenth century saw the advance of what contemporaries called commercial society at the expense of older modes of social organization, then both Switzerland and Scotland, though in some respects more 'advanced' than their large neighbours, could also figure as the mountainous refuges of old values and customs under threat from corrupt modern civilization. One might therefore expect the hackneyed opposition of the primitive and the refined, the rude and the polite, to take on a sharper edge in these societies. In the period between the publication of those two pillars of modern society, the French *Encyclopédie* and the *Encyclopaedia Britannica*, the debate on such issues passed to and fro between

Switzerland, France, Scotland and England. What were the politics and rhetoric of primitivism in these different environments?

My starting point must be the man who called himself simply the Citizen of Geneva.³ Living in Paris, Jean-Jacques Rousseau achieved fame with two discourses written for a polite French academy (that of Dijon): the first on the corrupting effect of the 'sciences and the arts', the second on the origins of the flagrant inequality of modern society. The discourses (particularly the former) are paradoxes, as contemporaries understood the word: the opposite of *doxa* or received opinion. Or perhaps it would be truer to speak of a preference for the less obvious of received opinions, for Rousseau's attack on modern corruption is to be placed in a long and powerful tradition, as are his idealized images of more primitive ways of life.⁴

Original or not, Rousseau was certainly influential in suggesting that the savage was to be preferred to the shopkeeper. Indeed he was widely misread as being more of a primitivist than he really was. Voltaire thanked him for his second discourse by saying, not without irony: 'On n'a jamais tant employé d'esprit à vouloir nous rendre bêtes. Il prend envie de marcher à quatre pattes quand on lit votre ouvrage'.⁵ But Rousseau did not really propose a 'return to nature'. The crucial Note 9 in the *Discours sur l'inégalité* compares the lot of 'l'homme sauvage' and 'l'homme civil', showing the life of the latter as a constant train of conflict and misery, whereas 'l'homme sauvage, quand il a dîné, est en paix avec toute la nature, et l'ami de tous ses semblables' (III, 203). But what lesson can we learn from this? 'Faut-il détruire les sociétés, anéantir le tien et le mien, et retourner vivre dans les forêts avec les ours?' (III, 207). No, says Rousseau, this is a parody of his thought ('conséquence à la manière de mes adversaires'); his own conclusion is much more measured and pessimistic. The ills of civilized man come from the institution of society itself, and this is irreversible. All that can be done, therefore, is to make the best of society, respecting its laws and using all the opportunities it offers to live a life of virtue. Later, in such works as *Emile, Du contrat social, La Nouvelle Héloïse*, and his political writings for Corsica and Poland, Rousseau was to propose ways in which enlightened social man can attempt to recover some of the advantages of the primitive independent state, without losing the benefits of the social state.

What he does, therefore, in the two discourses and elsewhere, is to paint tantalizing pictures of the lost state, a vanished paradise. The pictures serve firstly to expose the competitive complexities of commercial society. In the note I have just referred to, many of the ills of 'l'homme civil' are specifically associated with technical and economic progress. Agriculture and metallurgy were seen in the body of the discourse as the real agents of the enslavement of mankind; in this note Rousseau widens his attack to include the many branches of a commerce 'où la raison de chaque particulier lui dicte des maximes directement contraires à celles que la raison publique prêche au corps de la société, et où chacun trouve son compte dans le malheur d'autrui' (III, 202). His black tableau includes the grain merchants for whom a good harvest is a disaster, the arms salesmen, the fabricators of adulterated food, and all those whose profits come from the crippling work of mines and factories. Such evil trades flourish as a result of the growth of unnecessary needs in commercial society.

What then is the primitive state which is here set against such corruption? It is easy to be confused about this. Sometimes Rousseau writes of natural man, sometimes of the savage. But whereas all natural men are savages, not all savages are natural men. The first part of the *Discours sur l'inégalité* is devoted to images of a state of nature which preceded the establishment of society, a state in which solitary men and women wandered over the earth still 'abandonnée à sa fertilité naturelle, et couverte de forêts immenses que la Cognée ne mutila jamais' (III, 135). The image of green fertility makes this an appealing picture, but Rousseau does not disguise the fact that the state he is describing is a hypothetical one, 'un état qui n'existe plus, qui n'a peut-être point existé, et qui probablement n'existera jamais' (III, 123). Naturally then, he tends to shift his ground from this pure state of nature to that of the 'savages' who had been discovered in various parts of the world in the voyages of discovery of the preceding three centuries. For Rousseau, these people were no longer in the state of nature, since they all lived in societies, but being empirically attested, they provided a more telling illustration of the advantages of a primitive state. So, for instance, speaking of the superiority of natural man's sight, hearing and smell, he slides easily into a reference to early social man, the Hottentots of the Cape of Good Hope, who could see as well with the naked eye as the Dutch with their telescopes (III, 141).

In fact, apart from the first part of the *Discours sur l'inégalité*, Rousseau's pictures of a better, ruder state are almost always taken from existing examples of society, which are no longer in the state of nature, but are supposedly nearer to it than modern civilization. The *Discours* propounds a theory of social evolution which has something in common with the four-stage theory of the Scottish philosopher – historians, and at various points in his writing Rousseau highlights different moments in this process.[6] Thus the second part of the *Discours* includes a contradictory eulogy of what Adam Ferguson was to call the 'savage' state. This is already marred by the growth of self-love, competitiveness and aggression, which are inseparable from society, but even so it seems to have been the happiest and most durable stage in human history: 'L'exemple des sauvages qu'on a presque tous trouvés à ce point semble confirmer que le genre humain était fait pour y rester toujours, que cet état est la véritable jeunesse du monde' (III, 171).

It is of the same stage, one presumes, that Rousseau had written with equal nostalgia in the *Discours sur les sciences et les arts*: 'On ne peut réfléchir sur les mœurs, qu'on ne se plaise à se rappeler l'image de la simplicité des premiers temps. C'est un beau rivage, paré des seules mains de la nature, vers lequel on tourne incessamment les yeux, et dont on se sent éloigner à regret' (III, 22). 'Dont on se sent éloigner à regret': the verbs suggest a gradual, inexorable process, the ship carried off on the sea of history away from the original paradise, and it seems that Rousseau's efforts, here and in similarly eloquent passages, are directed at evoking in his enlightened readers an agonized sense of loss, lost happiness and lost innocence. The human race is seized by a movement which carries it too far forward, over-shooting the point where happiness might still be found. Sometimes, as on the first page of *Emile*, he seems to accept this movement,[7] but his usual desire is to halt the process. And this being so, since he was writing not for savages but for members of modern societies, it is natural that his lost paradises are more usually not among savages but in more developed states which might nevertheless be thought to share some of the virtues of tribal society.

Rousseau likes to refer to the simpler societies of antiquity, above all Sparta, 'cette cité aussi célèbre par son heureuse ignorance que par la sagesse de ses lois, cette république de demi-dieux plutôt que d'hommes' (III, 12). There is also the deliberately created rural paradise of *La Nouvelle Héloïse* and the simple world of *Emile*, for the child offers the perpetually new chance of regaining the happiness of the primitive state. These are the distant past and the imagined future, but there are also scenes from contemporary life, islands of simpler, if not exactly primitive, life. Rousseau's own existence offered some of these, notably the Ile de Saint-Pierre, where he could mimic the wise idleness of the unthinking savage. But as he says, such joys are fundamentally anti-social, and can only be allowed to a man cut off from active life by persecution. More often his pictures of rude simplicity show us those small old-fashioned societies which retained some of the good qualities lost in large-scale commercial society. While happiness is still a basic value, the stress in such cases is placed rather on virtue. Here the primitivist urge feeds into what has become known as the civic humanist tradition.

Corsica was one such society. Having said in *Du contrat social* that this island, fighting for its independence against the Genoese, was perhaps the only country in the world still capable of truly democratic government, Rousseau was invited by his Corsican admirer Buttafuoco to propose a constitution for the Corsicans. He responded with a plan, the whole thrust of which was to preserve the rude virtue of the islanders, to prevent them falling prey to the enervating effects of commerce. At the same period Rousseau's Scottish admirer James Boswell went to Corsica in search of ancient virtue, found it, and described it in his *Journal of a Tour to Corsica*, where a combination of savage and classical imagery is used to whip up British support for the cause of the modern Themistocles, Paoli.[8]

Nearer home than Corsica was Rousseau's native city, Geneva, the city of which he painted such a flattering image in the dedication to his *Discours sur l'inégalité*. Viewed optimistically, Geneva was an example to the modern world (and notably to France) of ancient simplicity and virtue. In the eighteenth century it was also a major centre of enlightenment, home of scholars, learned ministers of religion, and pirate publishers.[9] Traditional civic and religious values were married here with liberal enquiry and commercial expansion; the city belonged both to the old world and to the new. Rousseau himself, the expatriate citizen, who had thrown in his lot with the new (Diderot's *Encyclopédie*, the deism of *Emile*) wanted his native land to move no further along the road to modernity. In particular, in his *Lettre à d'Alembert*, he urged it to resist the temptation of that symbol of modern urban society, the theatre.

This is not the place to rehearse Rousseau's arguments against the theatre. What matter for my present purposes are his evocations of earlier, simpler manners. The first of these is that of the Montagnons, a peasant community outside Neuchâtel which he had briefly glimpsed in his youth. It reads now like a parody of an old-style American ideal. On a broad hillside each household occupies a roughly equal lot of land, where they all live lives of virtuous independence and self-sufficiency. Each man is his own locksmith and his own musician. They do have books, presumably written by outsiders in some cases at least, but this is almost the only intrusion of the larger world into their primitive autarky. What Rousseau does then is to imagine the effects, economic, social and moral, of the establishment of a theatre in this little world – and the same lesson will be repeated on a larger scale for Geneva. For the theatre is a symbol *par excellence* of polite society. Not only is it immoral in ways that had long been exposed to the censure of the church, but it also intensifies various undesirable features of modern city life: conspicuous consumption, confusion of male and female roles, unhealthy indoor living, and so on. Against such things Rousseau sets the almost mythical Montagnons, and also the old-style communal meetings of Geneva, whether it be the *cercles* (drinking for the men, sewing and chat for the women), the public balls, or the large-scale festivities which he sees (as his revolutionary disciples did some years later) as a potent social bonding mechanism.

Underlying all the details of Rousseau's case against the theatre is his hostility to the 'progressive' values of his former friends the Encyclopedists. The *Lettre à d'Alembert* is of course a reply to the article 'Genève' in the *Encyclopédie*, in which d'Alembert, acting as mouthpiece for Voltaire, had expressed surprise that the sophisticated Genevans still lacked a theatre. At the time of writing the *Lettre*, Rousseau had just broken with Diderot, editor of the *Encyclopédie* and a great believer in the social and moral importance of the theatre; this is no doubt one reason why his diatribe against modern manners has the sarcastic virulence of a recent convert. Not that he could be entirely opposed to the commercial society of which the *Encyclopédie* is the champion; indeed he makes the point that Geneva, having little in the way of natural resources, has to make its living by industry and commerce and that the theatre would deflect its people from the hard work necessary for economic survival. Sparta may figure as a model from time to time, but Rousseau has to admit that Geneva is no Sparta. Nor is he particularly optimistic about the future: 'Il ne faut point le dissimuler, les intentions sont droites encore; mais les mœurs inclinent déjà visiblement vers la décadence, et nous suivons de loin les traces des mêmes peuples dont nous ne laissons pas de craindre le sort.'[10]

In the light of such gloomy forecasts, the point of the eloquent evocations of the simple Montagnons or the Genevan *fêtes* is to awaken in the reader the desire to put a brake on the movement of progress. Is this an anti-Enlightenment position? Perhaps, if we identify the Enlightenment with the advance of commerce and refinement. But I think it would be truer to see in Rousseau's championing of older forms of society a defence of the values of humanity and citizenship which are central to a great deal of Enlightenment thinking – or perhaps, in the terms of Chapter 4 above, a plea for a new kind of politeness. The debate about rudeness and refinement was not a debate for or against the Enlightenment, but was internal to it.

The representation of 'rude virtue' clearly also meets a personal need of Rousseau's: to re-create in the imagination a world where he could be a happy member of the community. He had left Geneva for Paris, he had hobnobbed with tax-farmers, academicians, and Encyclopedists (representatives of the triumphant new world). He knew that there was no going back for him personally, any more than for the societies which had fallen victim to the corruptions of modernity. The eloquence which so impressed his first readers in his discourses and his subsequent works is fuelled by the knowledge that his ideal world is a lost world. Thus in *La Nouvelle Héloïse* the artificial charms and real miseries of Paris are set off against the crude but good life of the mountain people of Switzerland. The hero Saint-Preux writes: 'J'aurais passé tout le temps de mon voyage dans le seul enchantement du paysage, si je n'en eusse éprouvé un plus doux encore dans le commerce des habitants' (II, 79). Theirs is the simpler world that Rousseau longs for and that he re-creates time and again in his books: the only place of reconciliation.

It would be wrong, however, to see his representation of simpler social states merely as a reflection of his own personal predicament. The crucial point to be made here (and it serves to differentiate him from Diderot for instance) is that his primitivism, if indeed that is the word for it, is not only personal and moral but also political, a product of his historical situation. In the struggles that divided Geneva in the eighteenth century, Rousseau was on the side of the mass of the citizens against the patrician minority; his attack on the theatre is a defence of popular values against a Francophile elite. Eighteenth-century Geneva was no primitive community, but by linking it with Sparta and with the Montagnons, if not with the world of savages, he was setting the virtuous republic against its neighbour, the polite and corrupt monarchy of France. In this respect his critique of commercial society may be seen as comparable to that of certain Scots, especially Adam Ferguson.

The two *Discours* created a lasting image of Rousseau the eloquent enemy of polite society and defender of more primitive ways, the Diogenes of our time. This is how he was most often seen, admired, imitated, and refuted in England and in Scotland.[11] Scotland in the second half of the eighteenth century was undergoing a cultural revolution; in the century following the Union of 1707, this small poor country, which had lost its political independence, moved rapidly into the modern commercial world. Indeed, the loss of independence was a condition of the new prosperity, as the Edinburgh *literati* were well aware. But Scotland was more than the Enlightenment of Edinburgh and Glasgow. Since 1745 the Highlands had been the scene of a large-scale repression of a native population, who appeared like the representatives of a vanished world.[12] Scotland, more dramatically than Geneva, was poised between the 'rude' and the 'refined' states of society. The Highlands struck visitors from the South such as Samuel Johnson as a truly barbarous country, but one in which the old ways were being rapidly superseded, not necessarily for the good, by the values and habits of commercial society.[13] It is not surprising therefore that Rousseau's themes of corrupt civilization and lost virtue and happiness found an echo in the enlightened home of the *Encyclopaedia Britannica*.

His views on natural man, for instance, were enthusiastically adopted by Lord Monboddo, who showed a great interest in the earliest attested states of the human species and went one step further than the *Discours sur l'inégalité* by presenting the orang-utan as a kind of human being: 'a whole nation, if I many call them so, without the use of speech'.[14] Naturally, if not necessarily, this interest was accompanied by praise of the savage state. Boswell notes amusingly in his *Journal* how Monboddo, playing the part of country squire in his remote and uncouth estate, defends the Rousseauist line against Johnson: 'My lord and Dr Johnson disputed a little, whether the savage or the London shopkeeper had the best existence; his lordship, as usual, preferring the savage' (p. 210). It will be noted that the puny representative of the modern world is a shopkeeper; like Rousseau, Monboddo saw the development of commercial society as a decline from the republics of antiquity. This degeneration was visible in language; Latin and Greek showed a progress over the monotonous and excessively figurative language of barbarians, but the modern languages were barbarous compared with the perhaps more primitive classical tongues.

Monboddo is a rather eccentric figure; it is more interesting to see how some of the central figures of the Scottish Enlightenment viewed the relation between politeness and rudeness. How far were they prepared to go in setting up happier primitive states as a foil for the vices of commercial society? This is a vast question, and Hume, Smith, Millar and Ferguson (to name only a few of the outstanding figures) were far from speaking with one voice on it. Hume, in his essay entitled 'Of Refinement in the Arts' and in the first pages of the essay 'Of Commerce', sees nothing but good in the rise of modern

industry and trade and the development of city life; these have in-
creased the individual's security as well as the general sociability and
'humanity'. Adam Smith, despite his reputation as the champion of
laissez-faire economics, is more ambiguous. In his letter of 1755 to
the first *Edinburgh Review*, he presented the newly published *Discours
sur l'inégalité* as a more palatable development of Mandeville's cynical
Fable of the Bees, and in his own writing from time to time one finds
something of Jean-Jacques's historical pessimism. Thus, like the
Rousseau of the first *Discours*, he speaks of the loss of vigour, independence and martial spirit in the overspecialized worker produced
by the division of labour: 'The torpor of his mind renders him not
only incapable of relishing or bearing a part in any rational conversation, but of conceiving any generous, noble, or tender sentiment,
and consequently of forming any just judgement concerning many
even of the ordinary duties of private life.'[15] Elsewhere one hears a
note closer to that of the *Discours sur l'inégalité*. Even though commerce is seen as engendering greater freedom than previous modes
of production, Smith shows the inequality and oppression bred of
early capitalism:

In a civilized society the poor provide both for themselves and for the
enormous luxury of their superiors. [...] In a society of an hundred thousand
families, there will perhaps be one hundred who don't labour at all, and yet,
either by violence, or by the orderly oppression of law, employ a greater
part of the labour of the society than any other ten thousand in it. [...] On
the contrary those who labour most get least.[16]

But this page is immediately followed by a reminder of the 'superior
affluence and abundance commonly possessed even by this lowest and
most despised member of civilized society, compared with what the
most respected and active savage can attain to'. Smith's aim is not,
like Rousseau's, to set his readers dreaming of a happier state. It is
true that Book V of *The Wealth of Nations* suggests ways in which
earlier states in society may have had the advantage over commercial
society, but Smith does not paint these in alluring colours, nor is
there any sense that he is writing out of a sense of personal loss, as
Rousseau did.

    Similar notes of caution about the appropriate limits to 'improve-
ment' are to be heard in John Millar's *Origin of Ranks*, but for
something closer to Rousseau's out-and-out praise of more primitive
societies we must look to Adam Ferguson and his *Essay on the History
of Civil Society*, first published in 1767. It is true that Ferguson more
than once criticizes the *Discours sur l'inégalité*; indeed his book opens

with a fine demolition of the whole idea of the state of nature. Since man's nature is progressive, the 'passing stream' not the 'stagnating pool', it is vain to seek an original 'natural' state: 'If the palace be unnatural, the cottage is so no less; and the highest refinements of political and moral apprehension, are not more artificial in their kind, than the first operations of sentiment and reason' (p. 8).[17] This being so, the task of the philosopher, moralist or historian is to observe as accurately as possible the societies that are empirically known to us. Only such comparisons will allow us to know something of human nature, and perhaps to form judgements about the best ways of living. Ferguson preaches a splendid relativism which is rare in his times; some of his remarks read like anticipations of modern anthropology: 'Addicted to their own pursuits, and considering their own condition as the standard of human felicity, all nations pretend to the preference, and in their practice give sufficient proof of sincerity.' It follows that we may well be mistaken in our estimate of the happiness produced by a given social order. The apparently dirty, violent and insecure life of the savage or the barbarian may offer joys which civilized man cannot appreciate, and the savage, when offered the choice, 'droops and [...] pines in the streets of the populous city' and 'seeks the frontier and the forest' (p. 95).

Ferguson then, while adopting a scheme of history quite like the four-stage theory, does not subordinate this to any global assumptions about the superiority of either the 'rude' or the 'refined' state. His comparative picture of different societies is based on the normal sources available to his contemporaries: classical literature and modern travel books. In addition, since Ferguson was born on the Highland line, it is to be supposed that he made use of his first-hand observation of Scotland. Drawing on such sources, and spurred on by his concern for the health of his own society, he was led, like Rousseau, to present various primitive societies in an advantageous light.

The second part of his *Civil Society* is entitled 'Of the History of Rude Nations'. These are divided into two categories, the 'savage' and the 'barbarous', the former being mainly hunters and fishers who are 'not yet acquainted with property', the latter corresponding roughly to Smith's second and third stages of history, the pastoral and the agricultural. Both have their drawbacks and both their merits. In describing them, Ferguson is often led into something approaching Rousseau's eloquence, though his writing rarely has the nostalgic fervour of the Citizen of Geneva.

Dealing with the 'savage', he draws heavily on the recent accounts of North American Indians by Charlevoix, Lafitau, Colden and others. The picture is attractive; there are shadows, but they are easily outweighed by the light. Ferguson notes, for instance, that the male Indians confine themselves to warlike activities, leaving the economy to the women; this is 'a servitude, and a continual toil', but is to be preferred to actual slavery:

If in this destination of the sexes, while the men continue to indulge themselves in the contempt of sordid and mercenary arts, the cruel establishment of slavery is for some ages deferred; if in this tender, though unequal alliance, the affections of the heart prevent the severities practised on slaves, we have in the custom itself, as perhaps in many other instances, reason to prefer the first suggestions of nature to many of her after refinements.   (p. 83)

This is faint praise, damning by implication more modern developments (it may be compared with Rousseau's preference of Spartan slavery to modern despotism). But there are passages where Ferguson's tone is much warmer. This is particularly noticeable when he speaks of the sociability, the independence, and the martial qualities of the Indians. 'They are', he says, 'affectionate in their carriage, and in their conversations pay a mutual attention and regard [...] more tender and more engaging, than what we profess in the ceremonial of polished societies' (p. 88). As for their warlike qualities, 'the foundations of honour are eminent abilities and great fortitude, not the distinctions of equipage and fortune'. In his picture of these warriors, Ferguson rises to a hymn of praise:

They can, accordingly, trace a wild beast, or the human foot, over many leagues of pathless forest, and find their way across a woody and uninhabited continent, by means of refined observations which escape the traveller who has been accustomed to different aids. They steer in slender canoes, across stormy seas, with a dexterity equal to that of the most experienced pilot. They carry a penetrating eye for the thoughts and intentions of those with whom they have to deal; and when they mean to deceive, they cover themselves with arts which the most subtle can seldom elude. They harangue in their public councils with a nervous and figurative elocution; and conduct themselves in the management of their treaties with a perfect discernment of their national interests.   (p. 89)

This very male-centred celebration is in the great tradition that leads from Montaigne to Fenimore Cooper, and it is repeated or mocked in innumerable fictions throughout the eighteenth century.[18] It is echoed too in Rousseau's ideal education for a boy. But it is perhaps more unexpected that Ferguson finds subjects for praise in the nations he calls barbarous. Here, to be sure, there is a decline from the original

197

independence of mankind. If the first stage is 'on the eve of creating republics', the barbarous stage 'seems to exhibit the rudiments of monarchical government', and may well involve slavery: 'It is in this woeful condition that mankind, being slavish, interested, insidious, deceitful, and bloody, bear marks, if not of the least curable, surely of the most lamentable sort of corruption' (p. 103). Barbarians are fierce, vainglorious and predatory. Yet 'even under this description mankind are generous and hospitable to strangers, as well as kind, affectionate and gentle in their domestic society' (p. 101). And although 'we are generally at a loss to conceive how mankind can subsist under customs and manners extremely different from our own', Ferguson argues that 'we are apt to exaggerate the misery of barbarous times, by an imagination of what we ourselves should suffer in a situation to which we are not accustomed' (p. 105).

The strongest praise of barbarism is implied in a striking ironic set piece in Part IV. Here Ferguson imagines how an unprejudiced visitor from a more 'polished' society might have described the ancient Greeks. His traveller notes the insecurity and discomfort of life, the despicable smallness of the petty kingdoms, the lack of money, and the inadequate clothing of the natives: 'they come abroad barefooted, and without any cover to the head, wrapped up in the coverlets under which you would imagine they had slept' (rather like the Highlanders, one might add). And the traveller, having been informed of the high reputation of these people, remarks 'that he could not understand how scholars, fine gentlemen, and even women, should combine to admire a people, who so little resemble themselves' (p. 197). There is a fine paradoxicality about this passage, reminiscent of Nietzsche. Ferguson follows Lafitau, who had insisted on the similarity between the savages of North America and the Greeks of antiquity; his work chimes in well with the growing tendency to see Homer as a primitive. Compared with the barbarians, the inhabitants of modern commercial society appear selfish, pampered and degenerate.[19]

Indeed a good deal of Ferguson's account, like Rousseau's *Discours*, is devoted to the typically eighteenth-century notion of corruption. Using images of earlier societies as a foil, he argues once again that the division of labour reduces human beings to functions, and that the cash nexus loosens social bonds and diminishes the patriotic and warlike spirit. It is striking how much of his account of corruption is couched in military terms. He had been a chaplain in the Black Watch, and had been present at the battle of Fontenoy. In the 1760s, along with many of the Edinburgh *literati*, he was a vigorous advocate of a citizens' militia in Scotland, a passion he shared with the Rousseau of the *Lettre à d'Alembert* – though not with Adam Smith, who argued that in modern societies militias had no future against professional armies.

Ferguson's arguments for a militia are in fact not so much military as social. A militia is good for relations between members of a community, but it may not be the best form of national defence. He notes, twenty years after Culloden, that 'with all this ferocity of spirit, the rude nations of the West were subdued by the policy and more regular warfare of the Romans' (p. 106). And as one reads this, thinking of the place and date of composition, one cannot help wondering how much one should read through the images of savage, barbarous and ancient nations to the recent history of Scotland, where a ferocious and rude nation (as it seemed to contemporaries) had indeed been subdued (to put it mildly) by the 'regular warfare' of their more 'polished' neighbours. In Rousseau's writings the defence of more primitive ways is overtly connected with Geneva; how much should we see in the *Civil Society* a meditation on the recent history of Scotland?

It is hard to answer this question. The Scottish historians are rightly thought of as cosmopolitan, and Ferguson does not openly relate his argument to domestic concerns. He was, however, a Gaelic speaker, and he came from the edge of the Highlands. He was no Jacobite, but had witnessed the tragic aftermath of 1745. He was an Enlightenment figure, but his divided attitude to progress and politeness seems characteristic of his culture; it is expressed in a more memorable way in Scott's *Waverley*.[20] If Adam Smith can find kind words for the hospitality and valour of the Highlanders, then surely Ferguson, with his ready praise of the savage and the barbarian, must have found them worthy of admiration. But all this has to be read between the lines.[21]

If Ferguson's primitivism is a reflection of Scottish concerns, what then is the lesson for Scotland? It is here that we see the crucial difference between him and Rousseau. Where the Genevan writes with the fervent desire to halt the march of progress, the transformation of his native city into another Paris, Ferguson seems reconciled to the changes that Scotland has undergone. Polite, commercial society is here to stay, and it has obvious advantages.[22] Nor does it mean inevitable corruption, for the individual can always draw on his or her (but mainly his) inner resources and live a life of Stoic virtue: 'men of real fortitude, integrity, and ability, are well placed in every scene' (p. 280). This life of virtue is no doubt made easier by the contemplation of the more primitive societies which are presented so eloquently in parts of the *Civil Society*, but there is no future in the rejection of commercial society as such.

One aspect of primitive societies which Ferguson praises is their poetry. He is of course in no way original in writing in 1767 that 'when we attend to the language which savages employ on any solemn occasion, it appears that man is a poet by nature' (p. 172). The priority of poetry over prose was an opinion shared by Diderot, Condillac and Rousseau in the 1740s and it is spelled out, with the appropriate nostalgia, in Rousseau's *Essai sur l'origine des langues*. Like his contemporaries, Ferguson was a devotee of the primitive Homer, whose superiority appeared to derive from the simplicity of his society. In his view, the primitive poet possessed by nature the 'elegant propriety and just elevation' which becomes the difficult ambition of those who live in a society divided by rank and profession. So 'the artless song of the savage, the heroic legend of the bard, have some- times a magnificent beauty, which no change of language can im- prove, and no refinements of the critic reform' (p. 173).

It is not surprising then that Ferguson was one of the Edinburgh *literati* who backed James Macpherson in his re-creation of the nobly primitive Ossian. Ossian does not figure openly in the *Civil Society* any more than do the Highlanders, but he was surely not far from the author's mind when he wrote the lines quoted above. It is to Ferguson's friend Hugh Blair, however, that we must turn for a full treatment of the virtues of primitive poetry. And in Blair too we find the marriage of primitivism and enlightenment. The Ossianic poems were lauded not by the enemies of improvement, but by some of the central figures of the Enlightenment, whether in Edinburgh or in Paris.

Blair, the first Professor of Rhetoric and Belles Lettres at the University of Edinburgh, was no enemy of politeness. He spoke in his *Lectures* of 'that immense superiority which education and im- provement give to civilized, above barbarous nations', and equally above the 'rude and untaught vulgar'. But there may be loss as well as gain. Like Rousseau, Blair talks of the youth and old age of the world, and of the move from a primitive poetic eloquence to a more mundane plainness. He quotes the standard examples of primitive sublimity (Homer above all) and even gives an extract from a Red Indian harangue. This is 'figurative to excess' — in other words, childishly vulgar — and a long way from the 'natural and unaffected, easy and polite' style of the *Spectator*.[23] Even so, it too deserves our admiration.

How much more so the poems of Ossian! Like the stories which Perrault wrote down, these had supposedly come down from a primitive age in the speech and song of the 'untaught vulgar'. For Blair they were indeed the expression of a time when 'the face of rude nature' was not yet obscured by the 'refinements of society', and they owed their force to this. But it is worth noting that he contrasts the poems of Ossian with the old Scandinavian poetry which was being discovered at the same time. If the latter is a 'savage desert', the former is a 'fertile and cultivated country'.[24] The Ossianic poems may be 'abrupt' and even 'uncouth', but (not surprisingly given the circumstances of their discovery) they are also correct and in good taste. The reason Blair gives for this is not that they have been translated by an eighteenth-century Scot for an enlightened public, but that they were composed by a princely bard living in a great age before the Highlands declined into barbarity and ignorance (there is no continuous process of improvement here).

What we see in Blair's treatment of Ossian is the attempt to marry the primitive with the best of the modern. In the same way, Rousseau's Montagnons may not be highly civilized, but they are cultured (to use a distinction much beloved of a later period). And in Year II of the Revolution, Abbé Grégoire was similarly to speak of the proper language of free men, occupying a middle position between the powdered frivolity of aristocratic speech and the crude vulgarity of popular talk.[25] It is not possible to return to the ways of savage or barbarous societies, but it may be possible to draw inspiration from them, whether in morals (Ferguson) or in poetry (Blair).

At the same time, it seems that with Ossian (if not with Rousseau's Genevans) there is the characteristic move of modern society to consign its past to the museum. Since 1707 Scotland had lost its political independence. Ossian helped to provide cosmopolitan and progressive Scotland with a national identity, an identity rooted in a heroic past which placed Scotland on a par with Greece. In 1745, the wild Highlanders had struck fear into the hearts of the English and many of the Scots. By 1760, these primitives no longer presented a threat; they had been subdued and scattered, their social system had been dislocated, their weapons removed, and even the wearing of national costume was forbidden. At the same time, the *literati* of Edinburgh, followed by those of London, Paris and the rest of Europe, were enthralled by the melancholy grandeur of their poetry, which laments the passing of a heroic age.[26] Few of their enthusiastic readers would seriously have wished for the return of this lost past. The poems of Ossian are like an Indian reservation in European culture, and they are at the origin of the modern taste for the wild but unprofitable scenery of the depopulated Highlands.

In Rousseau, Ferguson and Blair, therefore, enlightenment and primitivism are plaited together in varying patterns. The Genevan is more eloquent than the Scots in his pictures of primitive virtue and happiness, for the subject is closer to his personal feelings of loss and desire. Even he, however, is no simple primitivist. There is also a modern Rousseau, the deist of the *Profession de foi*, the democratic theorist of *Du contrat social*. In different proportions, one finds the same combination in many of his contemporaries in Britain and France, the most notable case being Diderot, editor of the progressive *Encyclopédie*, translator of Ossian, and author of some of the most eloquent pages on the happiness of savage life and the discontents of civilization.[27]

Others, such as Hume or Voltaire, seem much more immune to the lure of the wild. Are we to say that these apostles of commercial society and critical philosophy are the true Enlightenment figures, and that in the other cases I have presented the praise of the primitive should be understood as a corrective to the excesses of Enlightenment reason? Or perhaps we should regard Ferguson, Rousseau and Diderot as caught in a contradiction? This does indeed seem to be true of Diderot at times: the final pages of his *Supplément au Voyage de Bougainville* show a writer torn between dream and reality, and his contributions to Raynal's *Histoire des deux Indes*, when brought together in the *Pensées détachées*, leap alarmingly from declamations about the joys of simple life to hymns of praise to commerce.

That is one way of looking at it, but there is another. In Diderot's writings, as in those of many of his contemporaries on both sides of the Channel, the savage and barbarian are often spokesmen of un-prejudiced reason. True enlightenment, in this view, will lead towards the primitive as well as away from it. Indeed, it is possible to envisage an ideal meeting point, as Diderot does in his texts for Raynal: 'Dans tous les siècles à venir, l'homme sauvage s'avancera pas à pas vers l'état civilisé. L'homme civilisé reviendra vers son état primitif; d'où le philosophe conclura qu'il existe dans l'intervalle qui les sépare un point où réside la félicité de l'espèce' (*Pensées détachées*, p. 141). As with Rousseau, it is the elusive mirage of a middle ground betwen the really primitive and the injustice and corruption of modern commercial societies. Many primitive societies exhibit the qualities and virtues that enlightened reason teaches us to value, even if the abuse of reason saps the exercise of these virtues. Paradoxically, enlighten-ment may lead us to see the merit of unenlightened states.

Enlightened primitivism

Finally, the examples of Rousseau and Ferguson point to the particular significance of primitivism in two small countries, both of them increasingly modern and cosmopolitan in the eighteenth century, but both conscious of a proud national identity. We can see in these writings a prefiguration of some characteristic problems of our own time, and in particular the need to preserve regional identity while lessening regional inequality. Rousseau's appeal to the primitive is a contribution to the international Enlightenment in the *Emile*, but elsewhere, and most clearly in the *Lettre à d'Alembert*, it is an urgent warning to Geneva not to go too far along the road taken by its more refined and corrupt neighbour. Ferguson is cooler, and less openly nationalist, but in his writing too one senses the desire to preserve in 'improved' society the older values which he may have seen embodied, then destroyed, in the Highlands. In both writers, as in their contemporaries, these threads of enlightenment and primitivism are interwoven in a way that makes generalizations wellnigh impossible. It is not a question of one or the other, but of both at once, in varying proportions, and in different degrees of tension and harmony.

12

FRONTIERS OF CIVILIZATION

The previous chapters have suggested that the confrontation between 'rudeness' and civilization has been a constant structuring principle in the European mind. The principle has operated mainly in the minds of the 'civilized', who define their society, manners and speech by opposition to what they call savage, barbarous, uncouth. This is often the language of imperialism, the language of the victors, whether they are happy with their victory or ashamed of it. Looking at the past, we rarely see what Nathan Wachtel, in his attempt to provide an indigenous view of the conquest of South America, called 'the vision of the vanquished'.[1]

For the European, then, the savage and the barbarian are the Other — like the madman. They easily become the objects of a mythologizing representation, through which the civilized subject of discourse can express in a potent form his or her fears and desires. European writing is full of the opposition between the rational civilized self and the wild Other, and not only writing, for some of the strongest images are visual. One need only think of the Western, which classically expresses the crusading ambition to establish a garden in the desert, a secure place where families can be raised, homesteads built — and then schools, banks, railroads, law-courts and the other institutions of civilized society. This settled order is threatened by the unruly, incomprehensible forces of Indian life, which must be tamed, driven back, eliminated.

Even in the Western, however, the image of the Indian is often not simply one of horror, fear and hate. Think of John Ford's *The Searchers*, where the character played by John Wayne, an unrelenting enemy of the Indians, is shown to share many of their characteristics; he is less at home in the garden than in the desert. And often the wild can be the object of fascination and desire. As one example among many of the willing espousal of the uncivilized, one might take Jules Michelet's defence of the Barbarians. Pierre Michel has described how the myth of the barbarian was used in nineteenth-century France (and is still used) to articulate an attitude of fear and hostility to the new 'dangerous classes'.[2] Michelet, however, wrote in *Le Peuple*: 'Souvent, aujourd'hui, l'on compare l'ascension du peuple, son progrès, à l'invasion des Barbares. Le mot me plaît, je l'accepte ... *Barbares*! Oui, c'est-à-dire pleins d'une sève nouvelle, vivante et rajeunissante'.[3] The whole of *Le Peuple* is based on the call for the barbarian (typically associated with the child as well as the common people) to give new life to a deadened civilization. It is an old theme with a long history in European culture.

Ignoble and noble savage, force of destruction and force of renewal – over the centuries the ubiquitous opposition has been given different colourings. Here I shall confine myself to a period when I think it is at its most interesting: the years between about 1760 and 1840. This is a time of rapid modernization in some parts of Europe, a time marked by the extension of European rule (including the Europeans of North America) at the expense of 'primitive' peoples, and also of course the time of Romanticism. What seems to me important is that the old opposition is here seen historically. Not so much an unending battle of cowboys and Indians as the onward march of humanity, which will leave behind or destroy previous modes of social life – just as the adult supposedly leaves behind the child. The savage is thus linked with the child; all of us have been savages, and the savage is our own past.

A crucial point in these visions of mankind's progress is the assumption of inevitability. Although Rousseau laments the decline of humanity through progress, he explicitly and repeatedly asserts that the process is irreversible. What is lost is lost, even if it may be possible to create conditions which will provide benefits equivalent to those we once enjoyed. Diderot, who shared so many of Rousseau's ideas, wrote of savage people in his contributions to Raynal's *Histoire des deux Indes*:

Le destin des peuples sauvages est de s'éteindre à mesure que des nations policées viennent s'établir parmi eux [...] Avant qu'il se soit écoulé trois siècles, ils auront disparu de la terre. Alors que penseront nos descendants de cette espèce d'hommes qui ne sera plus que dans l'histoire des voyageurs? Les temps de l'homme sauvage ne seront-ils pas pour la postérité ce que sont pour nous les temps fabuleux de l'antiquité? Ne parlera-t-elle pas de lui comme nous parlons des centaures et des lapithes?[4]

The confrontation of modern civilization and wildness is usually, and perhaps best, seen in the meeting of colonizers and natives in America and Africa. But the frontier with savage or barbarian life could be found nearer home. In his great work on the Mediterranean, Fernand Braudel, quoting Jules Blache, insists on the specificity of the mountains and their backward culture; 'la vie montagnarde semble bien avoir été la première vie de la Méditerranée dont la civilisation [...] "recouvre et dissimule mal des assises pastorales", qui évoquent un monde primitif de chasseurs et d'éleveurs'.[5] So the meeting of mountain and plain is often the meeting of two stages of European history. The late eighteenth and early nineteenth centuries saw what can be called the struggle of the civilization of the plains against primitive mountain cultures in a number of parts of Europe. I shall here look briefly at three of these, Scotland, Corsica and the Caucasus, examining how some important and intelligent writers represented and exploited the unequal struggle, how they explored the reality and shaped it into the characteristic myths of triumph and tragedy. The two main literary genres for this are the travel book and the novel.

Samuel Johnson's *Journey to the Western Islands* was published in 1773.[6] It is extraordinary that this cumbersome city-dweller, hammer of the Scots and eulogist of London, should have made this difficult journey in his sixty-fourth year. That he did so, to judge from his account, was partly due to a romantic urge which one does not always associate with him. His journey was to be a voyage into the past, to see 'savage virtues and barbarous grandeur' (p. 51), 'uncouth customs that are now disused' and 'wild opinions that prevail no longer' (p. 57). In fact he hoped, nearly thirty years after Culloden, to see the Highlanders of legend, the proud, brave, untamed mountaineers whose reputation had spread through Europe. He writes: 'To the Southern inhabitants of Scotland, [and *a fortiori* of England] the state of the mountains and the islands is equally unknown with that of Borneo and Sumatra' — a point repeated in many writings of the time.

It is not surprising therefore that the Highlanders sometimes figure as savages in the account of Johnson (and equally in that of James Boswell, who accompanied him in this journey). But generally this conscientious and clear-sighted observer was disappointed in his exotic desires. He found the Highlands in a state of rapid evolution:

There was perhaps never any change of national manners so quick, so great, and so general, as that which has operated in the Highlands, by the last conquest, and the subsequent laws. We came thither too late to see what we expected, a people of peculiar appearance, and a system of antiquated life. The clans retain little now of their original character, their ferocity of temper is softened, their military ardour is extinguished, their dignity of independence is depressed, their contempt of government subdued, and the reverence for their chiefs abated. Of what they had before the late conquest of their country, there remain only their language and their poverty.   (p. 51)

There were, it is true, relics of the old ways, and Johnson relished them, finding satisfaction in the persistence of feudal life on Raasay – though here he was only just in time, for in the early nineteenth century the island 'changed hands four times in sixteen years, and each time it lost some of its people'.[7]

Johnson was no simple primitivist, but he laments the loss of the old Highland virtues:

It affords a generous and manly pleasure to conceive a little nation gathering its fruits and tending its herds with fearless confidence, though it lies open on every side to invasion, where, in contempt of walls and trenches, every man sleeps securely with his sword beside him. [...] This was, in the beginning of the present century, the state of the Highlands. Every man was a soldier, who partook of national confidence, and interested himself in national honour. To lose this spirit, is to lose what no small advantage will compensate.
(pp. 82–3)

Of the commercial spirit which is displacing the older values and helping to drive the Highlanders into emigration, he writes bitingly: 'To make a country plentiful by diminishing the people, is an expeditious mode of husbandry; but that abundance, which there is nobody to enjoy, contributes little to human happiness' (p. 79).

In all this, Johnson is perhaps less a devotee of wildness than a conservative critic of the new improving forces in society, though it must be said that the two can be hard to distinguish. On the other hand, the Londoner is well aware of the advantages of civilization and picks on that feature of primitive peoples which so often acts as a focus for such considerations, their violence and love of revenge. Anticipating a widespread theme in modern culture, he writes: 'A man who places honour only in successful violence is a very troublesome and pernicious animal in time of peace' (p. 83). Like Adam Smith, he appreciates the great benefit bestowed by commercial society, the security that comes from observation of the law. In spite of some play-acting, there is nothing to suggest that he would have wished to preserve for himself the old life of the Highlands, but in this journey beyond the confines of modern civilization he found much to admire and regret as he noted down the tragic consequences of the destruction of a way of life.

Some forty years later, Walter Scott was to make the death of the old Highland order (or disorder) the theme of his first novel,

Waverley. Writing, as he puts it, of a time 'sixty years since', he observes in his postscript that 'there is no European nation which, within the course of half a century or little more, has undergone so complete a change as this kingdom of Scotland', and he cites in particular the 'effects of the insurrection of 1745', the 'destruction of the patriarchal power of the Highland chiefs', the 'abolition of the heritable jurisdiction of the Lowland nobility and barons', the 'total eradication of the Jacobite party' and the 'gradual influx of wealth and extension of commerce'.[8] All this has brought Scotland into the modern society described by Adam Smith.

Waverley is Scott's backward look at the beginning of the process, an attempt to come to terms with it. The romantic urge which we saw even in Johnson is here given to an impressionable young man, also an Englishman, visiting the Highlands and indeed Scotland for the first time. Young Waverley seems to represent something in Scott's own boyhood, his youthful Jacobitism – certainly the author is at pains to portray his hero as a dreamer. It is fitting therefore, from Scott's mature point of view, that he should be allowed to see the romantic Highlands of 1745, but in the end be disillusioned and return from the wild glens to the secure gardens of Southern England. In a way the novel is like *Northanger Abbey*, a comic tale of lost illusions and growing up – the savage state being the youth of the world.

What then does Waverley see in the Highlands? In the first place, scenes of primitive life which he is astonished to find in the 'otherwise well-ordered island of Great Britain'. The natives, with their moccasin-like brogues and their ability to track and to move silently through the dark, are compared more than once to Red Indians. The encampment of Donald MacBean is a 'Scythian camp' (p. 83), and the household of Fergus MacIvor is like something out of Homer, with its bard and great meat-feasts for retainers. Basing himself partly on Edward Burt's *Letters from the North of Scotland* (1754), Scott is giving a picture of the society that Johnson was too late to see. And though the hero's first view of this primitive life – in MacBean's cave – may be as awe-inspiring as the Cyclops's den, he also notices the grace of the people, as many travellers had commented on that of the Indians. Alice MacBean has a 'natural and rustic grace', not the 'sheepishness of an ordinary peasant' (p. 84). Fergus and his sister Flora have this quality to a far greater extent, and Waverley is captivated by this admirable pair, only gradually coming to see how in the case of Fergus the dignity of the chief is tainted with savage vindictiveness, selfish pride and a contempt for law which is precisely what the new Hanoverian order will seek to suppress.

Scott makes sure then – going much further than Burt at a distance of sixty years – that we can share his hero's enthusiasm for the manners and landscape of the Highlands. But he also sows seeds of disillusionment. The recurrent references to *Don Quixote* alert the reader to the comic side of things, the meanness of the cattle-rustling life and the petty politics hidden behind the tartan glamour. Moreover, Fergus himself is prepared to mock the 'barbarous ritual of our forefathers' (p. 102); he has lived at the French court and plays his primitive part with a certain cynicism. Above all, though, Scott makes it clear with the wisdom of hindsight that the Jacobite cause is a pathetic lost cause. For all the thrill of Prestonpans, the Highland fighters are, as Adam Smith noted, no match for the disciplined, though brutal, forces of the Hanoverians. The whole novel is indeed written to be read in the knowledge that these are 'old, unhappy, far-off things, and battles long ago'.

At the end, of course, the lost cause is given a tragic, Ossianic grandeur, as Fergus and Evan Dhu go to their deaths at Carlisle. This tragic scene was something which, according to the recent editor of *Waverley*, European audiences of 1814 were the more inclined to appreciate because of the Napoeonic wars in which they had 'watched the weaker nations of Europe submit to a conqueror – conquering in the name of the most improving principle' (p. xii). The trouble is, however, as the same editor notes, that this tragic scene is rapidly swallowed up in a happy ending where Waverley settles down to a life of civilized ease, marrying Rose, the sweet daughter of the harmless old Jacobite Bradwardine. Such a compromise corresponds well enough with Scott's own convictions, but hardly does justice to the aftermath of Culloden, the Clearances, and the destruction of the old disorder which is so rapidly evoked in the 'postscript'.

In this respect at least, one may prefer Dr Johnson's account, or indeed the harsher realism of Scott's own little story called 'The Two Drovers', one of the *Chronicles of the Canongate*, which are symbolically set between city and mountain, between present and past. In it the narrator (Croftangry) is at pains to keep the balance steady between his two heroes, the English and the Highland drovers. Seen from outside, the Highlander, with his comic speech, may look a pathetic character, but as he contemplates the revenge which his honour demands, we enter fully into his Gaelic-speaking mind and admire its poetic strength. The story ends with an expression of the author's balanced but ultimately 'civilized' view of the conflict between an old and a new code of values. Summing up the trial (in

209

England) of a Highlander who has avenged an insult by killing in cold blood, the English judge speaks as follows:

The country which he inhabits was, in the days of many now alive, inaccessible to the laws not only of England, which have not even yet penetrated thither, but to those to which our neighbours of Scotland are subjected, and which must be supposed to be, and no doubt actually are, founded upon the general principles of justice and equity which pervade every civilized country. Amongst their mountains, as among the North American Indians, the various tribes were wont to make war upon each other, so that each man was obliged to go armed for his own protection.

One can understand the Other, but 'the first object of civilization is to place the general protection of the law, equally administered, in the room of that wild justice which every man cut and carved for himself, according to the length of his sword and the strength of his arm'. And accordingly 'Robin Oig McCombich, *alias* McGregor, was sentenced to death' and, like Fergus MacIvor in *Waverley*, 'he met his fate with great firmness'.[9]

The question of revenge provides a bridge from Scotland to Corsica, which came to be regarded as the home of the primitive *vendetta*, a place which the civilizing power of France could never entirely reduce to order. The other link is James Boswell, who, before going to the Highlands with Johnson, had made his name as 'Corsica Boswell', the successful author of a *Journal of a Tour to Corsica* which fired enlightened opinion for the cause of the brave and primitive population of a mountainous island. If Boswell went to Corsica, it was partly because his idol Rousseau had written in the *Contrat social* that this wild, uncorrupted island was perhaps the only place in Europe still capable of true democratic government. Others had a lower opinion of the Corsicans, Lord Holland describing them as 'the vile inhabitants of one of the vilest islands in the world'.[10] Boswell, however, makes it clear that (like Waverley) he went to Corsica with high Romantic expectations. Unlike Waverley, he was not disappointed.

It is true that, like almost all his writing, Boswell's *Tour* contains an element of humour at the author's expense – partly deliberate, partly unconscious. He displays himself flaunting Corsican national costume and charming the natives with simple Scottish tunes on the flute. But such mildly comic interludes are subordinated to the heroic portrait of the freedom-loving islanders and their general Paoli, a portrait which draws amply on mythological traditions such as the pastoral Age of Gold and the mainly ideal of Sparta. In some ways this echoes other descriptions of rude nations, from the Indians of

America to the Highlanders of Scotland. Boswell notes for instance that 'the chief satisfaction of these islanders, when not engaged in war or in hunting, seemed to be that of lying at their ease in the open air, recounting tales of the bravery of their countrymen'.[11] But as compared with the images of Scotland to be found in Johnson and Scott, there are virtually no disadvantages here; indeed a long quotation from Gregory's *Comparative View of the State and Faculties of Man with those of the Animal World* is used to suggest that the Corsicans are at that 'period in the progress of society in which mankind appears to the greatest advantage' (p. 180). This is like the 'golden age' described in the second part of Rousseau's *Discourse on Inequality*.[12] It is true that Boswell is surprised that Paoli can bear to live in 'an island yet in a rude uncivilized state [...] instead of participating in *Attic* evenings', but the general assures him that in thirty years' time the island will have the 'arts and sciences' (pp. 174–6). What one glimpses here, as in Rousseau's *Contrat social* and some of his writings on Switzerland, is the possibility of having it both ways, preserving the 'manly' virtues and ancient simplicity of freedom-loving mountain people while cultivating the arts of civilization. To the enthusiastic Boswell the future of Corsica was bright with such hope, and his journal was meant to drum up support for this future.

Now if there was one feature of Corsican society which caught the attention of 'civilized' people, it was, as I have suggested, the *vendetta*. Most commentators on primitive societies noted the importance of revenge in them, and we have seen how in 'The Two Drovers' civilized society is seen to depend on the establishment of law. Boswell, however, with his idealized picture of Corsica, has little to say about the *vendetta*, remarking merely that Paoli is opposed to 'so barbarous a practice' (p. 193). Let us now consider a novel about Corsica which is in fact centred on this practice and which implies a much more ambiguous attitude to this primitive society, Mérimée's *Colomba*, published nearly eighty years later in 1840.[13]

Like Boswell's, Mérimée's is a tourist book, but the Corsica he visited was not Boswell's. Paoli's struggle for independence was defeated soon after the Scotsman's visit, the French took over from the Genoese, and early in the nineteenth century French rule was firmly established on the island (though there are still independence movements in Corsica, much more violent than those in Scotland). In his novel, Mérimée represents not only the primitive island, but various characters who represent stages on the road between the primitive and civilized, in particular the *préfet*, representative of

211

civilized French rule, who longs to be back on the mainland; Miss Lydia, the blasé young Englishwoman who is horrified and fascinated by the savagery of the island; and Orso, the islander who has lived on the mainland and half-adopted its values. As far as the English girl is concerned, her role is to allow Mérimée to mock the romantic appeal of his material (for the savage life of Corsica had been the subject of literary *images d'Epinal* in the years between Boswell's visit and Mérimée's). One is reminded of the way Waverley succumbs to the charm of the Highlands, but this time the mockery is cruder and the reader is not allowed to take Miss Lydia at all seriously when she is captivated by the Byronic fascination of the avenger.

All well and good; the satire is directed more against the civilized tourist's love of the wild than at the wildness itself. Mérimée laughs at himself, but through the veil of detachment his story still conveys the power and poetry of this barbarous, lawless society. This is done, as in his *Carmen* (and indeed *Waverley*) largely through a female figure. Colomba is beautiful and passionate; unlike the *brigands de l'Ambigu Comique*, whom the author is willing enough to ridicule, she has a wild dignity which is enhanced by her instinctive response to Dante (p. 159). She too is a poet, an improviser of songs and chants, and one may recall that sublime poetry and song is a distinguishing feature of idealized ancient society (much of Ossian's success seems to be due to the projected image of the tragic bard). When Colomba laments the dead and calls for revenge, Mérimée presents the scene in these terms:

A mesure qu'elle improvisait, sa figure prenait une expression sublime [...] C'était la pythonisse sur son trépied. Sauf quelques soupirs, quelques sanglots étouffées, on n'eût pas entendu le plus léger murmure dans la foule qui se pressait autour d'elle.   (p. 206)

Interestingly, Mérimée had himself produced a fake in this line, *La Guzla* (1827), purportedly a genuine collection of Illyrian folk poetry, which had taken in a good many readers, including Pushkin. The successful author of pastiche is what is called in *Colomba* an amphibian, living between two worlds. And Mérimée's attitude to his heroine remains mixed. In a first version he had apparently made her more scheming and self-interested at the end, but he removed the more sordid features in deference to the romantic taste of his friend Valentine Delessert; she had said of his original ending: 'L'alliance de sentiments si nobles avec des vues intéressées me semble impossible' (p. 127). Nevertheless, it is indeed this mixture that we see in *Colomba*, as in Scott's portrayal of Fergus MacIvor. Although Mérimée, to please his lady, 'exaggerated the passion of *vendetta*' in the final scene, in many other ways he belittles his subject, looking at the Corsicans, their habits and their customs with the disenchanted objectivity of the ethnographer. The first description of Pietranera sets the tone; the scene of the tragi-comedy is a miserable village. In the same way, the tragic events of the *vendetta* are shown to be founded on petty jealousies, and the means employed by the islanders, killing a pig in revenge for the mutilation of a horse's ear, rouse Orso's scorn: 'Vous n'êtes bons qu'à vous battre contre des cochons' (p. 234). Not primitive grandeur, but vindictive pettiness. What is more, Mérimée suggests that this old world is on the way out. It seems significant that early in the book he places his story in the vanishing past by having Orso disappear 'derrière les marécages remplacés aujourd'hui par une belle pépinière' (p. 178). At the end, the savage Colomba is becoming civilized, taking tea with an English colonel whose daughter her brother is to marry; intermarriage and travel break down the barriers between the wild and the tame.

It is in Orso that the conflict of old and new appears most clearly. Was it deliberately that Mérimée gave him a name like that of Orestes, the young son committed to a blood feud which (in Euripides's version at least) he finds hard to bear? As in the last play of Aeschylus's trilogy, we see here a struggle between primitive revenge and the rule of law. The Corsican who has lived in Europe is torn by conflicting urges and duties. He is the in-between figure, half-savage, half-civilized, who continues to exercise such a fascination over modern readers, no doubt because he stands for our own imperfect allegiance to the values of civilization. In his case, the story ends well; he is allowed the best of all words, satisfying the demands of *vendetta* as he kills his enemies in a spectacular way (with as little pain to the reader as in a classic Western), but shooting only in self-defence (the bad guy must draw first). And in the end, though less sadly than in *Waverley*, the savage world recedes into the distance, the story closes on the mainland near Pisa with strawberries and cream on the farm. 'Adieu les stylets', says Colomba, 'maintenant j'ai un éventail' (p. 273). The forests and mountains of Corsica, with their picturesque bandits, have been left behind, a place for holidays, novels or travel books, not a place to be taken seriously, and certainly not a threat to civilization.

Let me finally turn briefly to Russia and a third mountain frontier of civilization, the Caucasus. Here we meet the nearest analogy with the American frontier. The Russian armies were conquering and civilizing various non-Russian peoples who were racially and linguistically quite distinct from them, though in terms of the four-stage theory these were barbarians or farmers rather than savages. Now Alexander Pushkin,[14] the admirer of Mérimée's fake Illyrian poetry, wrote an article in 1836 about the memoirs of John Tanner, a white American who had been captured by the Indians as a child and lived among them for many years. In his article, Pushkin is sarcastic about Tanner's return to Yankee civilization – 'on which we congratulate him most sincerely' (VI, 191) – and speaks in by now familiar tones about the inevitable destruction of the Indians: 'One way or another, by fire and sword, or by rum and slander, or by more moral means, savagery must disappear as civilization advances' (VI, 165). Tanner's book, therefore, is a record of a disappearing race, 'the chronicle of illiterate tribes'. But what is most noticeable is that Pushkin insists equally on the dreary and brutish nature of Indian life, remarking that Chateaubriand and Fenimore Cooper have both embellished the Indians 'with the colours of their imagination' (VI, 166).[15] Such disenchanted realism is characteristic of the later Pushkin – and as one Soviet scholar has suggested, when Pushkin writes of America, he is also thinking of the Caucasus.[16]

Russia had been engaged in wars of conquest in this region for a long time by 1836, but the Caucasus became an important subject in Russian literature only after 1820, partly because of the Romantic taste for wild places and people, partly because a number of Russian writers went to these mountains not as tourists, but as exiles. Quite often this Caucasian writing is directly concerned with our present theme of the unequal meeting of ancient mountain wildness and new lowland civilization, a good example being the first story 'Bela' in Lermontov's *A Hero of our Times*. Often too, the question of revenge is present; in Bestuzhev Marlinsky's *Ammalat-Bek*, for instance, there is the same kind of conflict of values as in *Colomba*. Pushkin's writings show similar features.

Several of his works, apart from the specifically Caucasian ones, are concerned with the meeting of wild and tame. There is the long poem *The Gipsies* and the novel *The Captain's Daughter*, much influenced by Scott and showing Scott's fascination for primitive rebels, though coming down if anything more firmly on the side of civilized order. As far as the Caucasus is concerned, Pushkin wrote a popular long poem, *The Prisoner of the Caucasus*, in 1820, under the influence of his first visit, and in the 1830s, after the second visit, he produced a short travelogue, the *Journey to Arzrum*, an unfinished poem, *Tazit*, and a number of short lyrics.

Even more than Scott, Pushkin stresses the wild beauty of the mountains. To the Byronic outsider such scenes are a fitting spiritual home. So the Russian hero of the poem of 1820, a heartsick refugee from the salons of Petersburg, responds greedily to the glamour of the Circassian village where he is held prisoner. He admires too the beautiful picture of village life (III, 99–104). He observes the people's beliefs, customs, education, their simplicity and hospitality, their speed, strength, skill with weapons, love of fighting, bravery, horsemanship and beautiful clothes. Their bloodthirstiness is excused by a parallel with the different but equally cruel pastimes of the capital. But all of this is no use to him, nor is the love of the simple girl who befriends and rescues him. The Byronic hero is no longer capable of life and positive emotion. As a representative of modern Russia, he brings destruction, for he refuses the girl's love and she drowns herself. 'He understood it all', says the narrator blankly (III, 114).

It might seem then that the poem expressed the guilt of the civilized conqueror, but in fact this is hardly the case. For one thing, this is essentially the tragedy of the hero; the Caucasian world is seen only through his eyes, as the object of hopeless nostalgia for a world before the fall. Secondly, and paradoxically, Pushkin adds an extraordinary epilogue to his poem (III, 115–17). Here he speaks in his own name of the poetry both of the Caucasus and of conquest. His Muse has been captivated by the 'wild flowers' of the region and the 'severe people nurtured in war', but he will one day sing of 'that great hour when sensing the bloody conflict, our two-headed eagle rose over the turbulent Caucasus' and he looks forward to the day when the ferocity of the present will be a mere memory. 'The Caucasus will betray its forefathers and forget the voice of fierce battle', and 'the traveller will approach without fear the ravines where once you [the "proud sons of the Caucasus"] made your nests, and the obscure voice of tradition will tell of your ruin'. In other words, rather as in Scotland, tourism will mark the pacification of the unruly uplands. Once again the struggle between wild and tame is set in a context of inevitable historical development.

The Prisoner of the Caucasus is a confusing work, though it carries a sufficiently powerful charge to have generated imitations in the decades that followed and to have provoked Tolstoy's deliberately prosaic story of the same name. Pushkin also moved towards a more prosaic realism in the 1820s. His *Journey to Arzrum* in particular pulls the carpet from under the Romantic primitivism of much Caucasian writing. This short piece is apparently meant as a parody of Chateaubriand's *Itinéraire de Paris à Jérusalem*;[17] it mocks the clichés of such travel literature. As far as the Caucasus is concerned,

Pushkin provocatively includes in his first chapter a plain account in flat style of an unappetizing breakfast meeting with a Kalmyk girl:

> The young Kalmyk girl, who was not at all bad looking, was sewing and smoking tobacco. I sat down beside her. 'What's your name? – *** – How old are you? – Eighteen. – What are you sewing? – Gaiters. – Who for? – Myself.' She gave me her pipe and began eating her breakfast. The pot contained tea with mutton fat and salt. She offered me her dish. I didn't want to refuse and took a sip, trying not to be sick. I don't think any other national cuisine could produce anything more disgusting. (V, 417)

Later on, Pushkin laments the passing of the old military spirit of the area: 'Their spirit of wild chivalry has declined noticeably'; they hate the Russians because 'we have squeezed them out of their free pasturelands; their villages are destroyed, whole tribes have been wiped out' (V, 420). Even so, the author's perspective remains that of the conquerors. 'What is one to do with such a people?' he asks, having detailed their violent habits. He can only hope that civilization will have its effect:

> The influence of luxury may favour their subjugation; the samovar would be an important innovation here. There is another means, which is more powerful, more moral and more appropriate to the enlightenment of our age – the preaching of the Gospel. (V, 420)

It does not seem then that civilized man has anything to learn from the old wildness, though it may come as a refreshment to the tired soul of the blasé city-dweller. On the contrary, the new values of Christianity should conquer the old habits of plunder and revenge. This seems to have been Pushkin's viewpoint in his unfinished poem *Tazit*, which shows the inner struggles of a young man caught between the old Circassian code of behaviour and the new morality of civilization. His father curses him for his unmanly inability to fight, kill, steal and avenge himself like his ancestors. The hero, however, remains immobile and impenetrable. We guess his inner struggles, but from outside. Unlike Mérimée, Pushkin has not tried to represent directly the torn mind of the young man, no doubt because Tazit is still far closer to the old culture than is the cultivated Orso of *Colomba*.

As far as Europe is concerned, by the period that concerns us mountain wildness would appear to be a lost cause. It belongs to the past, which is being tamed and destroyed by the present and by the civilization of the plains. In mythical thinking, it is true, the plains themselves contain that other threat to order, the barbarian at the gates, always ready to invade and overturn the fragile work of civilization. These barbarian hordes find ever new incarnations in the yellow peril, communism, the young, the dangerous classes, and so on. They always represent the latent and perilous savagery in humanity. But this is not the same as the wild mountaineers, representatives of an earlier order which is being superseded, as Adam Smith might have said, by commercial society.

What happens, as we saw in Chapter 11, is that as polite civilization subdues its opposite, it both laments the loss and moves to preserve something of what is being destroyed. This was the function of Ossian. The writers and artists of modern society do not really prefer the older culture, but they recognize its strengths. They may indeed dream of a harmony between old and new – this is clearly the meaning of Boswell's vision of the civilized Paoli presiding over a Corsica which retains its Spartan virtues. Or even if no such ideal is envisaged, the civilized gain satisfaction from contemplating the vanished way of life – and playing with it. Scott writes of the pleasure to be derived from countries where the wilder hills meet the cultivated plain, and Johnson recalls the gratification he derived from enjoying the benefits of polite society against the wild backdrop of the Hebrides. One may well feel cynical about such tastes, noting that the life of 'primitive' people, when not obliterated, becomes the staple of national parks, reservations, folk museums and craft shops. Many modern city-dwellers go to the mountains because they want a solitude to play savages in, now that the savages have been civilized or destroyed.

We have moved a long way here from Perrault's re-creation of peasant naivety, but the same dialectic is at work. I do not wish to draw any moralizing conclusions, but simply to set before the reader the knot of conflicting attitudes to politeness and its opposites which seems to me so important in the culture of classical (and post-classical) France. Even for a detractor of modern politeness such as Jean-Jacques Rousseau, it was difficult to maintain a consistent position on such questions.[18] Let me conclude, therefore, with the ironic self-presentation of Rousseau's one-time disciple, Chateaubriand, as he remembers (or artistically re-creates) his first encounter with the savages of North America. The scene is set in a part of America which by the time he came to rewrite the episode in the *Mémoires d'outre-tombe* had been fairly completely 'civilized':

Lorsqu'après avoir passé le Mohawk, j'entrai dans les bois qui n'avaient jamais été abattus, je fus pris d'une sorte d'ivresse d'indépendance: j'allais d'arbre en arbre, à gauche, à droite, en disant: 'Ici, plus de chemins, plus de villes, plus de monarchie, plus de république, plus de présidents, plus de rois, plus d'hommes.' Et, pour essayer si j'étais rétabli dans mes droits originels je me livrais à des actes de volonté qui faisaient enrager mon guide, lequel, dans son âme, me croyait fou.

Hélas! je me figurais être seul dans cette forêt où je levais une tête si fière! tout à coup, je viens m'énaser contre un hangar. Sous ce hangar s'offrent à mes yeux ébaubis les premiers sauvages que j'aie vus de ma vie. Ils étaient une vingtaine, tant d'hommes que femmes, tous barbouillés comme des sorciers, le corps demi-nu, les oreilles découpées, des plumes de corbeau sur la tête et des anneaux passés dans les narines. Un petit Français, poudré et frisé, habit vert-pomme, veste de droguet, jabot et manchettes de mousseline, raclait un violon de poche, et faisait danser *Madelon Frisquet* à ces Iroquois. M. Violet (c'était son nom) était maître de danse chez les sauvages. On lui payait ses leçons en peaux de castors et en jambons d'ours. Il avait été marmiton au service du général Rochambeau, pendant la guerre d'Amérique. Demeuré à New-York après le départ de notre armée, il se résolut d'enseigner les beaux-arts aux Américains. Ses vues s'étant agrandies avec le succès, le nouvel Orphée porta la civilisation jusque chez les hordes sauvages du Nouveau-Monde. En me parlant des Indiens, il me disait toujours: 'Ces messieurs sauvages et ces dames sauvagesses'. Il se louait beaucoup de la légèreté de ses écoliers; en effet, je n'ai jamais vu faire de telles gambades. M. Violet, tenant son petit violon entre son menton et sa poitrine, accordait l'instrument fatal; il criait aux Iroquois: *A vos places!* Et toute la troupe sautait comme une bande de démons.

N'était-ce pas une chose accablante pour un disciple de Rousseau, que cette introduction à la vie sauvage par un bal que l'ancien marmiton du général Rochambeau donnait à des Iroquois? J'avais grande envie de rire, mais j'étais cruellement humilié.[19]

NOTES

Introduction

1 Norbert Elias, *Über den Prozess der Zivilisation* (Basel, 1939), tr. E. Jephcott, *The Civilizing Process*, 2 vols. (Oxford, 1978–82).
2 Clive Bell, *Civilization, an Essay* (London, 1928).
3 M. Foucault, *Histoire de la folie à l'âge classique*, 2nd edn (Paris, 1972).
4 Jean-Jacques Rousseau, *Œuvres complètes*, ed. M. Raymond and B. Gagnebin, 4 vols. to date (Paris, 1959–), IV, 251–2.
5 Victor Hugo, 'Réponse à un acte d'accusation', in *Les Contemplations*, ed. L. Cellier (Paris, 1969), p. 20.
6 Denis Diderot, *Œuvres complètes*, ed. H. Dieckmann, J. Proust and J. Varloot (Paris, 1975–), X, 402.
7 M. Bakhtin, *Tvorchestvo Fransua Rable*, translated into French by A. Robel, as *L'Œuvre de François Rabelais et la culture populaire* (Paris, 1970).
8 La Bruyère, *Les Caractères*, ed. R. Garapon (Paris, 1962), p. 82.

1 Hyperbole

1 Thomas Traherne, *Century II*, 52. I owe this quotation and many insights into the problem of hyperbole to the essay by Brian Vickers, 'The *Songs and Sonnets* and the Rhetoric of Hyperbole', in *John Donne; Essays in Celebration*, ed. A. J. Smith (London, 1972), pp. 132–74 (p. 148).
2 D. Bouhours, *La Manière de bien penser dans les ouvrages d'esprit*, 1715 edn (reprinted Brighton, 1971), p. 30. The first edition dates from 1687.
3 M. Allott, *Novelists on the Novel* (London and New York, 1959), p. 58.
4 André Gide, *Incidences* (Paris, 1924), p. 40.
5 Pierre Nicole, *Traité de la beauté des ouvrages d'esprit* (Paris, 1689), p. 38. This was translated from the Latin original of 1659; its republication was perhaps connected with the appearance of Bouhours's book two years earlier.
6 Quintilian, *Institutio oratoria*, ed. H. E. Butler (London, 1920–2), III, 338–45.
7 Vickers, 'The *Songs and Sonnets*' (p. 146), quotes Joseph Priestley's perceptive commentary in his *Course of Lectures on Oratory and Criticism*

219

(1777) on the Biblical hyperbole 'I will make thy seed as the dust of the earth', which helps the reader to imagine the unimaginable.

8 Bernard Lamy, *La Rhétorique ou l'art de parler*, 4th edn (1699, reprinted Brighton, 1969), pp. 284—5.

9 See J. Brody, *Boileau and Longinus* (Geneva, 1958).

10 See P. France, *Rhetoric and Truth in France: Descartes to Diderot* (Oxford, 1972), pp. 151—63.

11 Boileau, *Epîtres*, ed. C. H. Boudhors, 3rd edn (Paris, 1967), p. 58.

12 *Entretiens d'Ariste et d'Eugène* (1671), ed. F. Brunot (Paris, 1962), p. 42.

13 See for instance Du Marsais, summarizing the classical view of the matter in the following century in *Des tropes* (I quote from the third edition (Paris, 1775)): 'l'hyperbole est ordinaire aux Orientaux. Les jeunes gens en font plus souvent usage que les personnes avancées en âge' (p. 149). Hyperbole is thus connected with foreigners, young people, and, as we saw in the remarks of Nicole quoted above, with the plebs.

14 See, among many other works on the subject, J. M. Apostolidès, *Le Roi-machine* (Paris, 1981).

15 Vickers, 'The *Songs and Sonnets*', p. 148.

16 *Lettres portugaises, Valentins et autres œuvres de Guilleragues*, ed. F. Deloffre and J. Rougeot (Paris, 1962), p. 39.

17 Cyrano de Bergerac, *Lettres*, ed. L. Erba (Milan, 1965), pp. 37—9. It will be remembered that Boileau, in his *Art poétique*, while not going so far as to praise the by now outdated and unacceptable Cyrano, writes:

> J'aime mieux Bergerac et sa burlesque audace
> Que ces vers où Motin se morfond et nous glace.
>
> (IV, 39—40)

18 L. Spitzer, 'Die klassische Dämpfung in Racines Stil', *Archivum Romanicum*, 12 (1928), 361—472. Similar views are expressed in Karl Vossler's *Jean Racine* (Munich, 1926). I am aware of course that there is another equally (if not more) widespread view of Racine as the realistic painter of violent passions — but even in this tradition it is not common for there to be much reference to hyperbole.

19 On the question of myth and reason see below, Chapter 3.

20 F. Ogier, *Apologie pour Monsieur de Balzac* (Paris, 1627), pp. 117—65.

21 Later editions modify the final line to the more discreet:

> Lui seul peut arrêter les progrès d'Alexandre.

22 D'Aubignac, *La Pratique du théâtre*, ed. P. Martino (Paris, 1927), p. 353.

23 See for instance Boileau, *Satire VIII*, lines 99—112:

> Quoi! cet écervelé qui mit l'Asie en cendre? ...

2 Ogres

1 It is interesting to compare Turner's misty representation of a giant with Poussin's much more 'realistic' treatment in his *Blind Orion*.

2 See below, Chapter 3, pp. 44–50, for a discussion of this point and more generally of the *merveilleux* in French classical culture.

3 See R. Mandrou, *De la culture populaire en France aux 17e et 18e siècles* (Paris, 1964); G. Bollème, *La Bibliothèque bleue* (Paris, 1971) and *La Bible bleue* (Paris, 1975).

4 Perrault's texts are referred to in the following editions: *Contes*, ed. J. P. Collinet (Paris, 1981); *Parallèle des anciens et des modernes*, 4 vols. Paris, 1688–97). The *Contes* include both the three 'Contes en vers' and the eight more famous *Histoires ou contes du temps passé*, which are in prose. Perrault's *Contes* have been very interestingly discussed in Marc Soriano's *Les Contes de Perrault, culture savante et traditions populaires* (Paris, 1968). Many of Soriano's hypotheses have been disputed, but his book remains a mine of information and ideas. See also his *Dossier Perrault* (Paris, 1972) for material on various aspects of Perrault's career.

5 On the *Querelle des Anciens et des Modernes* see A. Adam, *Histoire de la littérature française au XVIIe siècle*, 5 vols. (Paris, 1948–56), III, 125–31 and V, 80–4.

6 See below, Chapter 3, p. 46.

7 On the Ancient Greeks as barbarians, see the quotation from Adam Ferguson below, Chapter 11, p. 198.

8 See Perrault, *Parallèle* III, 117 and 119–20, and Boileau, *Réflexions sur Longin*, ed. C. N. Boudhors (Paris, 1960), p. 75.

9 The consensus of critical opinion is that while the son wrote down versions of the stories, the father was responsible for the original telling and the final drafting of the text.

10 The introduction and notes by J. P. Collinet in his edition of the *Contes* contain some excellent pages on the relation betwen Perrault and La Fontaine.

11 For the passage from Marx's *Grundrisse* on the eternal childlike charm of Greek art, see below, Chapter 3, p. 46.

12 On the fairy story in the century following Perrault, see J. Barchilon, *Le Conte merveilleux français de 1690–1790* (Paris, 1975) and R. Robert, *Le Conte de fées littéraire en France de la fin du XVIIe à la fin du XVIIIe siècle* (Nancy, 1982).

13 See below, Chapter 3, Note 21.

14 P. Delarue and M. L. Ténèze, *Le Conte populaire français*, 3 vols. (Paris, 1957–77), I, 306–28.

15 In an interesting article 'The Making of Mother Goose' (*New York Review of Books*, 2 February 1984), Robert Darnton insists on the crude realism of the oral folk-tale in France.

16 Against La Fontaine and the 'connaisseurs', to remind oneself that Perrault's stories have not won universal praise, it is worth quoting the following remarks of a communard, as reported by Lucien Descaves in his *Philémon vieux de la vieille* (Paris, 1913): 'Mais il y a aussi merveilleux et merveilleux. Celui des légendes populaires est admirable, et celui de Perrault aussi stupide que les histoires de la mère Ségur. Si Peau d'Ane m'était conté, je n'y prendrai aucun plaisir' (pp. 320–1).

17 Quoted by Collinet in the introduction to his edition of the *Contes*, p. 28.
18 See the *Spectator*, nos. 21 and 25.
19 See L. Sainéan, *L'Influence et la réputation de Rabelais* (Paris, 1930).
20 Abbé de Villiers, *Entretiens sur les contes de fées* (Paris, 1699), pp. 108–9.
21 See below, Chapter 4, p. 67.
22 For a reversal of this theme from a mid-twentieth-century ecological and libertarian perspective, see Michel Tournier's story 'La Fugue du Petit Poucet' in his *Le Coq de Bruyère*. The hero here suffers from the destruction of trees, and the ogre is transformed into a life-loving, anti-authoritarian vegetable-eater.

3 Myth and modernity: Racine's *Phèdre*

1 Quoted in C. Brown, *Mandelstam* (Cambridge, 1973) p. 16.
2 Osip Mandelstam, *Sobranie sochinenii*, ed. G. P. Struve and B. A. Filipov, 2nd edn (New York, 1967–71), I, 50–1. The translation is mine; it is only a shadow of the original.
3 Subsequently included in *Sur Racine* (Paris, 1963), pp. 133–44.
4 G. Steiner, *The Death of Tragedy* (London, 1961).
5 I use the word 'myth' here principally to refer to the sacred systems and stories of earlier times. For the most part this means the so-called pagan mythology of Greece and Rome with its well-defined figures and legends, but the word should also be understood in the broader sense which has gained currency in the aftermath of such works as Frazer's *Golden Bough* (myths of death and rebirth, etc).
6 Mary Renault, *The Bull from the Sea* (London, 1962), pp. 242–3.
7 Robert Lowell, *Phaedra* (London, 1962), p. 23.
8 Tony Harrison, *Phaedra Britannica*, 3rd edn (London, 1976), p. 11.
9 For instance Barthes's assertion that 'les grands tableaux raciniens présentent toujours ce grand combat mythique (et théâtral) de l'ombre et de la lumière' (*Sur Racine*, p. 32).
10 Sainte-Beuve, *Port-Royal*, ed. M. Leroy, 3 vols. (Paris, 1952–5), III, 591.
11 A. W. Schlegel, *Vorlesungen über dramatische Kunst und Literatur*, ed. G. V. Amoretti (Bonn and Leipzig, 1923), II, 61.
12 The subject has been discussed at much greater length by (among many others) M. Delcroix, *Le Sacré dans les tragédies profanes de Racine* (Montreal, 1970) and R. Elliot, *Mythe et légende dans le théâtre de Racine* (Paris, 1969). See also R. C. Knight, 'Myth in Racine: A Myth', *L'Esprit Créateur*, 16 (1976), 95–104. This particular issue of *L'Esprit Créateur* is devoted to 'Myth and Mythology in Seventeenth-Century French Literature'.
13 On this subject, see V. Delaporte, *Du merveilleux dans la littérature française sous Louis XIV* (Paris, 1891).
14 J. Seznec, *La Survivance des dieux antiques* (London, 1940), p. 288.
15 B. Beugnot, 'Pour une poétique de l'allégorie classique' in *Critique et création littéraire en France au XVIIe siècle* (Paris, 1977), p. 417. See also

the discussion following this paper and the contributions to the same conference of B. Toccane, G. Hall and M. Fumaroli.
16 'Myth in Racine: a Myth'.
17 First published in Lyon in Latin in 1659. I quote here from Andrew Tooke's English translation, *The Pantheon, representing the Fabulous Histories of the Heathen Gods and most illustrious Heroes*, 29th edn (London, 1793).
18 *De l'origine des fables*, in Fontenelle, *Textes choisis*, ed. M. Roelens (Paris, 1966), p. 223.
19 See above, Chapter 2.
20 K. Marx, *The German Ideology*, ed. C. J. Arthur (London, 1970), pp. 148–51.
21 The words 'on dit' are used in a similar way by Théramène in his *récit* to refer to 'un dieu, qui d'aiguillons pressait leur flanc poudreux' (V, vi, 1540). In this way the intervention of Neptune in the death of Hippolyte is left uncertain; rational readers can distance themselves from Thésée and regard the whole thing as a catastrophic accident.
22 Racine, *Œuvres complètes*, ed. R. Picard, 2 vols. (Paris, 1950–2), II, 547.
23 Pradon is used as a whipping boy by A. W. Schlegel (*Vorlesungen*) among others. An interesting new look at Pradon and Racine is J. von Stackelberg, 'Racine, Pradon und Spitzers Methode', *Germanisch-Romanische Monatsschrift*, 19 (1969), 413–34.
24 Diluted in later editions to 'De la race du dieu, père de la lumière'. It is interesting to reflect on the possible reasons for this change.
25 See F. Orlando, *Lettura freudiana della "Phèdre"* (Turin, 1971).
26 W. McC. Stewart, 'Le Tragique et le sacré chez Racine', in *Le Théâtre tragique*, ed. J. Jacquot (Paris, 1962), pp. 271–85.
27 *The Allegory of Love* (Oxford, 1936), p. 83.

4 Polish, police, *polis*

1 On this topic and several other questions raised in this chapter, see Jean Starobinski, 'Le Mot civilisation', in his book *Le Remède dans le mal* (Paris, 1989), pp. 11–59.
2 For England, see L. E. Klein, *The Rise of Politeness in England, 1660–1715* (Baltimore, 1985).
3 Lord Chesterfield, *Letters to his Son and Others*, ed. R. K. Root (London, 1929), p. 171.
4 See J. C. Laursen, 'From Court to Commerce; David Hume and the French Vocabulary of "Politeness" in the Scottish Enlightenment', paper given at a conference on 'The Political Thought of the Scottish Enlightenment in its European Context', Edinburgh, August 1986.
5 Voltaire, *Œuvres complètes*, ed. W. H. Barber *et al.* (Geneva and Oxford, 1970–), VIII, 416.
6 Quoted in the *Oxford English Dictionary* under 'Politeness'.

7 Norbert Elias, *The Civilizing Process*, Vol. I: *The History of Manners*, tr. E. Jephcott (Oxford, 1978), pp. 3–34.

8 In this chapter I shall confine myself to the discourse of politeness, rather than attempting to study the way things actually worked in practice. The latter investigation is a vast undertaking; for some pointers, see *Histoire de la vie privée*, Vol. III, ed. R. Chartier (Paris, 1986).

9 La Bruyère, *Les Caractères*, ed. R. Garapon (Paris, 1962), p. 222.

10 N. C. J. Trublet, *Essais sur divers sujets de littérature et de morale*, 6th edn (Paris, 1768), II, 147. Trublet's essay on politeness was one of his first publications; it is confessedly a compilation of standard Parisian views on the subject. It first appeared anonymously in the *Mercure de France* in June 1731 under the title 'Réflexions sur la politesse', and was then included in his *Essais* (1735), which were several times reprinted, with additions and modifications.

11 Abbé Gédoyn, *Œuvres diverses* (Paris, 1745), p. 173.

12 J. B. Morvan de Bellegarde, *Réflexions sur la politesse*, 4th edn (Amsterdam, 1707), p. 35. This work was first published in 1698; together with its companion, *Réflexions sur le ridicule* (first published in 1696, quoted here in the 7th edn, Amsterdam, 1707), and a number of others on related subjects, it was several times reprinted in the years around 1700, and was translated into English.

13 M. Magendie, *La Politesse mondaine et les théories de l'honnêteté en France au XVIIe siècle, de 1600 à 1660* (Paris, 1926). See also V. Kapp, 'Attizismus und Honnêteté in Farets "L'honnête homme ou l'art de plaire à la cour"', *Romanistische Zeitschrift für Literaturgeschichte*, 1989, Heft 1/2, 102–16: and the article 'Honnête homme, honnêteté, honnêtes gens' in the *Handbuch politisch-sozialer Grundbegriffe in Frankreich 1680–1820*, Heft 7 (Munich, 1986).

14 See D. Roche, *Le Siècle des lumières en province: académies et académiciens provinciaux, 1680–1789* (Paris and The Hague, 1978).

15 On this concept see Starobinski, 'Le Mot civilisation', and more generally, the work of Norbert Elias (note 7 above).

16 See below, chapter 11.

17 R. Chartier, 'Distinction et divulgation: la civilité et ses livres', in his *Lectures et lecteurs dans la France de l'Ancien Régime* (Paris, 1987). I am much indebted to this valuable study, and to other work in the same field by M. Chartier.

18 Antoine Courtin, *Nouveau Traité de la civilité* (1671); J. B. de la Salle, *Les Règles de la bienséance et de la civilité chrétienne* (1703).

19 On *honnêteté* see Magendie, *La Politesse mondaine*; it is a word with both social and moral connotations. *Urbanité* is less used and is described by Richelet as 'écorché du latin'; see however the essay by Gédoyn referred to in Note 11 to this chapter.

20 Madame de Lambert, 'Avis d'une mère à sa fille' (1726), in *Œuvres morales*, ed. M. Lescure (Paris, 1883), p. 92.

21 See B. Munteano, *Constantes dialectiques en littérature et en histoire* (Paris, 1967), pp. 354–60.

22 *Mercure de France*, November 1731, p. 2559.

23 I am solely concerned in this chapter with the way politeness was viewed in the classical period. In more modern times, its different forms are studied by social scientists interested in the mechanisms of social control; it could also be interestingly related to the behaviour of other species, as outlined for instance in F. de Waal, *Peacemaking among Primates* (London and Cambridge, Mass., 1989).

24 Compare the musical analogy used for the 'commerce of the self' by Adam Smith, quoted below, Chapter 6, p. 103.

25 Pascal, *Pensées*, ed. L. Lafuma (Paris, 1952), p. 132.

26 On conversation, see C. Strosetzki, *Konversation. Ein Kapitel gesellschaftlicher und literaturischer Pragmatik im Frankreich des 17. Jahrhunderts* (Frankfurt, Bern, Las Vegas, 1978).

27 Quoted in Marivaux, *Journaux et œuvres diverses*, ed. F. Deloffre and M. Gilot (Paris, 1969), p. 729.

28 Marivaux, *Journaux*, p. 322. See also Chapter 5 below.

29 Rousseau was described as a modern Diogenes by contemporaries. It is interesting also to note the use of this figure in Diderot's *Neveu de Rameau*, where at first he is associated with Rameau, but in the end with the virtuous *philosophe*. See below, Chapter 7, pp. 127–8, and for a related case in Marivaux, Chapter 5, pp. 86–7.

30 Rousseau, *Œuvres complètes*, ed. M. Raymond and B. Gagnebin, 4 vols. to date (Paris, 1959–), III, 7.

31 Elias, *The Civilizing Process*, Vol. I.

32 O. Ranum, 'Courtesy, Absolutism and the French State', *Journal of Modern History*, 52 (1980), 426–51. It should be noted that the term *courtoisie* was perceived as an old-fashioned one by the dictionaries of the late seventeenth century.

33 See P. Bourdieu, *La Distinction, critique sociale du jugement* (Paris, 1979).

34 See R. Chartier, 'Distinction et divulgation'.

35 On taste, see M. Moriarty, *Taste and Ideology in Seventeenth-Century France* (Cambridge, 1988).

36 Daniel Gordon, '"Public Opinion" and the Civilizing Process in France: the Example of Morellet', *Eighteenth-Century Studies* 22 (1989), 302–28.

37 *Réflexions sur le ridicule*, p. 9. See also the quotation from Trublet in Chapter 6 below, p. 101.

38 See R. Zuber, 'Atticisme et classicisme', in *Critique et création littéraire en France au 17e siècle* (Paris, 1977), pp. 375–87.

39 See for instance the sentence from *Les Caractères* quoted above on p. 58. This definition of *la politesse* was much cited by later writers.

40 Voltaire, who was later to write that paradigmatic story of the civilizing of the savage, *L'Ingénu*, says in his dedication to *Zaïre* that politeness

is not 'une chose arbitraire, comme ce qu'on appelle civilité' but 'une loi de la nature qu'ils [les Français] ont heureusement cultivée plus que les autres nations'.

41 Marivaux, *La Vie de Marianne*, ed. F. Deloffre (Paris, 1957), p. 213.

42 On this subject, see my *Rhetoric and Truth in France: Descartes to Diderot* (Oxford, 1972), Chapter 3.

43 François-V. Toussaint, *Les Mœurs*, nouvelle édition (Amsterdam, 1759), p. 361.

44 Ch. Pinot Duclos, *Considérations sur les mœurs*, ed. F. C. Green (Cambridge, 1939). The *Considérations* were published in 1750.

45 On Rousseau's 'commerce' with his public see Chapter 6 below. Page references to *Emile* are to the *Œuvres complètes*, ed. M. Raymond and B. Gagnebin, Vol. IV.

46 See for instance the interesting pages by P. J. Hélias on ancient Breton peasant politeness in his *Les Autres et les miens*, Vol. I, *La Gloire des manants* (Paris, 1977), pp. 63–89.

5 The sociable essayist: Addison and Marivaux

1 David Hume, *Dialogues concerning Natural Religion*, ed. N. Kemp-Smith (Oxford, 1935), p. 158.

2 David Hume, *Essays, Moral, Political and Literary*, ed. T. H. Green and T. H. Grose (London, 1907) II, 367–70.

3 Page numbers in what follows refer to the classic edition of Donald F. Bond, *The Spectator*, 5 vols. (Oxford, 1965).

4 See N. Phillipson, 'The Scottish Enlightenment', in *The Enlightenment in National Context*, ed. R. Porter and M. Teich (Cambridge, 1981), pp. 19–40.

5 See A. Ross, 'The Rise of the Periodical in England', in *Literature and Western Civilization*, ed. D. Daiches and A. K. Thorlby, 6 vols. (London, 1972–   ), Vol. IV, *The Modern World*, Part 1, *Hopes* (1975), 625–49.

6 See Diderot's critique of Hélvetius's *De l'esprit* in his *Œuvres complètes*, IX, 263–312.

7 See Bond, I, xcviii–ciii.

8 On Bouhours see Chapter 1 above, pp. 13–17.

9 See Bond, I, xcvi.

10 References for Marivaux's journalism are to *Journaux et œuvres diverses*, ed. F. Deloffre and M. Gilot (Paris, 1969). I am much indebted to this excellent edition.

11 *The Idler* was of course the title chosen by Dr Johnson for one of his *Spectator*-inspired periodicals; there were also the *Lounger*, the *Rambler* and other titles of this kind.

12 On Diogenes see also Chapter 4, p. 62, and Note 29.

13 One may compare this figure with the free-speaking Arlequin of such comedies as *La Double Inconstance*, also a masked character. In stage

comedy, as in the essay, the use of the mask allows for the expressions of sentiments that may be repressed in social life.

14 'Bigarrure' is also the word used by Rousseau to describe the free and varied style he wanted in his *Confessions*; see the 1764 Neuchâtel preamble (*Œuvres complètes*, I, 1154).

15 On this question see the fascinating study by G. Bennington, *Sententiousness and the Novel* (Cambridge, 1985).

16 Much has been written about Marivaux's style, most notably by F. Deloffre, *Marivaux et le marivaudage, étude de langue et de style*, 2nd edn (Paris, 1967).

6 The commerce of the self

1 Nathalie Sarraute, *Les Fruits d'or* (Paris, 1963), p. 169.

2 When speaking of the orator I use the male pronoun because the theory and practice of eloquence in essentially a male province from Antiquity until the French Revolution.

3 Quintilian, *Institutes of Oratory*, tr. J. S. Watson (London, 1856), I, 255.

4 A useful introduction to this subject is R. L. Meek, *Social Science and the Ignoble Savage* (Cambridge, 1976). See also below, Chapter 11.

5 See G. Cayrou, *Le Français classique*, 6th edn (Paris, 1948), p. 162. In all quotations from older French texts the spelling is modernized.

6 See A. Hirschman, *The Passions and the Interests* (Princeton, 1977).

7 N. C. J. Trublet, *Essais sur divers sujets*, 6th edn (Paris, 1768), II, 171.

8 *The Theory of Moral Sentiments* is quoted from the edition of D. D. Raphael and A. L. Macfie (Oxford, 1976).

9 *The Wealth of Nations*, ed. R. H. Campbell, A. S. Skinner and W. B. Todd (Oxford, 1976), I, 25.

10 See L. Dickey, 'Historicising the "Adam Smith Problem"; Conceptual, Historiographical and Textual Issues', *Journal of Modern History*, 58 (1986), 579–609.

11 The treatment of the 'impartial spectator' is greatly expanded and strengthened in the sixth edition of 1790. Dickey suggests that this was because Smith had by then become less sanguine about the natural socialization that occurred in commercial society, and more convinced that 'for a commercial society to function properly [...] it would have to maintain a high degree of collective vigilance and "propriety" with regard to its morality' (*ibid.*, p. 608).

12 Jane Austen, *Northanger Abbey and Persuasion*, ed. J. Davie (Oxford, 1971), p. 318.

13 *Hume on Religion*, ed. R. Wollheim (London, 1963), p. 100. See also Chapter 5 above, p. 74.

14 See below, pp. 119–20.

15 Pierre Corneille, *Théâtre complet*, ed. P. Lièvre and R. Caillois, Bibliothèque de la Pléiade (Paris, 1950), I, 899.

16 Diderot, *Œuvres complètes*, XII, 177.
17 References to Rousseau's works are all to the Pléiade *Œuvres complètes*, ed. B. Gagnebin and M. Raymond, 4 vols. to date (Paris, 1959–   ). For Rousseau's attitude to politeness in general, see Chapter 4 above, pp. 69–72, and Chapter 11 below, pp. 188–93.
18 On the hostile reactions of early readers see the notes to this preamble in *Œuvres complètes*, I, 1231. For the opposite kind of reaction one could do worse than take these lines from William Boyd's *The New Confessions* (Penguin Books, Harmondsworth, 1988), describing the hero's first reading of the page in question: 'I have never read such an opening to a book, have never been so powerfully and immediately engaged' (p. 197).
19 Pascal's dictum is at once a condemnation of egoism and an allusion to the code of politeness which forbade too frequent reference to oneself.
20 Only apparent, because in fact some of Rousseau's hearers, like many other contemporaries, were far more favourably disposed towards him than he imagined.
21 On this point see Felicity Baker, 'Remarques sur la notion de dépôt', *Annales Jean-Jacques Rousseau*, 37 (1966–8), 57–93.

7 The writer as performer

1 References are to Boswell's *Life of Johnson* in the Oxford edition of R. W. Chapman (3rd edn, 1953), to *The Tour of the Hebrides* in the edition of F. A. Pottle and C. H. Bennett (Oxford, 1936) and to Gibbon's *Autobiography* in the edition of J. B. Bury (Oxford, 1907).
2 See the comments by Diderot's Rameau quoted in Chapter 6 above, p. 106.
3 G. Snyders, *La Pédagogie en France aux XVIIe et XVIIIe siècles* (Paris, 1964), p. 50.
4 See F. de Dainville, 'L'Evolution de l'enseignement de la rhétorique au XVIIe siècle', *Dix-septième siècle*, 80–1 (1968), 19–43.
5 References are to the third edition, entitled *De la manière d'enseigner et d'étudier les belles-lettres*, 4 vols. (Paris, 1775).
6 Marmontel's works are referred to in the following editions: *Mémoires* (*M*) ed. J. Renwick, 2 vols. (Clermont-Ferrand, 1972); other works in *Œuvres* (*O*), 7 vols. (Paris, 1819).
7 A particularly helpful discussion is that of Eva Katz, 'Marmontel and the Voice of Experience', *Studies on Voltaire and the Eighteenth Century*, 76 (1970), 233–59.
8 On polite conversation, see Chapter 4 above, in particular pp. 61–2.
9 See for instance Michelle Buchanan, 'Les *Contes moraux* de Marmontel', *French Review*, 40, 2 (1967), 201–12, and further cases reported in J. Renwick, *La Destinée posthume de Jean-François Marmontel* (Clermont-Ferrand, 1972), pp. 47–52.
10 Abbé Raynal, *Nouvelles littéraires* (1749), in Grimm's *Correspondance littéraire*, ed. M. Tourneux (Paris, 1877–82), I, 136.
11 Abbé Morellet, *Mémoires* (Paris, 1821), I, 239.

12 Diderot, *Correspondance*, ed. G. Roth and J. Varloot (Paris, 1955–70), IV, 203.

13 *Correspondance littéraire* V, 377.

14 See his illuminating article, 'Jean-François Marmontel: The Formative Years', *Studies on Voltaire and the Eighteenth Century*, 76 (1970), 139–232.

15 *Correspondance littéraire*, VII, 248–54. See also Diderot, *Correspondance*, VII, 57.

16 See P. France, *Rhetoric and Truth in France: Descartes to Diderot* (Oxford, 1972), pp. 235–64.

17 Rousseau, *Œuvres complètes*, ed. B. Gagnebin and M. Raymond, 4 vols. to date (Paris, 1959–) I, 1013. On Rousseau's 'commerce of the self', see above, Chapter 6, pp. 107–12.

18 *Mémoires*, I, 68–9.

19 *Correspondance littéraire*, IX, 417–24.

20 References for Helvétius are to his *Œuvres complètes* (including a biographical account by Saint-Lambert) (Paris, 1795, reprinted by Georg Olms Verlag, Hildesheim, 1969).

21 Diderot, *Œuvres complètes*, XII, 118.

22 Questions of literary expression are also the subject of many of the youthful manuscript notes published by A. Keim, *Notes de la main d'Helvétius* (Paris, 1907).

23 See his edition of *Le Neveu* for the Editions Sociales (Paris, 1972).

8 Beyond politeness? Speakers and audience at the Convention Nationale

1 Having been neglected, this subject is now attracting more attention. Among recent work, see H. U. Gumbrecht, *Funktionen parlamentarischer Rhetorik in der französischen Revolution* (Munich, 1978); Lynn Hunt, 'The Rhetoric of Revolution in France', *History Workshop Journal*, 15 (1983), 78–94; J.-C. Bonnet, 'La Sainte Masure', in *La Carmagnole des Muses*, ed. J.-C. Bonnet and P. Roger (Paris, 1988), pp. 185–222; and in particular, for a clear account of the conditions of speech and the workings of the assemblies, Patrick Brasart, *Paroles de la Révolution: les assemblées parlementaires* (Paris, 1988).

2 A. Aulard, *Les Orateurs de l'Assemblée Constituante* (Paris, 1882); *Les Orateurs de la Législative et de la Convention*, 2 vols. (Paris, 1885–6).

3 On La Harpe, see P. Roger, 'The French Revolution as Logomachy', in *Language and Rhetoric of the Revolution*, ed. John Renwick (Edinburgh, 1990), pp. 4–17.

4 H. Taine, *Origines de la France contemporaine; II. La Révolution*, 3 vols. (Paris, 1882–5), I, 147.

5 F. Brunot, *Histoire de la langue française; Vol. X, Part 1, La Langue classique dans la tourmente* (Paris, 1939), p. 72.

6 See R. Garaudy, *Les Orateurs de la Révolution française*, Classiques Larousse (Paris, 1939).

7 *Littérature française*, ed. C. Pichois; Vol. XI, B. Didier, *Le XVIIIe Siècle* (Paris, 1976), p. 54.

8 L.-S. Mercier, *Le Nouveau Paris*, new edn (Paris, 1862), I, 275–80, 'Sur la Convention et son style'.

9 C. Nodier, *Œuvres* (Paris, 1832–7), VII, 228. This is a variant on a classical topos: that the health of a nation's eloquence depends on political liberty. It is interesting to note that in a manual published shortly before the fall of the Bastille (*De l'éloquence des orateurs anciens et modernes*, 1789), J.-L. Ferri asserts once again that despotism has stifled political eloquence in France.

10 Peter Gay rightly underlines the partisan nature of most representations of revolutionary eloquence in his *The Party of Humanity* (London, 1964), Chapter 6, 'Rhetoric and Politics in the French Revolution'.

11 P. France, 'Eloquence révolutionnaire et rhétorique traditionnelle: étude d'une séance de la convention', *Saggi e ricerche di letteratura francese*, 24 (1985), 143–76.

12 See in particular the editions of Danton's speeches by A. Fribourg (Paris, 1910) and the *Œuvres complètes* of Robespierre (Paris, 1950–67).

13 In what follows I generally quote from the *Archives parlementaires* (*AP*), references being to Vol. 52 (Paris, 1897) unless otherwise indicated. The relevant volume of the *Réimpression de l'Ancien Moniteur* (Paris, 1840), is Vol. 14.

14 B. Kazansky, 'Rech Lenina', *LEF*, 5 (1924); this volume contains a very interesting set of studies of Lenin's eloquence by the principal Russian formalist critics.

15 On the rhetorical theories of the Revolution, in addition to the works already quoted, see P. Trahard, 'Le Recours à l'éloquence' in his *La Sensibilité révolutionnaire* (Paris, 1936), pp. 175–92.

16 Pétion, newly elected President of the Convention, declared on 21 September: 'Nous ne perdrons jamais de vue que nous tenons dans nos mains les destinées d'un grand peuple, du monde entier et des races futures' (*AP*, 68).

17 David Williams, *Incidents in my Life*, ed. P. France (Brighton, 1980), p. 27. On the make-up of the Convention, see Lynn Hunt, *Politics, Culture and Class in the French Revolution* (University of California Press, 1984), Chapter 5.

18 Quoted by Brasart, *Paroles*, p. 84.

19 See *Moniteur*, XX, 662.

20 On this and other related questions see the useful book of P. D. G. Thomas, *The House of Commons in the Eighteenth Century* (Oxford, 1971).

21 The essential source, for this and for pathos, is Aristotle's *Rhetoric*, together with Quintilian's *Institutes*. On *ethos*, see also Chapter 6 above.

22 Bonnet, 'La Sainte Masure', p. 215.

23 The reference to Molière's Alceste is a very frequent one during this period, as indeed throughout the eighteenth century. In Fabre d'Eglantine's

comedy *Le Philinte de Molière* (1790), the tables are turned on the partisans of polite moderation, the moderate Philinte being seen as the real misanthrope, whereas the virtuous Alceste emerges as positive hero. This was of course the way Rousseau put the matter in his *Lettre à d'Alembert sur les spectacles.*

24 The *Moniteur* gives a somewhat different text according to which Buzot says: 'j'y conserverai mon âme indépendante' and 'moi qui vivait au sein de ma retraite, dans mon département'.
25 See P.-J.-B. Buchez and P.-C. Roux, *Histoire parlementaire de la Révolution française*, Vol. XIX (Paris, 1835), p. 70.
26 *Procès-verbaux du Comité d'Instruction Publique de l'Assemblée Législative*, pp. 200–3.
27 See Bonnet, 'La Sainte Masure', pp. 200–2.
28 Quoted by Brasart, *Paroles*, p. 31.
29 Here again the *Moniteur* gives an interestingly different version: instead of 'nous avons trop de confiance ...' we read: 'vous devez avoir confiance dans la justice du peuple'.
30 That the deputies might not feel so sure of their eminence is suggested by the sort of mockery we find in this counter-revolutionary song: 'Comme ils sont faits! / Cela fait pitié, je vous jure / Comme ils sont faits! / On les prendrait pour des jokais / Ils en ont la tournure / L'accoutrement et la coiffure / Comme ils sont faits!'
31 The words 'de philosophes' are missing from the *Moniteur*'s account of this speech.

9 Translating the British

1 See J. F. Lafitau, *Mœurs des sauvages américains comparées aux mœurs des premiers temps* (Paris, 1724).
2 On the 'querelle d'Homère' see Noémi Hepp, *Homère en France au 17e siècle* (Paris, 1968), Part 4.
3 George Steiner, *After Babel* (Oxford, 1975).
4 Jean Starobinski, 'Diderot et la parole des autres', *Critique*, 28 (1972), 3–22.
5 J.-P. Seguin, *Diderot, le discours et les choses* (Paris, 1978).
6 J. Proust, *L'Objet et le texte* (Geneva, 1980).
7 References to Diderot are to his *Œuvres complètes*, ed. H. Dieckmann, J. Proust and J. Varloot (Paris, 1975–).
8 See J. Proust, 'Diderot et les problèmes du langage' in *L'Objet et le texte*, pp. 15–37.
9 Lord Shaftesbury, *An Inquiry concerning Virtue, or Merit*, in *Characteristics*, ed. J. M. Robertson (New York, 1964), I, 338.
10 See P. Van Tieghem, *Ossian en France* (Paris, 1917); and J. Chouillet, 'Diderot, Poet and Theorist of the Homer and Ossianist Revival', *British Journal for Eighteenth-Century Studies*, 5 (1982), 225–32.
11 In his preface to the 1773 edition, Macpherson writes: 'Through the

medium of version on version they retain in foreign languages their native characters of simplicity and energy' (*The Poems of Ossian*, ed. M. Laing, 2 vols. (Edinburgh, 1805), I, lxviii).

12 *Fragments of Ancient Poetry* in *The Poems of Ossian*, II, 385.

13 Edward Moore, *The Gamester* in *Poems, Fables and Plays* (London, 1756), p. 459.

14 See also the beginning of the *Eloge*: 'Tout ce que Montaigne, Charron, La Rochefoucauld et Nicole ont mis en maximes, Richardson l'a mis en action' (XIII, 192). In this way the English novelist joins the ranks of the French moralists.

15 See G. Goggi, 'Diderot et Médée dépeçant le vieil Eson', *Colloque international Diderot*, ed. A. M. Chouillet (Paris, 1985), and in particular the translation from Hobbes's *De cive*.

16 See P. France, 'Translation and Eloquence', *Journal of European Studies*, 11 (1981), 1—8.

17 E. Audra, *Les Traductions françaises de Pope (1717—1825): Etude de bibliographie* (Paris, 1931).

18 See A. Gunny, *Voltaire and the English, Studies on Voltaire and the Eighteenth Century*, 177 (1979).

19 See R. C. Knight, 'Anne Dacier and Gardens: Ancient and Modern', *Studies on Voltaire and the Eighteenth Century*, 185 (1980), 119—29.

20 Voltaire, *Lettres philosophiques*, ed. G. Lanson (Paris, 1915), II, 136.

21 See R. G. Knapp, *The Fortunes of Pope's 'Essay on Man' in Eighteenth-Century France, Studies on Voltaire and the Eighteenth Century*, 82 (1971).

22 See P. Van Tieghem, 'La Prière Universelle de Pope et le déisme français au XVIIIe siècle', *Revue de littérature comparée*, 3 (1923), 190—212.

23 See J. de la Harpe, 'Le *Journal des Savants* et la renommée de Pope en France au dix-huitième siècle', *University of California Publications in Modern Philology*, 16 (1933), 173—215.

24 Alexander Pope, *Œuvres complètes* (Paris, 1780), 8 vols.

25 Virgile, *Œuvres complètes*, tr. Abbé P.-F.-G. Desfontaines (Paris, 1743), I, xxx.

26 Earl of Roscommon, *An Essay on Translated Verse* (London, 1684).

27 Voltaire, *Œuvres complètes*, ed. L. Moland (Paris, 1877), VIII, 319.

28 See Knapp, *The Fortunes of Pope's 'Essay on Man'*, pp. 22—32.

29 Pope, *Essais sur la critique et sur l'homme*, tr. E. de Silhouette (London, 1737), p. 13.

30 Abbé Goujet, *Bibliothèque française*, new edn (Paris, 1755), VIII, 232—75.

31 See La Harpe, 'Le *Journal des Savants*', p. 180.

32 See M. Edwards, 'A Meaning for Mock-Heroic', *Yearbook of English Studies*, 15 (1985), 48—63.

33 Voltaire, *Lettres philosophiques*, ed. G. Lanson (Paris, 1915) II, 137.

10 Jacques or his master? Diderot and the peasants

1 An exception is provided by Emmanuel Le Roy Ladurie, whose major contribution to Volume II of the *Histoire de la France rurale* draws heavily on Restif de la Bretonne's *La Vie de mon père*. He justifies this use of 'qualitative' material as follows: 'Toute étude agraire, sur le dernier siècle de l'Ancien Régime, resterait abstraite, si ne s'y glissait l'irremplaçable regard que l'homme rustique personnellement jette sur lui-même, sur les autres, et sur son monde' (see his *Le Territoire de l'historien*, Vol. II (Paris, 1978), p. 337.

2 George Sand, *François le champi* (avant-propos). See also Michelet's *Le Peuple* (introductory letter to Quinet) for a critique of contemporary novelists' biased depictions of the peasantry and of the common people in general.

3 P. Goubert, 'Sociétés rurales françaises du XVIIIe siècle. Vingt paysanneries contrastées', in *Conjoncture économique; structures sociales. Hommage à Ernest Labrousse* (Paris and The Hague, 1974), p. 378.

4 Saint-Lambert, *Les Saisons*, 5th edn (Amsterdam, 1773), p. 3.

5 R. Mandrou, *La France aux XVIIe et XVIIIe siècles* (Paris, 1967).

6 *Lettres à Grégoire sur les patois de France, 1790–1794*, ed. A. Gazier (Paris, 1880, reprinted Geneva, 1969), p. 222.

7 See M. de Certeau, D. Julia, J. Revel, *Une Politique de la langue; la Révolution française et les patois* (Paris, 1975).

8 On the relation between elite and popular culture see R. Muchembled, *Culture populaire et culture des élites dans la France moderne (XV–XVIIIe siècles)* (Paris, 1978); P. Burke, *Popular Culture in Early Modern Europe* (London, 1978).

9 On regional and *patois* literature in eighteenth-century France, see however the pages by M. Piron and A. Berry in *Histoires des littératures, III: Littératures françaises, connexes et marginales*, ed. R. Queneau (Paris, 1958), pp. 1428–38 and 1475–88.

10 From a letter to Tabureau provoked by a popular uprising in Lyon in 1769, quoted by R. Mortier, 'Voltaire et le peuple', in *The Age of Enlightenment. Studies presented to Theodore Besterman*, ed. W. H. Barber *et al.* (Edinburgh and London, 1967), pp. 137–51 (p. 144).

11 On Diderot's political attitudes and opinions see A. Strugnell, *Diderot's Politics* (The Hague, 1973).

12 On the word 'peuple' see for instance the contributions to a conference held in Aix-en-Provence in 1969, *Images du peuple au dix-huitième siècle* (Paris, 1973).

13 Diderot's works are referred to by the following abbreviations:
AT: *Œuvres complètes*, ed. J. Assézat and M. Tourneux (Paris, 1875–7).
CORR: *Correspondance*, ed. G. Roth and J. Varloot (Paris, 1955–70).
OC: *Œuvres complètes*, ed. H. Dieckmann, J. Proust and J. Varloot (Paris, 1975–).
POL: *Œuvres politiques*, ed. P. Vernière (Paris, 1963).

14 On this connection see Angus Martin, 'Diderot's *Deux Amis de Bourbonne* as a Critique of Saint-Lambert's *Les Deux Amis, conte iroquois*', *Romance Notes*, 20 (1980).

15 Diderot discusses Homer's language in the *Lettre sur les sourds et muets* (*OC*, IV, 180).

16 On Diderot and Ossian see J. Chouillet, 'Diderot, Poet and Theorist of the Homer and Ossianist Revival', *British Journal for Eighteenth-Century Studies*, 5, 2 (1982), 225—32. See also Chapter 9 above, pp. 158—9.

17 On levels of language in *Jacques* see D. J. Adams, 'Style and Social Ideas in *Jacques le fataliste*', *Studies on Voltaire and the Eighteenth Century*, 124 (1974), 231—48.

18 See J. Proust, *L'Objet et le texte* (Geneva, 1980), pp. 245—76, for an interesting comparison of the rendering of lower-class speech in *La Nouvelle Héloïse*, *Les Liaisons dangereuses* and *Clarissa*.

19 On the possible implications of the names Bigre and Boule see the edition of *Jacques* by S. Lecointre and J. Le Galliot (Paris and Geneva, 1976), p. 456.

11 Enlightened primitivism

1 Throughout this discussion I use the term 'primitivism' in a deliberately broad sense, to signify a preference for earlier, more primitive states. Primitivist ideals are of course present in innumerable fictional writings of the time; see for instance Lois Whitney, *Primitivism and the Idea of Progress in English Popular Literature of the Eighteenth Century* (Baltimore, 1934).

2 See N. Phillipson, 'The Scottish Enlightenment', in *The Enlightenment in National Context*, ed. R. Porter and M. Teich (Cambridge, 1981), pp. 19—40.

3 On Rousseau and politeness see also Chapter 4 above. References to Rousseau's works are to the *Œuvres complètes*, ed. B. Gagnebin and M. Raymond, 4 vols. to date (Paris, 1959—   ), unless otherwise indicated.

4 For a summary of the 'noble savage' question, see J. Franco, 'The Noble Savage', in *Literature and Western Civilization*, ed. D. Daiches and A. K. Thorlby, 6 vols. (London, 1972—   ), Vol. IV, *The Modern World*, Part I, *Hopes* (1975), 565—94. For the 'civic humanist' tradition of attacks on corruption, see J. G. A. Pocock, *The Machiavellian Moment* (Princeton, 1975). Rousseau's debts to earlier writers are explored in the edition of the *Discours sur les sciences et sur les arts* by G. Havens (New York, 1946).

5 Voltaire, *Correspondance*, ed. T. Besterman, definitive edn (Geneva, 1968—77), XVI, 259.

6 On the four-stage theory see R. L. Meek, *Social Science and the Ignoble Savage* (Cambridge, 1976). The stages are: (a) hunting and fishing, (b) pastoral, (c) agricultural, (d) commercial.

234

7 'Notre espèce ne veut pas être façonnée à demi', words not without a charge of bitterness.

8 On Boswell, see Chapter 12 below, pp. 210–11.

9 See S. S. B. Taylor, 'The Enlightenment in Switzerland', in *The Enlightenment in National Context*, pp. 72–89.

10 *Lettre à d'Alembert*, ed. M. Fuchs (Paris and Geneva, 1948), pp. 149–50.

11 See H. Roddier, *Jean-Jacques Rousseau en Angleterre au 18e siècle* (Paris, 1950), especially pp. 128–32. As for Rousseau's knowledge of the Scots, he was for a time close to Hume, but does not seem to have been aware of what is now called the Scottish Enlightenment. His conversations with Boswell and his letters suggest that he shared a commonly held vision of the Scots as an ancient and valorous people (the barefoot Scots at Fontenoy). For a brief period in 1765 he thought of seeking asylum and freedom in Scotland on the estate of Earl Marischal Keith (who had suggested that he write a life of the Scottish patriot Fletcher of Saltoun).

12 William Robertson, Principal of Edinburgh University, said in a sermon of 1755 that in the Highlands and Islands of Scotland 'society still appears in its rudest and most imperfect form' (see R. L. Meek, *Social Science and the Ignoble Savage* (Cambridge, 1976), p. 132).

13 On Johnson's visit to the Highlands, see Chapter 12 below, pp. 206–7.

14 *Of the Origin and Progress of Language*, 6 vols. (Edinburgh, 1773–92), I, 174.

15 *The Wealth of Nations*, ed. E. R. A. Seligman, 2 vols. (London and New York, 1910), II, 264.

16 Quoted in Donald Winch, *Adam Smith's Politics* (Cambridge, 1978), pp. 88–9.

17 Quotations are from Duncan Forbes's edition (Edinburgh, 1966).

18 See for instance Voltaire's story *L'Ingénu*, published in the same year as Ferguson's *Civil Society*.

19 Compare Rousseau's teasing motto, twisted from its original meaning in Ovid: 'Barbarus hic ego sum, quia non intellegor illis' (I am a Barbarian here because I an not understood by these people).

20 On *Waverley*, see Chapter 12 below.

21 Duncan Forbes is much more positive in his introduction to the *Civil Society* (pp. xxxviii–xxxix).

22 Unlike Rousseau, Ferguson was a supporter of the establishment of a proper theatre in his city.

23 *Lectures on Rhetoric and Belles Lettres*, 2 vols. (London, 1783), I, 19, 114.

24 *A Critical Dissertation on the Poems of Ossian* (London, 1763), p. 11.

25 See Chapter 8 above, p. 135.

26 Among the first translators of Ossian were those champions of the French Enlightenment, Turgot and Diderot. See P. Van Tieghem, *Ossian en France* (Paris, 1917) and Chapter 9 above, pp. 158—9.

27 See in particular his *Supplément au Voyage de Bougainville* (1772) and the closely related pages 'Sur les nations sauvages' in his *Pensées détachées: contributions à l'Histoire des deux Indes*, ed. G. Goggi (Siena, 1976), pp. 122—64.

12 Frontiers of civilization

1 N. Wachtel, *La Vision des vaincus* (Paris, 1971), tr. B. Reynolds and S. Reynolds, *The Vision of the Vanquished* (Hassocks, Sussex, 1977). For another such vision, which shows how wild the city of Canberra appeared to the aboriginal inhabitants of the supposedly savage lands of Australia, see Rhys Jones, 'Ordering the Landscape', in *Seeing the First Australians*, ed. Ian and Tamsin Donaldson (Sydney, London and Boston, 1985), pp. 181—209.

2 P. Michel, *Un Mythe romantique: les Barbares (1798—1848)* (Lyon, 1981).

3 J. Michelet, *Le Peuple*, ed. L. Refort (Paris, 1946), p. 24.

4 D. Diderot, *Pensées détachées: contributions à l'Histoire des deux Indes*, ed. G. Goggi (Siena, 1976), pp. 160—61.

5 F. Braudel, *La Méditerranée et le monde méditerranéen à l'époque de Philippe II*, 2nd edn (Paris, 1966), I, 46.

6 Page numbers for quotations to Johnson's *Journey* refer to the edition by R. W. Chapman (Oxford, 1930), which also includes Boswell's *Journal of a Tour of the Hebrides*.

7 J. Prebble, *The Highland Clearances* (Harmondsworth, 1969) p. 251.

8 W. Scott, *Waverley*, ed. C. Lamont (Oxford, 1981), p. 340. All references are to this edition.

9 W. Scott, *The Waverley Novels*, Dryburgh edn (London and Edinburgh, 1894), XX, 346—7.

10 See W. Dowling, *The Boswellian Hero* (University of Georgia Press, 1979), pp. 21—2.

11 J. Boswell, *Journal of a Tour to Corsica*, in *Boswell on the Grand Tour*, ed. F. Brady and F. A. Pottle (London, 1955), p. 184. Subsequent references are to this edition.

12 See above, Chapter 11, p. 190.

13 All references are to P. Mérimée, *Romans et nouvelles*, ed. M. Parturier, 2 vols. (Paris, 1967), Vol. II.

14 References are to Pushkin's *Sobranie sochinenii v desyati tomakh* (Moscow, 1959—62).

15 It is worth noting that Chateaubriand, for all the beautifying of his North American experience, does present a comically self-deprecating account of his first meeting with savages; see below, pp. 217—18.

16 See B. S. Vinogradov, *Kavkaz v russkoi literature 30-ikh godakh XIX. veka* (Grozny, 1966), Chapter 2.

17 See V. L. Komarovich, 'K voprosu o zhanre *Puteshestiviya v Arzrum*', *Pushkinsky Vremennik 3* (Moscow–Leningrad, 1937), 326–38.

18 A symptomatic passage is the account in the seventh of the *Rêveries du promeneur solitaire* of his discovery of a stocking mill in a wild place in the mountains. It may be compared with the passage from Chateaubriand quoted at the end of this chapter.

19 *Mémoires d'outre-tombe*, ed. M. Levaillant (Paris, 1948, reprinted Paris, 1982), I, 290–1.

INDEX

Index

Index

Index

Index

Index

Cambridge Studies in French

General editor: MALCOLM BOWIE

244

245